NORTHAMPT
AIRFIEL
IN THE SE
WORLD \.₋₋₋

ERRATUM SLIP

We apologise to readers for three errors to the captions of pictures in this book:

(a) Page 33 –   Photo is of a Miles Master II Advanced Trainer
                  and should have appeared on page 34.

(b) Page 34 –   Photo shown is a duplicate from page 29
                  (Airspeed Oxfords).

(c) Pages 175 and 177 – Captions are transposed.

NORTHAMPTONSHIRE
AIRFIELDS
IN THE SECOND
WORLD WAR

Graham Smith

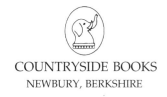

COUNTRYSIDE BOOKS
NEWBURY, BERKSHIRE

First Published 1998
© Graham Smith 1998

COUNTRYSIDE BOOKS
3 Catherine Road
Newbury, Berkshire

ISBN 1 85306 529 3

The cover painting by Colin Doggett shows
a B-17G of the 401st Bomb Group
taking off from Deenethorpe.

Designed by Mon Mohan

Produced through MRM Associates Ltd., Reading
Typeset by Techniset Typesetters, Merseyside
Printed by Woolnough Bookbinding Ltd., Irthlingborough

CONTENTS

ACKNOWLEDGEMENTS

I am, again, greatly indebted to a number of people for assisting me during the preparation of this book, especially with the provision of illustrations: Norman G. Richards of the Archives Division of NASM, Chris and Mavis Parker, James Beckett of BRDC Archives, the staff of Northamptonshire Central Library, Northamptonshire Record Office and the City of Peterborough Museum. As usual I am grateful for the willing help of the staff of Galleywood Library.

It has not been possible to fully express the individual bravery of each and all the Allied airmen, who operated from the county's airfields, and it is to those airmen that this book is humbly dedicated.

Graham Smith

NORTHAMPTONSHIRE'S WORLD WAR II AIRFIELDS

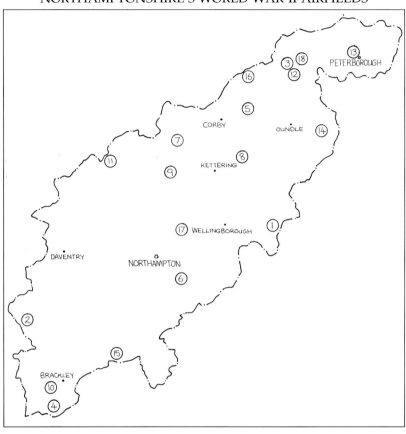

KEY TO MAP

1 Chelveston
2 Chipping Warden
3 Collyweston
4 Croughton
5 Deenethorpe
6 Denton
7 Desborough
8 Grafton Underwood
9 Harrington

10 Hinton-in-the-Hedges
11 Husbands Bosworth
12 King's Cliffe
13 Peterborough
14 Polebrook
15 Silverstone
16 Spanhoe
17 Sywell
18 Wittering

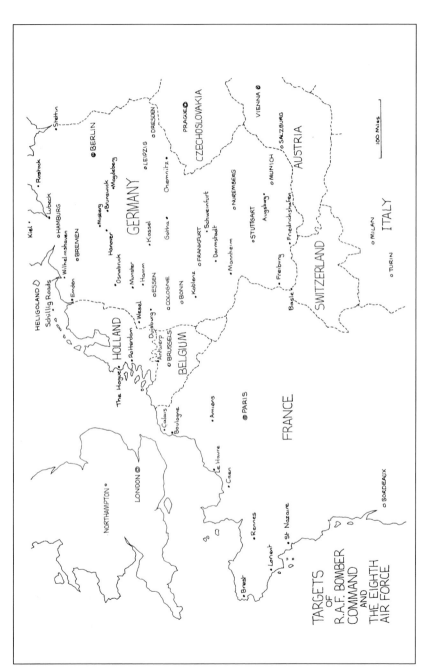

TARGETS OF RAF BOMBER COMMAND AND THE EIGHTH AIR FORCE

I
SETTING
THE
SCENE

The origins of Service flying in Northamptonshire can be traced back almost to its inception, an aviation heritage that few counties can better. In late September 1913 units of the Royal Flying Corps were engaged in the Army's autumn manoeuvres and a large grassed field near Lilbourne was used as the Corps' main base, with several other advanced landing fields being used throughout the county. During the month HM King George V and Queen Mary took the opportunity to inspect their embryonic Corps and its pioneer airmen. The Royal Flying Corps had only been constituted in April 1912 and formed the following month. Its frail and rather rudimentary aircraft that were lined up for inspection at Lilbourne were in stark and striking contrast to the large and thunderous B-17s (Flying Fortresses) of the United States' Eighth Air Force that would fill the county's skies less than 30 years later, a clear demonstration of the rapid progress of aviation in less than three decades.

Lilbourne became the first Service aerodrome to open in the county, although its early aviation history has now been largely forgotten. In June 1916 No 55 Reserve squadron arrived to take up residence at the grass surfaced field, which was situated alongside the A5 road or Roman Watling Street. The aerodrome was provided with a few hangars, administrative buildings and living quarters, and soon became involved in flying training for the RFC. The word 'aerodrome'

BE (Blériot Experimental) 2a near Badby on 24th September 1913. (Northamptonshire Libraries & Information Services)

was derived from the Greek meaning 'aerial racecourse', and the name was used in this country until well into the Second World War when the 'airfield' – an American term – came into general use in the Service.

Since the outbreak of the war the Corps had grown rapidly and in 1916 comprised 31 squadrons with over 420 aircraft, most of which were operating in France. There was an urgent need to train pilots for the planned new squadrons as well as to replace the high losses of airmen on the Western Front; during the Battle of the Somme almost 500 airmen were either killed, wounded or missing in action. The first airman to be awarded the Victoria Cross hailed from Spratton Grange near Northampton. He was Second Lieutenant W. B. Rhodes-Moorehouse, who had received his pilot's certificate in October 1911. In April 1915 he was serving with No 2 squadron at Merville, France, and on 26th April he returned mortally wounded from a bombing sortie over the railway station at Courtrai. His bravery on this mission resulted in the posthumous award.

From 1915 onwards, as the threat of enemy aerial bombardment materialised in the shape of the dreaded Zeppelin airships, it was recognised that a special Home Defence Force was needed to afford the country some protection from these air attacks. One of the new squadrons formed for this Force, No 38, was based at Melton Mowbray but it was decided that one of its Flights, 'A', would move, in October 1916, into a large site alongside the A1 or Great North Road. It is rather surprising to find that as early as 1912 it had been established that military aerodromes, whenever possible, should be placed next to Roman roads, because 'the straight roads would aid location from the air'! Another requisite was that the field should be able to give runs of 500 to 600 yards in any direction. The new aerodrome, which was situated close to the village of Wittering, was first named Stamford from the nearby town. A Major Arthur T. Harris had been given the task of forming the squadron and locating suitable landing fields for its Flights. He will be eternally remembered as Air Chief Marshal 'Bomber' Harris, the wartime Commander-in-Chief of RAF Bomber Command.

By mid-1917 the organisation of flying training, of sheer necessity, had greatly progressed especially as six months earlier the Army Council had rather reluctantly agreed to a massive expansion of the RFC. In July Stamford became No 1 Training Depôt, effectively three training squadrons with an establishment of over 30 aircraft, and three months later another small landing ground at Easton-on-the-Hill opened, also to be used for flying training. It later became No 5 Training Depôt, though mainly undertaking advanced instruction. Twenty-three years later this airfield would reopen as Collyweston, and become intrinsically linked with its neighbouring airfield at Wittering. Both the Depôts would house airmen of the 831st Aero Repair Squadron of the United States Army Air Service, the county's first and early association with American airmen that would be so strongly renewed during the Second World War.

The immediate post-war, heady days of peacetime Britain saw many squadrons disbanded and most of the Service aerodromes closed down. Lilbourne, which had been latterly engaged in training flying instructors, closed in July 1919, and it never reopened as an airfield. Its landing field was later taken over by the General Post Office as a wireless telegraph station. Easton-on-the-Hill also ceased but Wittering, as Stamford had been renamed on 10th April 1918, survived on a care and maintenance basis. The future of the nascent Royal Air Force, which had been formed on 1st April 1918, looked decidedly bleak. Its saviour proved to be its first Chief of Air Staff, Sir Hugh (later Lord) Trenchard. He not only fought most doggedly for its very survival in the face of severe opposition from the other two Services, but he also managed to build a Service which, although small, was nevertheless well trained, professional and highly motivated. Trenchard thoroughly deserved the title of 'The Father of the RAF'; the Service that entered the Second World War bore his indelible imprint.

11

In 1924 it was decided, largely as a result of the Defence Review, that Wittering would be developed into a major RAF aerodrome. Construction work by J. Laing & Co started in July of that year but it would be another two years before the new permanent station was ready for occupation. The Central Flying School, then at Upavon, completed its move to Wittering by October 1926. It was commanded by Group Captain W. R. Freeman, who later in the war, as the Air Member for the Research, Development and Production on the Air Council, ordered the first 50 Mosquitos from de Havilland against strong Service opposition. In its early days before it had proved itself as a superb and versatile aircraft, the Mosquito was known as 'Freeman's Folly'!

The CFS, as it was always known in Service circles, had originally been purely a flying training school but developed into a School of Special Flying whilst stationed at Gosport, and it had become dedicated to the training of flying instructors. The school was said to have 'turned the art of flying into a science' and in the process had inculcated excellent flying procedures and techniques, which were enshrined in a small booklet, *Flying Instruction*. These principles and practices slowly filtered through to operational squadrons and down to the other flying training schools, ensuring that the quality of flying training in the RAF was of the highest standard. During its time at Wittering the CFS, although it was a relatively small unit of some 230 airmen, had justifiably gained a fine and high reputation as a centre of excellence, with many of the Service's luminaries passing through its doors either as instructors or students or indeed both. Basil Embry and David Acherley were two examples of the latter. On the first course at Wittering, which commenced on 19th October 1926, Flying Officer F. Victor Beamish attended as a student. He was destined to become one of the legendary figures of the RAF during the Second World War.

But perhaps the school's most valuable contribution to service flying was the introduction and development of instrument flying into the RAF during the early 1930s, which was a remarkable achievement that was to have far-reaching effects on operational flying. Flight Lieutenant W. E. Patrick Johnson was the major motivator of this revolutionary flying technique, and his Flight was given the task of introducing blind flying or 'cloud flying', as it was called in the syllabus, to existing pilots and flying training schools, all within two years. The Avro 504K became the RAF's first instrument trainer with six of the school's Avros being fitted with blind flying hoods and special turn and bank indicators.

Avro 504K of No 1 FTS. (RAF Museum)

It was this ubiquitous aircraft, also known as 'The Immortal 504', that was most likely to be seen in the county's skies during the 1920/ 30s. It dated back to 1913 and had given sterling service as a bomber and Zeppelin destroyer during the First World War, before becoming one of the classic trainers of all time and operating as such until replaced in 1933. The aircraft had been produced in such numbers during the war that a vast number had survived. Many were purchased by private individuals, giving them their first experience of piloting and of offering 'joy rides' to the public, who were more than eager to discover all the excitement and thrills of flying. The fast growing public interest in this new form of transport can be gauged by the number of spectators, over 3,000, who attended the first Air Pageant organised by Northampton Aero Club and held at Sywell aerodrome in September 1928. Sywell was the first private aerodrome to open in the county and over 70 years later it is still thriving and successful.

In August 1932 a new Service aerodrome opened at Westwood, about one and a half miles to the north-west of Peterborough. A couple of weeks before it opened officially, Sir Alan Cobham was given permission to stage one of his National Aviation Days there. This was just one of over 100 shows his famous Flying Circus mounted during

The inspection of RAF Wittering by HM King Edward VIII in July 1936.
(RAF Museum)

the year; indeed, it was so successful that he returned in September 1933 to give a repeat performance. Sir Alan was one of the most celebrated airmen of the time, famed for his various pioneer flights and his tireless efforts to popularise flying. He also conducted a personal crusade to persuade local authorities to provide municipal aerodromes, though it must be admitted that very few town councils responded to his call, and certainly Peterborough City Council was no exception!

It was during the mid-1930s that all three airfields in the county became engaged in flying training. Brooklands Flying School was formed at Sywell in September 1933 at the newly enlarged aerodrome to offer private flying tuition, and in June 1935 it was given a contract to provide elementary flying instruction for Service and Reserve airmen as a result of the rapid expansion of the RAF. In the same year Peterborough (as it was now officially known), which hitherto had been an Aircraft Acceptance Park and later redesignated No 1 Aircraft Storage Depôt, became the first home of No 7 Flying Training School (FTS) providing student pilots with the main stage of their flying training. In September 1935 the CFS left Wittering and was replaced by No 11 FTS. The importance of flying training in the rapidly expanding Service was recognised in July 1936 when King Edward VIII made an

Sywell Aerodrome in pre-war days. (Sywell Aerodrome Ltd)

inspection of the School at Wittering. He was accompanied by his brother the Duke of York (later King George VI) and Air Chief Marshal Sir Edward L. Ellington, the Chief of the Air Staff. The King had learned to fly some five years earlier and had previously predicted that Britain would soon possess 'a great air organisation on the same lines as our mercantile marine'!

Just a month earlier the RAF had been comprehensively reorganised into four separate and functional Commands – Fighter, Bomber, Coastal and Training – each divided into a number of Groups. In May 1938, Wittering passed from Training Command into the control of No 12 Group of Fighter Command to become an operational station, and two fighter squadrons arrived to take the place of No 11 FTS. The other two aerodromes continued with their flying training duties, as they would do throughout the war.

On that fateful Sunday morning of 3rd September 1939 when most people in the country clustered around their wireless sets to listen to the tired and doleful voice of the Prime Minister intone the dire news that 'we are now at war with Germany', there were just two RAF stations in the county, with Sywell formally coming into the Service's fold in January 1940. In that year four new airfields came into operation, Croughton, Denton, Hinton-in-the-Hedges and Collyweston. All operated as satellites for larger airfields and, except for

15

Collyweston, were engaged in some form of flying training.

In 1941 Wittering gained a second satellite – King's Cliffe – and three new airfields opened at Polebrook, Chipping Warden and Chelveston. The following year was notable for the arrival of the United States' Eighth Air Force, first at Grafton Underwood and Polebrook, and later Chelveston and King's Cliffe would also pass over to American control. During 1943 five new airfields came 'on stream' with Silverstone, Husbands Bosworth, Desborough and Harrington all engaged in operational training and Deenethorpe housing another Eighth Air Force Group. The final wartime airfield to open in the county, in early 1944, was Spanhoe from where C-47s (Dakotas) of the United States' Ninth Air Force transported Allied troops to the major airborne operations of 1944/5.

In purely operational terms the Eighth Air Force played the major role in the county's air war. Wittering was situated too far north to be actively engaged in the Battle of Britain but its night-fighter squadrons played a successful part in the air defence of the country. The other RAF airfields were mainly heavily engaged in servicing the RAF's massive flying training commitment, from elementary to advanced and finally onto operational instruction. To appreciate the vital contribution made by these Northamptonshire airfields during the Second World War, it is necessary to examine Fighter Command's night-defence of the country, the work and objectives of RAF Flying Training Command, and the operations of the USAAF's Eighth Air Force.

Fighter Command

Early in May 1940, shortly before he became Prime Minister, Winston Churchill warned the House of Commons with quite remarkable prescience, 'We must be careful not to exhaust our Air Force in view of the grave dangers which might open on us at any time.' Within months Fighter Command had reached its 'finest hour' during the Battle of Britain, when its brave pilots achieved a narrow but vital victory despite quite overwhelming odds. However, the Command's protracted battle against the night-bombing offensive has received far less publicity and recognition, and yet from the autumn of 1940 until March 1945 its pilots and night-fighter crews waged a long, gruelling and often frustrating battle against the Luftwaffe. In the early days they

Blenheim If of No 25 squadron, involved in the early trials of AI.

fought with unsuitable aircraft and rather inadequate equipment, gaining scant success despite all their valiant efforts.

At the outbreak of the war the air defence of the country was based on the concept that the bombing offensive would be conducted by day, and thus the Command was largely equipped with day-fighters – Hurricanes and Spitfires – with just a token force of night-fighters, merely six squadrons of Bristol Blenheim Ifs. This aircraft had been designed as a light bomber back in 1935 but had been superseded by the improved Mark IVs, so about 200 Blenheim Is were hastily converted to night-fighters despite the fact that they were slower than most contemporary German bombers! They had been adapted for their new role by the simple expedient of bolting a pack of four Browning machine guns onto the underside of the fuselage. However, they would in due course be equipped with the new and highly secret AI (Airborne Interception) radar sets.

In February 1936 Robert Watson-Watt of Radio Direction Finding fame (RDF was later known as Radar), came up with a proposal for airborne radar as opposed to ground installation radar. The project was given a low priority rating as the main and essential task was to establish the ground RDF system, but after satisfactory trials the AI sets were put into production and before the outbreak of the war the first Mk.1 sets were installed in Blenheims of No 25 squadron. They were quite primitive, cumbersome and prone to error and failure. Nevertheless, Airborne Interception was continuously developed and became the Command's major weapon in the night-defence of the country throughout the war. The first success came on the night of 22/23rd July

1940 when a Blenheim from the Fighter Interception Unit (FIU) claimed the first enemy aircraft to be destroyed with the assistance of Airborne Interception.

Airborne Interception worked on the principle that radio beams sent out would create an echo when they hit another aircraft. The two small radar tubes or screens in the intercepting aircraft could then compute the range and bearing once contact had been made. It had a detection scope of a maximum of some three miles and a minimum of some 600 yards, but visual contact had to be made before the pilot engaged the target as it could have been a 'friendly' aircraft. The actual practical application proved to be vastly different to the theory and the early failures of the system only proved that a much better apparatus was needed.

In June the Luftwaffe launched several night-bombing operations and the day-fighters, along with Blenheims, opposed them. The Spitfires and, to a far lesser extent, the Hurricanes were not really suited to night-fighting and their pilots had little or no experience of such operations. They were compelled to continually patrol until an enemy aircraft had been coned by searchlights, and then they could move in to engage. It was rather a hit or miss affair, and despite the thousands of searchlights in operation little success was achieved. On 18/19th June Flight Lieutenant Adolph 'Sailor' Malan, DFC, of No 74 squadron, who became one of the finest fighter pilots of the war, managed to destroy two Heinkel IIIs, although it must be admitted that double successes at night would be very rare occurrences. Another three aircraft were shot down for the loss of four RAF fighters; maybe a Pyrrhic victory but at least it demonstrated that day-fighters were capable of inflicting some damage on the Luftwaffe at night.

However, even this modest success proved to be rather illusory as the Luftwaffe soon operated at higher altitudes and used evasive tactics to reduce the effectiveness of the searchlights. Sir Hugh Dowding, the Commander-in-Chief of Fighter Command, who was a dedicated supporter of AI, fully acknowledged the problems faced by his pilots and night-fighter crews: 'our task will not be finished until we can locate, pursue and shoot down the enemy in cloud by day and night, and AI must become like a gun sight.'

From September 1940 onwards the Luftwaffe, because its day operations had proved too costly, concentrated its bomber resources into a night assault on London, provincial cities, towns and seaports. As Adolf Hitler had stated: 'When they declare that they will attack our cities, then we shall wipe out their cities.' The almost incessant nightly armada of Luftwaffe bombers stretched the Command's meagre night-force close to breaking point, and Boulton Paul Defiants were hastily brought into the night-fighting role. These unique turreted, single-engined fighters had suffered heavily in August and had been quickly withdrawn from the Battle of Britain. Nevertheless the Defiants, when provided with VHF radios and AI Mk.IV sets in 1941, proved to be a valuable addition to the country's night-defence, and during the winter of 1940/1 their crews recorded more 'kills' than any other night-fighters.

After the Battle of Britain, squadrons of Spitfires and Hurricanes became increasingly involved at night, though many pilots felt that they had been 'relegated to night-flying'! These squadrons were known as 'cat's eyes' because they did not have the advantage of AI radar. The pilots found their nightly patrols to be most frustrating, as they flew around in the darkness in the vain hope of locating the enemy bombers. They also brought about a crop of flying accidents, largely due to night-landings at ill-equipped airfields and in poor weather conditions. Squadron Leader Peter Townsend, DFC, who commanded a Hurricane squadron, No 85, that had been diverted to night-operations, thought it 'a most difficult and hazardous occupation'!

November proved to be a particularly harsh month with London and, of course, Coventry taking the brunt of the heavy night blitz. In the whole of the month only 29 enemy aircraft were shot down, with just three falling to night-fighters. In the following month 'Fighter Nights' were introduced, day-fighter squadrons making night patrols over certain areas and above an agreed altitude with instructions to shoot at any aircraft with more than one engine. These nightly operations lasted for about an hour, during which time the AA batteries were silenced. The Air Ministry freely admitted that 'they were not an ideal method of night interception ... but should be operated whenever weather conditions or visibility were good'!

In September 1940 a new night-fighter had entered the fray – the Bristol Beaufighter. This heavy, pugnacious and reliable fighter was armed with four 20 mm cannons and six .303 inch machine guns, and had first flown in July 1939. Just twelve months later the first aircraft were being tested at the FIU and they showed such promise that they were rushed into production. One pilot described the Beaufighter as 'sturdy, powerful and fearsome', and certainly the various marks of Beaufighters would operate very successfully throughout the war, mainly in the night-fighter role. They were equipped with the improved AI Mk.IV sets, in which many of the earlier problems had

An artist's impression of the new night-fighter – Bristol Beaufighter.

been resolved. Flight Lieutenant John Cunningham, DFC, of No 604 squadron claimed the first of his many victories with a Beaufighter on 19/20th November. He and his radar operator, C. F. 'Jimmy' Rawnsley, became the most successful night-fighter team of the war, Cunningham personally ending with 20 victories.

Towards the end of December a special night-fighting Operational Training Unit (No 54) was formed at Church Fenton, although at first it only produced twelve pilots a month, and No 3 Radio School at Prestwick began training specialist AI operators. Although modest, they were steps in the right direction. Also by the end of 1940 there were six Beaufighter squadrons formed, but not all fully operational because of delivery delays due to enemy action; these squadrons would not really begin to make their mark until March 1941. The total night-fighter force had only destroyed 35 enemy aircraft in the previous six months. The Luftwaffe's loss rate was well under 1%, a figure that would have delighted Bomber Command as their operational losses were running at 2%. This was despite the Luftwaffe being as equally unprepared for a night-bombing offensive, and it should be noted that as yet its night-fighter crews did not have any radar aids.

Fighter Command moved onto the offensive in December when the first night-intruder missions were mounted. These were long-range patrols over the near Continent with the intention of attacking the Luftwaffe bombers as they returned to their bases; the philosophy being that the best form of defence was attack. Blenheims and Beaufighters of No 23 introduced these operations, followed by other squadrons in 1941. The Luftwaffe also operated a night-intruder force, the Fernnachtjäger, which during the first two months of 1941 destroyed eight RAF aircraft and damaged another nine.

In January 1941 Sir Archibald Sinclair, the Secretary of State for Air, stated: 'Night-fighting is the most intense and important battle of those on which we are now engaged.' During the first months of the year six Ground Control Interception (GCI) stations had become operational, each associated with a Sector Control station. They had a range of about 50 miles and were able to plot both the enemy aircraft and the fighters, thus enabling more accurate fixes to be reported to the crews. They were also able to identify the aircraft, obviating the need for visual contact. The first combined AI/GCI success inevitably fell to John Cunningham on February 15/16th although many weeks would pass before another similar victory was recorded. The art and skill of the GCI controller was to position the fighter some six or so miles behind the enemy aircraft and on a parallel track at the same altitude. In April the first of twelve mobile GCI stations or AMES (Air Ministry Experimental Stations) became operational and soon most areas of the country would be screened by GCI.

The night-fighter forces were slowly beginning to make some inroads into the Luftwaffe. From just three victories in January and four the following month, they increased to 48 in April, a figure that was doubled the following month. Now at long last they were

Ground Control Interception Mobile Station. (via G. Evans)

destroying more enemy aircraft than the AA defences. On 10th May when London suffered a major night blitz with over 1,400 civilians killed and heavy damage sustained, the night-defences accounted for 28 enemy aircraft, of which two fell to Douglas Havocs, the new night-fighter. This American-built A20/DB – 7B had been originally designed as a light bomber but it had been adapted and renamed by the RAF to operate as a night-fighter. Subsequently, Havocs became very effective on night-intruder operations and were also used in the Turbinlite experiments during 1941/2 when they were equipped with a large airborne searchlight.

The Luftwaffe night-offensive began to lessen from May onwards because most of their bombers were withdrawn in preparation for the Russian offensive. By June only about 210 were left in Western Europe compared with over 1,400 a few months earlier. Since the autumn of 1940 the Luftwaffe had launched over 130 major bombing operations or 'mass raids' as they were termed, with a countless number of smaller raids, and most cities, towns and seaports in the country had suffered to a greater or lesser degree. Enormous and widespread damage to property had been caused and almost 42,000 civilians had lost their lives – about 60% of the total civilian fatalities in the war. Fighter Command, along with the British public, were not aware that the worst of the night blitz was over, and its night-fighter force was now stronger than ever, 18 squadrons in operation or in the process of being formed. They were mainly equipped with Defiants and Beaufighters, but three had a mixture of Hurricanes and Defiants. One of these 'hybrid' squadrons, No 151, had the most successful Hurricane night-fighter pilot of the war – Flight Lieutenant R. P. Stevens, DSO, DFC Bar – but more of him under Wittering. Besides John Cunningham, other night-fighter 'aces' were Squadron Leader John R. D. Braham, DFC Bar, who would also serve at Wittering with No 141 squadron, and Squadron Leader Roderick 'Rory' Chisholm, DFC, of No 604 squadron.

The first de Havilland Mosquito NF Mk.IIs entered the Service in January 1942 when No 157 squadron and its crews began trialling an improved AI set – Mk.V. Another squadron, No 151, at Wittering was also re-equipping with this remarkable and versatile aircraft, which proved to be probably the most outstanding night-fighter ever produced. So successful were Mosquitos in this role that by the end of 1942 there were six squadrons in operation, and they also proved to be ideally suited to both day and night-intruder operations. The night-fighter version of the aircraft was constantly developed throughout the war. The final mark – NF38 – was produced in November 1950 and they subsequently gave way to the Gloster Meteor jets.

During April to October 1942 the Luftwaffe launched a bombing offensive against cathedral cities, the so-called 'Baedeker' raids in retaliation for Bomber Command's heavy attack on Lubeck in late March. In the five months to August the night-fighters claimed over 220 enemy aircraft shot down, almost half falling to Beaufighter crews. Other provincial cities and towns were bombed during the summer, especially Birmingham which suffered three consecutive night raids at the end of the month, and 16 bombers were destroyed. The Air Ministry was now able to report: 'the night-fighters are exacting a

23

Dornier 217E-4, mainly used in the 'Baedeker' bombing offensive. (via R. Hughes)

steady and mounting toll of enemy raiders over this country ... they ensured that a heavy and sustained air offensive by the Luftwaffe against the United Kingdom was temporarily out of the question.' The Mosquitos had also proved to have a speed advantage over Focke-Wulf 190s that were being increasingly used on intruder operations and 'tip and run' raids over the coastal towns of southern and eastern England.

At the beginning of 1943 Fighter Command had 20 squadrons of night-fighters with Beaufighters still in the majority. The Luftwaffe continued to operate at night albeit in rather a spasmodic manner, in addition to making many intruder raids both by day and night. However, in the last six months of the year when almost 1,000 sorties had been launched by Fighter Command, the Luftwaffe had lost 66 aircraft mainly to Mosquito night-fighters. In November, Fighter Command was robbed of almost two-thirds of its squadrons when they were moved into the 2nd Tactical Air Force, formed to provide air to ground support for the Allied armies in the planned invasion of Europe. The name Fighter Command also disappeared and was replaced by The Air Defence of Great Britain – a name redolent of the RAF in the early 1930s.

The ADGB, under Air Marshal Roderic M. Hall, CB, MC, AFC, comprised just ten day and eleven night-fighter squadrons tasked with the air defence of the country, as well as providing defensive cover for the mass of men and equipment gathering in southern England in

Mosquito NF Mk.II of No 157 squadron: the first to be equipped with this remarkable night-fighter.

preparation for the forthcoming invasion. Nevertheless, the air defence of the country was in an excellent state. The squadrons were equipped with the latest marks of Spitfires, Beaufighters and Mosquitos were in operation, a superb ground radar screen was operational and radar-guided AA and searchlight batteries were all in place. Just how effective and destructive all these defences had become was shown in the early months of 1944.

On 21/22nd January the Luftwaffe launched its final major bombing offensive – Operation Steinbock – and for the next four months the Baby Blitz, as it became known, continued, mainly directed against London. The Luftwaffe used their new heavy bombers, the Junkers 188 and Heinkel 177, as well as employing Düppel, their anti-radar foil similar to the British Window, which did create a little confusion to the GCI system. As the bombing offensive progressed the Luftwaffe suffered increasingly heavy losses, mainly to the Mosquito squadrons, and as it drew to a conclusion at the end of May over 300 enemy aircraft had been destroyed, which amounted to about 60% of the Luftwaffe's total bomber force.

Faced with such a crushing and crippling defeat of its conventional bombers the German High Command turned to its Vergeltungswaffen or 'revenge weapons' – the V1 and V2 rockets – for a last desperate aerial bombardment of London, East Anglia, and the south-east. Other areas of the country suffered from air-launched V1s. RAF pilots managed to destroy over 1,900 V1s or 'divers' as they called them, just slightly more than the AA batteries. Nevertheless, the Luftwaffe still made minor incursions over central and eastern counties, mainly using its twin-engined Messerschmitt 410Bs – Hornisse or Hornets – which was its closest equivalent in performance to the Mosquito. This aircraft was a match for most Mosquito marks except for the NF Mk.XXX – the ultimate in wartime night-fighters. Another minor problem caused by the Me 410s was their striking resemblance to Mosquitos, which often caused errors in aircraft identification with unfortunate results.

The night-battle still continued with the Luftwaffe making intruder raids over bomber and training airfields. From March to June 1944 over 30 Allied aircraft were destroyed with another ten being damaged by enemy action. The worst day was 22nd April when 14 Eighth Air Force bombers were shot down or wrecked in crash-landings after being attacked whilst returning from a daylight bombing operation to Hamm. In October, the title Fighter Command was reinstated for the home-based fighter squadrons.

The Luftwaffe launched its final offensive in March 1945. On 3rd/4th of the month Operation Gisela, as it was code-named, was mounted and, coming at this late stage of the war, it managed to achieve an element of surprise. About 70 enemy aircraft roamed around the skies of eastern England seeking out aircraft as well as bombing and strafing airfields. Only seven enemy aircraft were destroyed by the defences, although another twelve crashed in bad visibility on return to their bases. The final enemy action over Britain came on 20th March, with the last aircraft, a Junkers 188, being shot down by a Mosquito NF Mk.XXX of No 125 squadron.

For five long years the night-fighter squadrons, from Blenheims, Hurricanes, Defiants, Beaufighters and Havocs to Mosquitos, had waged a bitter war in the night skies over Britain and they had finally achieved their hard fought victory. Nearly 3,700 airmen of Fighter Command had been killed with just over 1,200 wounded; one-fifth of these casualties came in the Battle of Britain, but exactly how many airmen lost their lives or were wounded in the night-defence of the country is not known.

Flying Training Command

In the early 1930s the Royal Air Force was often described, somewhat unjustly, as 'agreeably amateur and the best flying club in the world'. Perhaps this cosy image had been fostered to some extent by the many air pageants or air displays mounted by the Service in the inter-war years when 'pretty flying' or aerobatics seemed to be the order of the day. The opening of a number of permanent airfields to the public on Empire Air Days from 1934 only strengthened this impression. Their striking and aesthetically pleasing buildings created an ambience of a comfortable and somewhat elitist club, whose privileged members dashed about the skies in aircraft that had little changed from those of the First World War.

And yet the cream of this select flying club – the pilots – were very much in the minority. In 1935 they made up only 2% of the Service's total manpower, and even including the pilots of the Auxiliary Air Force and Reserve squadrons they still did not exceed 5%. A common fallacy was that the pilots were largely the products of public schools and the Cranwell College (the 'University of the Air'). Although many were, almost 40% were Non Commissioned Officers, a considerable number of whom had entered the Service as boy apprentices, whereas others had come into the Service via the Volunteer Reserve. These airmen radically changed the social structure of the RAF that entered upon its biggest challenge in 1940; indeed, in the Battle of Britain over 40% of 'The Few' were Sergeant pilots.

These pilots had received about 150 hours of flying training before being posted to a first line squadron to receive further in-house training. Up until 1933 they were trained on aircraft that had been in service since the First World War, mainly the stalwart Avro 504s, but these had been replaced by Avro Tutors. Navigation hardly merited a mention, though map reading did; air navigation became the art of following railway lines, known as 'Bradshawing' from the famous railway timetable. Gunnery and bombing training and practice were very minor elements of the course and, as yet, instrument flying was in its infancy. There was a heavy importance placed on tight formation flying and aerobatics. The fighter tactical lessons acquired in the bitter and costly combat flying during the First World War had been largely abandoned and had to be re-invented from harsh experience during the Battle of Britain.

The build-up of the RAF in the late 1930s resulted in an almost threefold increase by 1939. This rapid expansion did, of necessity, demand a large increase in the number of pilots as well as other aircrew categories. In those days it took almost two years to train a pilot up to full operational readiness, and with the failure or wastage rate in the region of 30%, flying training became a major priority. In late 1935 Air Commodore Tedder, who in 1944 became the Deputy Supreme

The start! A student pilot climbs into a Tiger Moth.

Commander of the Allied Expeditionary Force, was appointed to reorganise flying training, and to make full use of all available resources. The number of Service Flying Schools doubled to ten in 1937 and more would have been formed but for a dearth of flying instructors. Private flying schools were given contracts to provide basic flying training to both regular and Volunteer Reserve airmen, and by 1937 there were 13 such schools with another seven solely devoted to VR pilots. By the summer of 1940 46 Elementary & Reserve Flying Training Schools were in operation, spread almost evenly throughout the country but mostly situated close to large towns. These schools were a great success, they indirectly brought back many experienced instructors who had been trained whilst previously serving in the RAF.

With the reorganisation of the Service in 1936, a Training Command was set up with its headquarters at Market Drayton, controlling all Service training under four Groups. However, early in 1937 another new Command – Reserve – was formed and it took over the responsibility for the E&RFTSs. Despite (or maybe because?) of this large and rapid increase in flying training facilities, there were still failings in the system. Even in late 1939 some fighter pilots were arriving at operational squadrons without having ever flown a

Pupil pilots practise formation flying with their Airspeed Oxfords. (Imperial War Museum)

monoplane, and at the outset of the Battle of Britain, in the summer of 1940, many newly trained pilots had not received any instruction or practice in air gunnery. It was not until January 1939 that the Air Ministry really began to tackle the status of aircrew other than pilots. For instance it was not until December that air gunners were made full-time, given the rank of sergeant and their half-wing 'AG'.

Bomber Command was forced to borrow some navigators from Coastal Command for their first bombing operation, and because a low priority was given to navigation and night-flying during training, this serious deficiency manifested itself in Bomber Command when it was forced to change to night-bombing operations in 1940. One of the reasons given for the number of 'Nickel' (dropping propaganda leaflets) operations in 1940 was that they gave crews valuable experience of night navigation. This problem should not have come as a surprise because in the immediate pre-war years there had been no less than 450 forced landings in Great Britain at night due to the crews losing their way! The AOC of Bomber Command stated that 40% of his crews 'were unable to find a target in a friendly city in broad daylight'! Although a School of Air Navigation had been established in 1933 and expanded in early 1938, the aircrew category of Air Observer was only reintroduced in December 1937, and their first specialist schools had opened. It would be some time before a sufficient number of specially trained navigators filtered through to operational flying or as training instructors. However, fortnight-long 'crammer' courses for bomber pilots and flight commanders were held to introduce them to the skills of aerial navigation.

Until early 1940 the student pilot spent some eight weeks on ground instruction at an Initial Training Wing followed by up to ten weeks at the Elementary Flying Schools before moving on to one of the 14 Service's Flying Schools for advanced training and flying practice, which could last four months or so depending on the time of year. At the end of this stage of training the qualified pilots were now in possession of their coveted 'wings' – a badge that represented months upon months of mental and physical effort. They would then be sent to one of the Commands' Group Pools, to receive 'conversion and operational' training on the types of aircraft they would fly operationally. This final period of training could vary from four to six weeks, by which time they would have logged perhaps 160 flying hours, which had effectively taken at least twelve months or longer.

Although the period of flying training had been shortened, the flow of trained pilots was still insufficient to cope with the demands of the Service, especially for Fighter Command. The biggest problem during the Battle of Britain was not the supply of replacement aircraft but rather the number of trained pilots to fly them. The shortfall in trained aircrew was made up by the so-called amateur or weekend pilots of the Volunteer Reserve and the University Air squadrons, who made such a vital contribution to the Battle of Britain. The other 'weekend pilots' of the Auxiliary and Reserve squadrons had already been absorbed into the Service. Another welcome addition for Fighter Command was the number of already qualified pilots from the Commonwealth and enemy occupied countries that served in the Battle (about 20%). Throughout the Second World War there was always a steady influx of airmen from the Commonwealth and European countries that ensured that the RAF became a most cosmopolitan Air Force.

In April 1940 it was decided that operational training for pilots and crews would be placed on a more regular and formal basis, so the existing Bomber Command Group Pool squadrons were reorganised into Operational Training Units (OTUs). The Command had, in September 1939, allocated 14 operational squadrons out of its already slim resources to this training role. It now absorbed these squadrons into eleven OTUs under the control of No 6 Group, although it was shortly followed by another Group, No 7. In 1941 Fighter Command

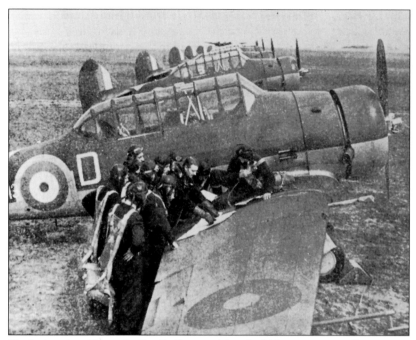

North American Harvards: Pupil pilots receiving final hints on map reading.

had four OTUs, including one devoted to night flying, with three such Units formed for the crews of Coastal Command.

The following month Training Command *per se* was officially disbanded and replaced by two separate Commands – Flying Training and Technical Training. Air Marshal Sir Arthur Longmore, who had been in charge of Training Command since July 1939, moved out to Egypt as the Commander of RAF Middle East. Sir Arthur was one of the earliest qualified pilots in the Service, having gained his licence in April 1911! He was replaced by Air Marshal L. A. Pattinson, CB, DSO, MC, DFC, who controlled six Groups, Nos 21, 23, 25, 50, 51 and 54. Each was specialised in character, responsible for a particular type of training, for instance No 21 was solely engaged in training pilots, whereas No 25 was for armament and gunnery training. There were over 80 Flying Training Schools and over 3,000 aircraft engaged in flying training, from Tiger Moths, Magisters, Oxfords, Audaxes, Ansons, Masters, and Harvards right up to current operational aircraft such as Blenheims, Whitleys, Wellingtons, Hampdens, Spitfires, Hurricanes and Defiants in the OTUs. It was reported that there were

56 different types of aircraft involved in training! Most of them bore yellow colourings on the underside of the fuselage. This colour was the International Flag Code for Quarantine – in other words a warning to other aircraft to stay away – although the aircraft in OTUs were finished in the same markings as the other aircraft in their various Commands.

In order to try to keep pace with the ever increasing requirement for pilots and aircrews the Air Ministry had been negotiating with the various Dominion countries to organise flying training courses. In May 1940 the Empire Air Training Scheme came into being, though in June 1942 the scheme was renamed the 'British Commonwealth'. The first school opened at Belvedere near Salisbury in Southern Rhodesia on 24th May, followed shortly by the first flying training schools being transferred to Canada; throughout the war more airmen received their training in Canada than any other Commonwealth country.

It was not quite such a novel expedient as it appeared because even in pre-war days No 4 Service Flying School had been based at Abu Sueir in Egypt, where it had been found that the better weather conditions and clearer skies enabled the courses to be completed on time. A wide variety of flying training schools were later established in Canada, Australia, New Zealand, South Africa, Southern Rhodesia and India, and by the end of 1942 there were over 130 such schools offering flying training for pilots from elementary through to advanced, as well as specialised instruction for the other aircrew categories. The pilots would then return to the United Kingdom for refresher and acclimatisation courses before continuing their training at OTUs and finally at Heavy Conversion Units (HCUs).

The first trained pilots under the scheme arrived back in November 1940. In the summer of 1942 basic flying training was conducted at six private flying schools under contract to the USAAF, and ultimately 14,000 RAF airmen received much of their flying training in the United States. The British Commonwealth Air Training Scheme proved to be a salvation for Flying Training Command. It greatly eased the pressure on British airfields, its crowded airspace and trained aircrew, as well as supplying a regular flow of trained pilots and aircrew – over 168,000 passed through the scheme, almost half of them pilots, and with the majority being trained in Canada.

As the three operational Commands grew at quite an alarming pace during 1941/2, there was an almost insatiable demand for pilots and aircrew, not only to man the newly formed squadrons but also to replace aircrew either killed or missing in action or those who had

'The Faithful Annie' – Avro Anson – a reliable training aircraft.

completed their operational tours. And yet despite enemy night activity over training airfields, which delayed training schedules, Flying Training Command still managed to produce over 17,000 trained aircrew during 1941. About a half of this figure were Wireless Operators/Air Gunners. Bomber Command, especially, were experiencing rather heavy losses during these years, but the training situation was slightly eased when, in March 1942, it was decided that heavy bomber crews would only contain one pilot rather than two as had previously been the practice, with flight engineers effectively becoming second pilots.

By February 1942 there were 17 OTUs operating in Bomber Command, based at 28 airfields mostly in the counties of what could be considered as middle England. The introduction of four-engined bombers into the Command had resulted in the formation of the first Conversion Flights – a further stage of training for aircrews before they were considered ready for operational flying. In the following year another five new OTUs were formed and now there were ten fully fledged HCUs under the control of the Command's three operational training Groups – Nos 91 to 93. Most OTUs were equipped with Vickers Wellingtons in a variety of marks, whereas the HCUs had Short Stirlings, Handley Page Halifaxes and Avro Lancasters. Later Lancaster Finishing Schools would be established to provide about twelve hours additional flying training on these aircraft. In the other two operational Commands there were another 23 OTUs. The flying hours for aircrews had now increased to almost 350 before an operational standard was achieved and the whole process lasted almost two years. Sir Arthur

Miles Master II Advanced Trainer.

Harris, C-in-C of Bomber Command, later maintained that 'the education of a bomber crew was the most expensive in the world; it cost some £10,000 for each man, enough to send ten men to Oxford or Cambridge for three years'!

Since 1942 the responsibility for flying training had rested with Air Marshal Sir Philip Babington, KCB, MC, AFC, and at the end of 1943, which was the wartime peak for flying training, almost 24,000 aircrew qualified in all categories. And there were over 150 flying schools and training units in the United Kingdom, without those operating in the Commonwealth countries. No type of flying training could be undertaken without accidents and since OTUs had been introduced in 1940 well over 2,000 aircraft had been lost in training accidents, and this figure does not include all the losses at the Elementary and Advanced Flying Schools, where accidents tended to be more numerous if of a less serious nature.

The manpower and resources devoted to flying training in all aircrew categories were immense. In Bomber Command alone over one-third of its operational aircraft were engaged in training and 55% of the Command's flying hours were devoted to training. Besides purely basic flying instruction and operational training there were a myriad of other specialised schools and flying training courses, such as

Beam Approach Flights, Pathfinder Flights, Glider Pilots, Flying Instructors, Air Gunners, Observers ... et al. The majority of aircrew personnel when they had completed their operational tours ended up as training instructors, either at OTUs, HCUs or other specialist training establishments such as the Central Navigation School and the Air Armament School.

By January 1945 Flying Training Command had grown to seven Groups, and there were another six Groups in the three operational Commands that were solely devoted to operational and conversion training. The RAF's commitment to flying training during the Second World War was a massive undertaking conducted on a grand scale, which produced the most highly trained pilots and aircrew of the Second World War – almost 100,000 aircrew of all categories were trained in the United Kingdom. It should also be remembered that all of the RAF aircrew personnel were volunteers, at no period of the war did the Service have to resort to conscription for flying duties. Many of the wartime airfields in Northamptonshire played their small but essential part in this great flying training enterprise. It is rather appropriate then that two memorial stones, one at Silverstone and the other at Sywell, should record this contribution for posterity.

United States Army Air Force

The first USAAF airmen appeared in Northamptonshire during May 1942 when about 500 personnel of the 15th Bomb Squadron (Light) arrived at the picturesque village of Grafton Underwood to take up residence at the nearby airfield. Their squadron would become the first flying unit of the Eighth Air Force to operate from the United Kingdom, but they proved to be merely birds of passage because within a month they had moved away to Molesworth. Nevertheless, they were the harbingers of a flood of American airmen that would ultimately take up residence at seven airfields in the county.

They were speedily replaced by the members of the 97th Bomb Group, who settled into the airfield and Polebrook to prepare the bases and to await the arrival of their charges – Boeing B-17s. On 6th July the clamorous roar of Wright Cyclone engines once again echoed around the countryside, heralding the arrival of the first B-17s of the Eighth Air Force to operate from the United Kingdom. The sight and sound of

Major General Carl Spaatz and Brigadier General Ira C. Eaker at a presentation of decorations at Polebrook, December 1942. (National Archives & Records Administration)

these large and almost elegant aircraft were not totally unfamiliar to the locals at Polebrook because twelve months earlier RAF Flying Fortresses had operated from the airfield. However, the spectacle of these powerful bombers leaving and returning to their bases would become a commonplace sight over the next three years. It was from Grafton Underwood, on 17th August, that the Eighth set out on its first heavy bombing mission of the war, although by then another Group of B-17s had taken up residence at Chelveston. These three airfields were in the vanguard of the Eighth's tentative early bombing operations.

This Air Force was a mere babe-in-arms compared with RAF Bomber Command, its cohort in the Allied bombing offensive. The Eighth had only been formed in January 1942 specifically to provide air support for an Allied invasion of North Africa, but when this operation was postponed, Major General Carl A. Spaatz, the USAAF Commander in Europe, arranged for the embryonic Force to be moved to the United Kingdom to form the nucleus of the USAAF in Europe. Brigadier General Ira C. Eaker, the Eighth's Bomber Commander and its overall

Commander from December 1942 until January 1944, arrived in
England in February with a mere handful of officers with the express
purpose of establishing the new Air Force in Britain.

These officers were faced with a herculean task. The Eighth was
scheduled to number 60 operational Groups comprising over 3,500
aircraft and all planned to be in place by April 1943 – the original target
date for the invasion of Europe. The sheer volume of logistics necessary
to assemble, accommodate, equip, train, service and operate such a
massive organisation was formidable in the extreme. And yet, by June
1944, the Eighth had developed into a powerful Air Force just short of
its original target, fully justifying its cognomen 'the Mighty' not solely
on account of its size alone but also because of the brave and valiant
deeds of its crews. Without doubt the Eighth Air Force owed a deep
debt of gratitude to General Eaker and his small band of officers for
their indefatigable efforts whilst working under severe handicaps and
their fortitude in the face of heavy setbacks.

The Eighth was utterly dedicated to a high altitude heavy bombing
offensive using its B-17s and B-24s (Liberators) solely by day. These
aircraft had been designed for this type of operation, with the
advantages of 'superior' oxygen and heating systems, and equipped
with the highly secret and 'wonder' Norden bomb-sight, which was
thought to be deadly accurate even from such high operational
altitudes (20,000 feet and above). Furthermore the USAAF had
complete confidence in the self-defensive capabilities of their large
and tight heavy bomber formations, although the evidence of three
years of operational experience by the RAF would suggest that this
type of operation was a little unwise. However, the Eighth Air Force
was determined to prove that daylight precision bombing could be
undertaken successfully. In August a Joint Allied Directive was issued
stating that in the first phase of the Eighth's operations 'American day
bomber forces under British fighter protection reinforced by American
fighter forces ... will attack suitable objectives within the radius of
British fighter cover.' In the coming twelve months the Eighth's total
commitment to daylight bombing would be severely tested, almost to
breaking point.

The USAAF entered the European air war on 29th June when one
crew of No 15 Bomb Squadron in a borrowed RAF aircraft flew in an
RAF operation from Swanton Morley. Five days later (appropriately
Independence Day) six American crews operated with six RAF crews
on a low level mission over Holland. Sadly two of the American crews
failed to return, the first American airmen to be lost in action in the

Tremblin' Gremlin *of 384th Bomb Group following two 303rd B-17s through flak. This B-17 was lost over Hamm in September 1944. (Imperial War Museum)*

European Theater of Operations (ETO).

The Eighth's first daylight, high level heavy bombing mission was mounted on 17th August by twelve B-17s of 97th Bomb Group from Grafton Underwood. It was led by Colonel Frank Armstrong, the Group's Commanding Officer, and General Eaker also took part flying in a B-17 named, appropriately, *Yankee Doodle*. The B-17s were escorted by RAF Spitfires, and all arrived back safely. Air Chief Marshal Harris, the C-in-C of Bomber Command, who had struck up a good working and personal relationship with Eaker, sent him a congratulatory message, '*Yankee Doodle* certainly went to town and you can stick another well-earned feather in his cap'! The first two Fighter Groups of the Eighth, Nos 31 and 52, saw action the following day. Both were equipped with Spitfires, and the 31st Group lost eight aircraft operating over Dieppe. It was not until 6th September when 75 B-17s (there were now three operational Bomb Groups) attacked an aircraft factory at Meaulte in France that the Eighth lost their first heavy bombers in action.

On 9th October the Eighth was able to send out over 100 heavy bombers on a mission for the first time because of the introduction of B-

24s into the Force; four aircraft were lost and another two were so badly damaged that they were written-off. The bomber formations had been strongly opposed by enemy fighters and the gunners returned with claims of 25 fighters shot down. This was an early example of the overly high claims made by the Eighth's gunners (and fighter pilots) throughout the war, although all claims were rigorously examined by intelligence officers. It is now thought that only eight enemy aircraft were destroyed on the day. Nevertheless, the Eighth's bombers had shown that they could at least defend themselves without suffering too heavily, thus raising hopes that would unfortunately be cruelly dashed in 1943.

It would be the spring of 1943 before the Eighth Bomber Command would be in a position to send out another hundred heavy bombers. In November the Eighth lost two experienced Bomb Groups and four Fighter Groups to the Twelfth Air Force then engaged in Operation Torch – the invasion of North Africa. General Eaker was, once again, faced with the slow and patient task of rebuilding what he now called 'his piddling little Force'! By 27th January 1943 he felt confident enough to authorise the Eighth's first attack on German targets – Vegesack and Wilhelmshaven. On this operation the crews encountered the most severe fighter opposition so far and although 'only' three aircraft were lost, it did not augur well for their future operations over Germany.

The Eighth had found that the European winter conditions had greatly hampered their operations, and their bomber formations were not quite as secure and self defensive as had originally been thought. During the next few months it became increasingly clear that without an adequate fighter escort, their losses would mount, especially over German targets. The only Fighter Group operating in early 1943 was the 4th, which had been formed out of the three RAF Eagle squadrons, and its pilots were still flying their RAF Spitfires. The P-38s (Lightnings), then the best long-range fighters, had been diverted to the North African campaign, and would not rejoin the Eighth until the late autumn. Their replacements were P-47s (Thunderbolts), which although strong and very destructive fighters, did not, originally, have the necessary range to operate beyond the German frontier.

In May the Eighth Air Force's light/medium bombers, B-26 (Marauders), entered operations for the first time and not too successfully. General Eaker was never convinced that they were an integral part of the Eighth's Bomber Command, and he used them in a support role until they could be transferred to the Ninth Air Force later in the year. The B-26s actually developed into one of the most successful strike forces with the lowest operational losses in the USAAF overall.

Throughout the early summer the Eighth continued to wage their daylight bombing campaign with great courage and determination despite sustaining heavy losses on some operations. On 17th April whilst attacking the Focke-Wulf factory at Bremen 16 bombers were lost (14%), the heaviest operational loss so far. By the middle of June the Eighth was attacking a variety of targets according to the Pointblank directive. This was a combined Allied bombing policy, which had been agreed in the Casablanca Conference back in January. The primary targets were listed in order of priority as U-boat yards and bases, the German aircraft industry, ball bearing plants and oil refineries. The intermediate objectives were the Luftwaffe fighter strength, followed by synthetic rubber plants and military transport factories. Although the priority given to these targets would change during the long bombing offensive, they nevertheless remained the main targets for both the Eighth and Bomber Command for the rest of the war.

During the last week of July the Eighth and Bomber Command joined forces for the first time in a combined bombing campaign directed against Hamburg. The Eighth attacked the city on two successive days after the first RAF night operation. It was not a great success because the dense smoke from the fires started by the RAF's night-bombing caused the American crews considerable difficulties, and in future the Eighth were loath to follow immediately on RAF night raids because of this problem. The six daylight raids conducted by the Eighth became known as 'Blitz Week' and it was their most sustained bombing offensive so far. Over 1,700 sorties were flown for the loss of 88 bombers (5.1%) – the Eighth Air Force can certainly be said to have now come of age.

The growing strength and power of the Eighth Air Force had forced the German High Command to vastly increase its day-fighter forces. Units were brought back from other war fronts and by August the Luftwaffe's day-fighter strength had doubled to over 600 and in the autumn would become even more powerful. Also their pilots had, from harsh battle experience, developed very effective tactics to counter the concentrated fire-power of the American bomber formations. Thus the scene was set for a long and major air-battle of attrition between the Luftwaffe and the Eighth's gunners and fighter pilots, which continued almost unabated until the final months of the war.

On the anniversary of the Eighth's first heavy bombing operation –

17th August 1943 – it received a crushing blow when the joint attack on Regensburg and Schweinfurt resulted in 60 heavy bombers being lost (15.9%), three times the tolerable loss rate. And matters would not improve as more heavy losses were just over the horizon. In one disastrous week in October almost 150 bombers were lost in action, including another 60 when the Eighth returned to Schweinfurt. Such horrendous losses were difficult to bear and they cast very serious doubts on the whole concept of daylight bombing. Back in July tentative plans had been made to convert six B-17 Groups to night operations, but eventually only one squadron co-operated in some of the RAF's night operations. Eaker and his commanders held their nerve, and continued with daylight bombing. General Curtis LeMay, the Commander of the 4th Bomb Wing, put it succinctly, 'The more Fortresses we have the shorter the war is going to be and the more fighters we have to protect the Forts, the smaller the losses will be.'

Some comfort was near at hand, as within four days of the Schweinfurt disaster P-38s again became available for escort duties. Then in early December the first P-51s (Mustangs) appeared, although at first in a ground attack role with the Ninth Air Force, which had arrived in England in October 1943. This aircraft soon demonstrated its true metier – as a superb long-range pursuit fighter. When a sufficient number of P-51s became operational they turned the scales in favour of the Eighth and in the process it became one of the classic fighters of the Second World War.

The onset of the Eighth's second winter in Europe brought only further strains on the crews. All had to get used to the cold and damp weather conditions of eastern England. Ground crews found the routine of servicing, bombing and arming the aircraft a thankless task. Flying at high altitudes even during the summer months was no mean feat but northern European winters made operational life much more uncomfortable, and placed quite intolerable physical strains on the aircrews. Sweat bands froze, icicles formed inside oxygen masks, and frost-bite was quite common. Winter conditions, such as ice, snow and freezing fog, only produced additional hazards both in the air and on the ground, and the incidence of accidents greatly increased during the winter months.

Early in January 1944 Eaker was replaced as Commander of the Eighth by Lieutenant General James H. Doolittle, who remained in charge until the end of the war. Not only was Doolittle an excellent pilot but he also proved to be a very fine tactician and resolute leader. Until then perhaps his greatest claim to fame was that he had led the

All three American fighters of the Second World War can be seen in this photograph. P-51 Gentle Annie was the personal aircraft of Lt. Col. Harold Rau, CO of 20th Fighter Group. (Smithsonian Institution)

first American bombing mission to Tokyo. Within days of his arrival the Eighth suffered heavily whilst attacking German aircraft industry targets; for the third time in its short existence it had lost 60 aircraft on a single mission.

Since the previous November a combined Allied bombing offensive against the German aircraft industry had been planned under the codename Argument, which finally took place in the third week of February. It proved to be a costly offensive for both Air Forces with almost 300 Allied bombers lost, more than half of them American. Although expensive in terms of aircraft and airmen, the Eighth could now well sustain such heavy losses as replacement crews and aircraft were arriving almost daily from the States. The American war machine had gained momentum and was now in full swing.

As the RAF's long and bitter Berlin offensive was drawing to a close, the Eighth Air Force attacked the German capital for the first time in early March, and in the four operations mounted in the month its crews discovered, like their RAF counterparts, that it could be a most fearsome target. In Bomber Command's winter campaign against Berlin, over 620 bombers were lost with over 3,300 airmen killed. In the total of the Eighth's operations to the German capital some 350 bombers went missing, but with higher crew fatalities than those suffered by Bomber Command in 1943/4 because of the larger crew complements on B-17s and B-24s.

The Eighth Air Force took its share of the bombardment of V1 rocket sites under Operation Crossbow – a combined Allied air offensive. It had also been allocated 24 of the 80 specific targets detailed in the Allied Transportation Plan, which was a concentrated bombing campaign of road/rail installations, bridges, marshalling yards, airfields and strong points, mainly situated in central and northern France and Belgium, as an essential prelude to the forthcoming invasion. The Transportation Plan had caused a certain friction between Winston Churchill and President Roosevelt, who had expressed deep concern about the possibility of heavy civilian casualties. Churchill reassured the President that 'all possible care will be taken to minimise this slaughter of friendly civilian life.' The Eighth's heaviest raids came in May over Saarbrucken, Brussels and Troyes.

Also in May, the Eighth's bomber crews began their long and most determined assault on the German oil industry, which would ultimately have a critical influence on the demise of the Luftwaffe as a fighting force. For the next seven months oil targets figured large in the Eighth's operational schedules. This offensive proved to be very costly as no single priority target caused the loss of so many American airmen. The Merseburg refinery at Leuna near Leipzig was the largest synthetic oil plant in Germany, and it was attacked 18 times in 1944 by the Eighth for the loss of over 100 crews

The final months of 1944 saw the Eighth's huge fighter force, now with P-51s in the preponderance, engaged in a desperate battle with the Luftwaffe not only in the skies but also on the ground as the fighter pilots became most expert in ground-strafing. The appearance of the Luftwaffe's rocket-propelled Me 163s and later the turbo-jet Me 262 jet fighters ensured that the Eighth's final victory in the air was delayed until April 1945. The Eighth Air Force continued their bombing operations on a colossal scale, their largest air strike of the war coming on Christmas Eve when over 2,000 bombers attacked airfields and rail and road communications in western Germany in support of the American ground forces battling in the Ardennes. Also on the day, 850 fighters acted as escorts, and this massive phalanx was achieved despite two Fighter Groups being fogged in at their bases!

The Eighth's final bombing mission of the war took place on 25th April when almost 1,200 bombers and fighters were in action over targets in Czechoslovakia and south-east Germany and seven aircraft failed to return. In less than three years the Eighth Air Force had mounted over 950 missions, in addition to hundreds of other smaller operations – photo-reconnaissance, weather scouting, air-sea rescue and dropping supplies and agents over enemy occupied territories. From mid-1945 onwards there was a massive exodus of aircraft and

The final resting place of so many B-17s and B-24s. (San Diego Aerospace Museum)

Brookwood Cemetery where many of the Eighth's personnel killed during the first year were buried. (Smithsonian Institution)

airmen back to the States. Over 2,000 bombers were ferried back. They normally carried ten passengers in addition to the crews, and most were routed through RAF Valley in Anglesey. Ultimately hundreds upon hundreds of these bombers ended up in the deserts of the southern States.

The Eighth Air Force had fought a bitter and costly air offensive, with over 43,000 airmen killed or missing in action. The sacrifice of these gallant American airmen has certainly not been forgotten. The American Military Cemetery and Memorial at Madingley near Cambridge, which was opened in 1948, is a splendid memorial to these men; although most of the Eighth's personnel killed in Britain were originally buried in the cemetery at Brookwood in Surrey. The American Memorial Chapel in St Paul's Cathedral contains a Roll of Honour and there is a Book of Remembrance in St Clements Dane, the central church of the RAF, listing the names of American airmen lost whilst serving in the United Kingdom during the Second World War. At the American Air Museum at Duxford there is a most impressive memorial sculpture, 'Counting the Cost', which records on glass panels

45

the losses of all Groups of the Eighth and Ninth Air Forces. Nearer to hand, each American airfield in Northamptonshire has its own special memorial dedicated to all the airmen who served at the base, and there are memorial windows in the churches at Grafton Underwood and Weldon to commemorate the two Bomb Groups that served from the nearby airfields.

The Airfields

In 1925 there were only 27 RAF aerodromes in the United Kingdom, but by the outbreak of the war the number had risen to 116. If this increase seems to be large it was minor when compared with the number of Service airfields just five years later – over 660! A situation that fully justified the description of Britain as 'a vast aircraft carrier anchored off the north-west coast of Europe'! Northamptonshire made a modest contribution to this massive expansion by increasing its number of airfields from just three in 1939 to 18 by 1944, a total that would have been slightly greater had the proposed airfield sites at Culworth, Finedon and Yardley Gobion been further developed.

The two permanent pre-war stations at Wittering and Peterborough were built to quite a high standard, at least when compared with the airfields constructed in great haste during the early war years. Most of the buildings were of brick construction and provided with central heating, although at Peterborough the airmen's accommodation was rather more functional and spartan – wooden huts! Many of the administration blocks and mess halls were built on neo-Georgian lines and were pleasing on the eye, especially for military buildings. They have become a lasting testimony to Sir Edwin Lutyens, who had been involved in their design working under commission for the Air Ministry Aerodromes Board. The officers, especially, were provided with a fair degree of luxury and many of their elegant messes have survived to the present day. The airmen's accommodation tended to be more functional but by the standards of the day it afforded no small comfort, and even the guardhouses betrayed some architectural merit. These stations were all provided with ample sporting facilities, and the roads within the confines of the station were invariably tarmacked or concreted, thus avoiding the constant bane and irritation of wartime-built airfields – mud, mud and more mud! Those American airmen who were fortunate enough to be stationed at such permanent RAF airfields, were known as 'the country-club set' by their colleagues who were based at other very basic wartime airfields.

Pre-war permanent stations were normally sited well away from large towns for obvious safety reasons, and they became virtually self-contained and independent communities. As far as was possible this policy was continued during the wartime construction programme, hence one of the reasons why so many wartime airfields were situated in rather secluded and remote places. Nevertheless, all these airfields did have a most decided impact on the surrounding countryside and the local communities. Not only did they offer opportunities of a variety of work for the local civilian population, but their very presence left indelible and lasting marks on the landscape. The sheer bulk and size of the large hangars, the high and gaunt water towers, allied to all the flying activity ensured that the locality would never be the same again. The traffic and bustle of an airfield that could accommodate up to 3,000 airmen meant that the peace and tranquillity of the countryside was shattered for the foreseeable future.

The method of selection of airfield sites was begun by a close examination of the one inch Ordnance Survey maps to identify areas of sufficient flat land that was relatively free of obstructions. The terrain, if possible, should be close to sea level or at least not above 600 feet because of the greater incidence of hill fog and low cloud. The distance from existing or planned airfields was also considered, and although three miles was recommended, five miles was more normally used as a rule of thumb. Indeed, an airfield site had been planned for Culworth, but because it was 'midway between Chipping Warden and Silverstone, it is recommended that it be resited farther to the north.' Once a promising site had been identified, it was then inspected field by field with consideration given to the flight paths and any obstructions, either natural or man-made, as well as the nature of the subsoil. If the site still seemed suitable, steps were taken to requisition the land and the planning stage was set in motion. The most frequent objections to airfield sites came from the Ministry of Agriculture and Fisheries on account of the loss of valuable farming land, but invariably the Air Ministry prevailed. However, in the case of a proposed airfield site at Finedon, the War Department refused to give up land which was used as a tank training area, and the site was not developed.

Most of the pre-war airfields were grass surfaced and they normally offered four grass strips, the main one some 1,300 yards long and maybe 400 yards wide, with the other three measuring 1,000 yards and

Laying concrete runways. (John Laing plc)

possibly half as wide as the main strip. It is rather strange to recall that concrete runways, which are now considered a major feature of wartime airfields, were relatively late onto the scene. Even in 1937 it was recognised that the new generation of aircraft that were beginning to enter the expanded Service would require hard runways. In that year the new Commander-in-Chief of Bomber Command, Air Chief Marshal Sir Edgar Ludlow-Hewitt, had voiced the opinion that his Force 'would only be able to operate in dry weather'! The main objection to hard runways was on the grounds of cost, but it was also thought that they would create camouflage problems and furthermore it was considered that they 'did not possess the natural braking powers of grass.'

In May 1939 it was decided that all future bomber airfields should be provided with 'firm' runways 800 yards by 50 yards, which would be connected by a perimeter track some 50 feet wide. This road invariably followed the boundary of the airfield, at least as far as the contours of the land would permit. Originally most of these runways were constructed of tarmacadam, hence 'Tarmac' came into general use to describe the aprons in front of hangars and sometimes the runways. It had already been conceded that eight priority fighter airfields would also be provided with runways, though the work had been completed at only two airfields by the outbreak of the war. By December 1940 it was planned that all new bomber airfields would have three concrete runways, with the main one of a length of 1,400 yards and two at 1,100 yards and placed as near 60° to each other as possible. During the next twelve months the ideal runway dimensions had increased to 2,000 yards for the main one with two subsidiaries each 1,400 yards long and they were invariably laid down in the shape of a letter A. These sizes effectively became the template for what became known as Class A standard airfields, and most of the ten wartime airfields in the county were either built to this specification or later lengthened to conform with the standard. Wherever possible the main runway was aligned in a north-east, south-west direction.

From February 1939 it had been official policy to disperse aircraft around the perimeter of the airfield and from this ruling so developed the provision of concrete dispersal points or hard standings. Either in 'spectacle' or 'loop' shapes, these became familiar and recognizable features of all wartime airfields. By 1942 Bomber Command had decreed that 50 hard standings should be the standard number, but many of the airfields occupied by the US Eighth Air Force had an extra number added due to the larger complement of aircraft in their Bomb Groups. This wartime concrete, although often laid in a great hurry, has seemed more impervious to the passage and ravages of time and strips of runways, perimeter roads and hard standings can be still be discovered throughout the countryside.

The hangars at the wartime airfields were perhaps the most prominent features. In the early flying days they were known as sheds; the word 'hangar' came from the French and it was originally

Chelveston's 'J'-type hangar still survives.

49

used to describe a covered space for a carriage. Some of the wartime airfields were provided with at least one of either the 'J' or 'K' type hangars, which had been introduced in 1939. They were made predominantly of metal and brick with a curved roof of steel plate and measured some 300 feet long with a span of half that distance, and had a maximum door height of 30 feet. A well-preserved 'J' type hangar can be seen in a field near Chelveston. But perhaps the most ubiquitous hangars were the 'T' types, which stood for Transportable and they were manufactured by Tees-Side Bridge and Engineering Works. These hangars were of an all metal construction and were quick to erect; their lengths could vary, though 240 feet seemed to be the normal supplied. They had an opening span of 90 feet with a door height of 25 feet, and they were often placed at opposite sides of the airfield. Also the rather basic 'Over Blister' hangars were frequently provided for smaller airfields; they were of a simple curved-steel sheet construction and were normally placed around the perimeters of the airfields.

One of the most important buildings on an airfield was the watch office or control tower; the latter name, which came into general use during the war, was of American origin. They were often sited on the inner side of the perimeter track or road. The control tower housed the

The control tower at Silverstone, November 1997. (BRDC/James Beckett)

flying control and weather offices and was packed with radio, radar and teleprinting equipment. By 1942 it had become of a standard design – a very functional two-storied brick building rendered with concrete and provided with a railed balcony on the first floor as well as railings on the roof. On the departure of an operation the building became the hub of the airfield and some hours later the railed balcony would be thronged with officers anxiously waiting for the returning aircraft. Not many of the wartime control towers have survived throughout the country, although some have been used for aviation museums with the odd one being converted for residential use. Two derelict control towers at Hinton-in-the-Hedges and Deenethorpe managed to survive 50 years or so but unfortunately they have now been demolished. However, the control tower at Silverstone is still standing despite the development of the famous race circuit.

Close to the control tower would be the airfield's unique wartime identification code – two large white letters. These codes really originated from the pre-war flying days when the name of each airfield was displayed in letters that could be seen from at least 2,000 feet. For obvious security reasons this system was changed at the outbreak of the war and the two letter code was introduced. Most of the codes bore some relation to the name of the airfield, for instance 'GU' for Grafton Underwood and 'WI' for Wittering but some airfields, because their obvious letters were already in use, were allocated other codes that had no apparent relation to their names, such as 'AW' for Croughton. For night identification purposes a mobile beacon unit known as a 'pundit' was used to flash in red the identity letters in morse code, thus they became more generally known as the 'pundit code'. With so many airfields clustered together in central and eastern England, the pundit codes became an essential and speedy means of identification. Indeed, trainee pilots were given a number of pundit codes to identity the airfields from the air as a night-flying exercise.

The airfield itself comprised a myriad of administrative and technical buildings from the armoury through to the vehicle repair shops. Most of these buildings would be constructed of precast concrete slabs – 'Orlit' or 'Maycrete' huts seemed to be the more prevalent – and others were built of timber and plasterboard. The operations room was usually set aside from the main site, and constructed of concrete with no windows in order to offer the maximum protection from bomb damage. The bomb stores, a series of narrow roadways protected by earth bankings, were positioned, if possible, in a wooded area well away from the main buildings and usually on the opposite side of the

Polebrook Airfield in late 1944. (Smithsonian Institution)

airfield. Two large and partially underground aviation fuel tanks, each containing 72,000 gallons, were placed close to the perimeter road. Some of the multiplicity of airfield buildings have managed to survive the ravages of time and are still in use for a variety of purposes, most notably at Chelveston, Chipping Warden, Desborough and Silverstone.

Behind the main airfield buildings and dispersed some distance away in the surrounding countryside were the accommodation huts, mess halls, communal sites, and sick quarters in separate sites about six to twelve in number. It was here that the omnipresent Nissen huts in spans of 16, 24 and 30 feet could be found. These famous or infamous curved sheet constructions perhaps more than any other single feature epitomise these wartime airfields, and are often fondly remembered by wartime airmen despite their reputation for being bitterly cold in the winter and oppressively hot in the summer – perhaps the distance of time has lent enchantment to the memory! They originated from the First World War and had been first designed by Colonel P. Nissen, who received the DSO for his invention. Although Colonel Nissen died in 1930, his huts were still being used by the military in the Falklands conflict. The American airmen especially seemed to find them less than comfortable, they knew them as 'Quonsets', from Quonset Point,

Rhode Island, where they were first built. Their distance away from the main airfield sites often made a bicycle an essential and treasured necessity. Though many airmen recalled that during the winter, the presence of thick mud meant that they spent more time carrying their bikes than riding them!

Most of the Northamptonshire wartime airfields conformed to this general pattern, even Harrington, which was the only airfield in the county to be built by US Army Aviation Engineers. Some now famous household names were involved in the massive airfield construction programme. John Laing and Son Ltd, Taylor Woodrow Ltd, George Wimpey & Co Ltd, John Mowlem, W. & C. French Ltd and Tarmac Ltd were all engaged in the construction of some of the county's airfields, helped, of course, by hundreds of large and small sub-contractors. In 1942, which was the peak of airfield construction, no less than 125 new airfields were opened and the total cost in that year alone was £145 million, with a labour force of some 130,000 involved in this quite staggering building project. It was estimated that £600 million was spent on airfield construction and improvements during the five years of war; each standard wartime airfield cost on average £1 million. It was also estimated that over 160 million square yards of concrete was laid, said to be 'sufficient to complete a 9,000 mile road 30 feet wide from London to Peking'!

Besides the 18 airfields, Northamptonshire also had four practice bombing ranges that were used by the various OTUs operating in and around the county. For quite obvious safety reasons these ranges were sited in fairly secluded and isolated parts of the countryside, and required little more than the provision of a large white target circle at each range and maybe one or two tall brick-built quadrant towers overlooking the target area. It was in these towers that an observer would stand to take bearings on each practice flash bomb burst, fix the position and radio back the result to the aircraft's crew. There were bombing ranges at Bearshanks Wood near Brigstock, Pilton, Shutlanger and Preston Capes, and it is at the latter range that a solitary quadrant tower has survived. It now looks rather gaunt and forlorn overlooking the surrounding farmland.

Wittering and Sywell are still prospering in their separate ways, but many of the other airfields have long since returned to farming or disappeared under industrial or housing development, with the old airfield site at Silverstone perhaps gaining the most post-war fame – as an international motor racing circuit. Hinton-in-the-Hedges and Deenethorpe are still used for private and club flying and Husbands

The quadrant tower at Preston Capes, that now looks rather gaunt and forlorn.

Bosworth is a most active gliding centre. Croughton, which remained a grassed airfield throughout the war, is now in the hands of the USAF.

2
CHELVESTON

Although it falls to Chelveston to start the story of Northamptonshire's wartime airfields, it barely scrapes into the county because it was situated right alongside the boundary with Bedfordshire. The airfield was built by Taylor Woodrow Ltd during 1940/1, opening in August 1941, and for almost twelve months it provided a temporary residence for a variety of flying units, both RAF and USAAF.

Chelveston was originally allocated to No 2 Group of Bomber Command under the control of RAF Polebrook, but within weeks it became an independent station within No 8 Group, which had just been re-formed to control light bomber units. In fact the Group did not become operational and was disbanded in January 1942, although about twelve months later it would be reactivated to control the famous Pathfinder Force. Nevertheless, it was decided to extend the airfield's three existing concrete runways to bring them up to Class A standard. Early in November the construction work was put in hand, and in the following May the improved airfield was allocated to the USAAF.

Whilst the building work was still progressing, the RAF's Central Gunnery School arrived from Northern Ireland in December to mark time until its permanent base at Sutton Bridge in Lincolnshire became available. The CGS, as it was known, was responsible for the training of gunnery leaders for Bomber Command, although it subsequently devolved into two Wings – Bomber and Fighter – and was later commanded by Wing Commander A. G. 'Sailor' Malan, DSO Bar, DFC Bar, of Battle of Britain fame. The School left Chelveston for its new station on 31st March 1942.

For a month or so the airfield was devoid of aircraft but with airfield space at such a premium it was destined not to stand empty and idle for very long. On 5th May 'A' Flight of the Airborne Forces

Experimental Establishment arrived from Ringway near Manchester, to continue its trials on the capabilities of Stirling and Halifax bombers to tow gliders. The concept of landing airborne troops by gliders was in its infancy with only a small cadre of glider pilots; the Glider Pilot Regiment had only been established in February, so it was truly 'experimental' work that was conducted at Chelveston during the summer of 1942. The three British gliders of the war – Hotspur, Horsa and Hamilcar – could be seen around the airfield. The latter glider had been designed and built by General Aircraft, and had flown for the first time on 27th March – a genuinely 'rara avis' at this time. Ultimately over 400 were produced, and the Hamilcar proved to be the largest Allied glider of the war, the only one capable of transporting a light tank (about seven tons in weight).

Early in July, whilst the Flight was still in residence, the first USAAF aircraft landed at Chelveston – Douglas C-47s (Skytrains, or better known as Dakotas). They became the best known transport aircraft of all time, and more information on them will be noted in the chapter on Spanhoe. The C-47s belonged to the 60th Troop Carrier Group and their ultimate destination was a new airfield at Aldermaston in Berkshire. On 7th August over 50 aircraft moved off to their new base, but this also was a transitory home because in November they left with airborne troops for North Africa, where the Group would serve with the Twelfth Air Force.

Two days later the first B-17Fs of 301st Bomb Group (Heavy) began to land at Chelveston, ending a long transatlantic flight via Greenland, Iceland and Prestwick in Scotland. B-17s would become the hallmark of the Eighth Air Force's Bomber Command throughout its time in the United Kingdom, and they would eventually be operated by 26 Groups providing a massive concourse of power and destruction. The aircraft had first flown in July 1935 as Model 299, Boeing's response to the US Army Air Corps' requirement for a high altitude and heavily armed bomber, and the first YB-17s – as they were known – entered the Service two years later.

The all-metal, sleek four-engined monoplane was a revolution in aircraft design. It was a large and heavy aircraft, almost 75 feet in length with a wing span close to 104 feet and weighing 20 tons. With an operational speed of almost 200 mph carrying a bomb load of 4,000 pounds, the early B-17s were certainly far in advance of other contemporary bombers. But it was the bristling array of armament – eleven or twelve .50 inch machine guns in the model Fs – that captured the press and the public's imagination and it was soon dubbed 'The

Flying Fortress', a name which stuck throughout its operational life. In combat it proved most durable, able to sustain considerable damage and still survive. The aircraft was universally admired by its crews, who had an unbounding faith that their 'ship' would bring them back home. General Eaker considered it 'the best combat airplane ever built', though I am sure that Air Chief Marshal Harris and all his Lancaster crews would have other thoughts on that subject!

The B-17Fs were first produced in April 1942 and although outwardly the same as the earlier 'E' models they had over 400 design modifications, and were the first to be provided with extra fuel cells in their wings. These were known as 'Tokyo Tanks' in the erroneous belief that the aircraft could bomb Tokyo from mainland America. The tanks greatly increased the aircraft's range, enabling it to reach targets the length and breadth of Germany. Some 3,400 B-17Fs were produced and they equipped most of the Eighth's Groups until late 1943.

Each Group comprised four squadrons giving a total aircraft complement of 36 with some spares in reserve, a figure that would later greatly increase as the monthly production of B-17s at the factories of Boeing, Douglas and Lockheed-Vega accelerated from a 'mere' 120 in August 1942 to almost 600 in March 1944. In the Eighth's early operations it was not necessarily the number of serviceable aircraft on hand that dictated how many would be despatched on a mission but rather the number of combat crews available to man them. Like all of the Eighth's Groups in the county the 301st was placed in the 1st Bomb Wing, which was upgraded to the 1st Division in September 1943.

By September 1942 the American airmen were in sole occupation of the airfield, 'A' Flight having returned to Ringway. The Group's Commanding Officer, Colonel Ronald R. Walker, considered that twelve crews were now ready for their first operation – to the Sotteville railway yards at Rouen on the 5th of the month. They joined 25 crews of 97th Group from Grafton Underwood, and all the aircraft returned safely. After just two more missions the 301st was transferred to the Twelfth Air Force although it continued to operate under the Eighth until early November.

It was on its fourth mission that the first aircraft was lost to enemy action. Whilst returning from the Fives locomotive works at Lille, a damaged aircraft was forced to ditch in the English Channel about a mile off North Foreland. All of the crew escaped from the aircraft before it sank – it was thought that a B-17 would float for about $1\frac{1}{2}$ minutes. On this occasion all ten airmen were picked up, which was the first successful air/sea rescue of an Eighth bomber crew. During the

HM King George VI visits Chelveston, November 1942. (Smithsonian Institution)

war 450 of the Eighth's bombers ditched and over 1,500 airmen were rescued, or a survival rate of about 35%, although in the early days the numbers of airmen rescued were considerably fewer.

The 301st returned to Lille on 8th November for its eighth and final operation with the Eighth. Five days later HM King George VI paid a visit to Chelveston to inspect the Group before its departure to North Africa on the 24th of the month, although the ground personnel did not leave until early December. They were quickly replaced by one of the most famous Bomb Groups in the Eighth, 305th, which adopted and richly deserved the sobriquet 'Can Do'. It had been occupying Grafton Underwood since mid-September and had already been blooded in battle. The 305th, along with three other Groups, became known as 'The Pioneers', as it was their crews that led the way and suffered during the difficult early months of the Eighth's bombing offensive. They also initiated and developed combat formations and bombing techniques that would later become standard operational procedures in the Eighth.

The Group was led by Colonel Curtis E. LeMay, a tough, brusque but most determined Commander who was known as 'Old Ironpants' or 'Hard Ass'! He proved to be an astute tactician, and the many innovations developed by the Group over the coming months were instigated by him; under his strong and positive leadership the 305th developed into a very effective fighting unit. During the winter of

1942/3 the U-boat pens along the French Atlantic coast became the first priority for the Eighth as the Battle of the Atlantic reached a critical stage. On the last mission of 1942, the Group lost its second aircraft in action over Lorient, and another two went missing in the four missions in January – to St Nazaire, Lille, Brest, and Wilhelmshaven.

In February No 102 Provisional Combat Bomb Wing was established, comprising 305th and 306th Groups, with its headquarters at Chelveston; LeMay was appointed to command the Wing. The month's operations were again frustrated by bad weather with only five being flown, but the Luftwaffe was now beginning to take the Eighth's daylight offensive more seriously, and for the first time the bombers were opposed by twin-engined fighters (Me 110s and Ju 88s). It proved a more costly affair with seven aircraft lost in the month, three over Wilhelmshaven on the 26th. Major J. J. Preston, who led the Group on this mission, considered that they had encountered the strongest fighter opposition so far. It was estimated that about 70 enemy fighters were in action and they pressed their attacks with some determination, claiming six bombers in total.

On 4th April the Eighth attacked the Renault motor works at Billancourt near Paris. About 75 FW 190s opposed the formations over the target area, making numerous and sustained head-on frontal attacks in force rather than singly. It was the first time that the Luftwaffe had employed this tactic. They also sought out the most unprotected squadron in a combat wing for special attention; in this instance the Group's 364th squadron was exposed and flying in the vulnerable low wing position and half of its six B-17s were shot down. One, *Dry Martini IV*, fought back with great determination and its gunners claimed ten fighters destroyed, which was then an Eighth record for a single bomber. Despite the severe fighter opposition and heavy flak, over 250 tons of bombs were accurately dropped and extensive damage was inflicted on the works with a considerable loss of production. It was probably the Eighth's best bombing performance to date and the Group was awarded a Distinguished Unit Citation for their part in this successful mission. The USAAF reserved this highly-prized commendation for a Group's meritorious achievement on a single mission or a succession of operations. Only 27 were awarded by the Eighth throughout the war, so they were greatly prized and were formally presented to the Group with full and due ceremony.

During May the 305th suffered the loss of 13 aircraft, all but one going down in four missions to U-boat yards at Kiel, Lorient and St Nazaire. With such steadily increasing operational losses, a crew's

Hell's Angels *of 305th Bomb Group over Huls, June 1943. (Imperial War Museum)*

chances of surviving an operational tour of 25 missions, maybe seven months or more of combat flying, were in theory very slim indeed. Yet about a quarter of the crews did manage to survive and 'go back States-side', though few returned for a second European tour; like their RAF counterparts they ended up on training duties. In May Colonel LeMay left to command the new 4th Bomb Wing, which ultimately became the 3rd Division. He would gain fame in leading his Wing to Regensburg and on to North Africa on that fateful August day. In 1944 he was transferred to the 20th Air Force in the Pacific to lead the B-29 (Super-Fortress) force against Japan, and had a most distinguished post-war career ending up as the Chief of Air Staff. LeMay's replacement was Lieutenant Colonel Donald K. Fargo, who was the first Eighth Air Force officer to be awarded the British DFC.

One of the features of the Eighth's aircraft – both bombers and fighters – was the strange and sometimes exotic names that they had been given by their crews and pilots. The names were invariably accompanied by a pictorial representation painted on the nose, and this 'nose art' rightly became famous, with many depicting scantily clothed

Captain Bruce Bairnsfather beneath B-17 Old Bill, *at Chelveston. (USAF)*

young ladies in the style of Vargas, the famed 'pin up' artist. Some of the names of B-17s that served at Chelveston were *Any Time Annie, Southern Comfort, Wolfess, Wham Bam, We the People, Target for Tonite* and *Old Bill*. The latter had been copied from Captain Bruce Bairnsfather's well-known First World War character; Bairnsfather was then contributing cartoons to the US Army Forces' newspaper the *Stars and Stripes*.

In July 1943 the Eighth planned to equip and train six B-17 Groups to join in the RAF's night operations. However, the 422nd squadron at

Chelveston was selected to act as a guinea pig, so their B-17s were duly modified and night-flying training began early in August. Unfortunately on the 31st *Eager Eagle* was on a night-training flight when it collided with an RAF Beaufighter; nine of the crew were killed including an RAF officer. On 8/9th September just five crews joined an RAF operation against a long-range gun battery at Boulogne. Another seven operations were mounted with two B-17s lost in action, before it was decided that the necessary B-17 modifications and the enormous task of training the crews in night-flying made it an unpractical proposition.

Rather than waste the crews' valuable night-flying experience, the 422nd was given the task of delivering propaganda leaflets and newspapers over mainly enemy occupied countries. Their first leaflet operation went out on 7/8th October to Paris; usually the squadron despatched up to six B-17s on its nightly operations. Major Earle J. Aber, the squadron's commander, was responsible for much of the expertise and was instrumental in the development of a special leaflets bomb (T1) in 1944. It contained 80,000 leaflets and was time-fused to explode at about 2,000 feet, with each aircraft carrying on average twelve of these leaflet bombs. The squadron was redesignated the 858th on 24th June and moved away to Cheddington in Buckinghamshire.

The first infamous Schweinfurt operation in August 1943 passed tolerably well for 305th considering the resultant mayhem; they lost two crews. But the costly mission to Stuttgart on 6th September had a vastly different outcome. Heavy clouds frustrated attacks on the briefed targets, and the weather also caused the formations to become separated, a situation that was capitalised on by the Luftwaffe. The 1st Bomb Wing lost 27 B-17s or 15%. Over half came from the 102nd CBW with the Group losing five – a quarter of the aircraft that had left Chelveston. The total losses of the Eighth were 45 in action, and another ten written-off in crash-landings due to battle damage or shortage of fuel. It was a disastrous operation, especially coming less than a month after the Schweinfurt/Regensburg losses.

The first of the Eighth's Pathfinder (PFF) aircraft came into operation on 27th September on a mission to Emden. The B-17s were equipped with the RAF's airborne radar sets – H2S. The ultimate intention was to train enough crews to provide one PFF squadron for each Division, then one per Wing and finally a PFF squadron in every Group. By 22nd March 1944, No 422 squadron had twelve PFF aircraft operating with H2X, which was the American version of H2S and was quickly dubbed

The town flag of Schweinfurt was presented to the Group. (Smithsonian Institution)

a 'Mickey' set by the American airmen. For about two months or so the squadron provided PFF aircraft for the other Groups in the Division, but by the end of 1944 each Group would have at least twelve PFF aircraft on strength to lead the operations.

October 1943 turned out to be the blackest month of the war so far for the 305th. On the 14th the Eighth decided to return again to Schweinfurt and the Group despatched 18 aircraft but three crews returned early because of mechanical defects with their aircraft. Of the remaining B-17s only three survived the massive Luftwaffe fighter onslaught to reach the target and just two crews managed to make it back to Chelveston. It was a disaster of some magnitude – 13 aircraft and 130 airmen lost on a single mission, the heaviest loss sustained by any Group over this notorious target. When Schweinfurt was captured by American forces in 1945, its flag was sent to the Eighth Air Force headquarters, who presented it to the Group in recognition of its crews' sacrifices.

The losses over the previous three months had resulted in morale sinking to a low ebb throughout the Eighth Air Force. Perhaps rather fortuitously, poor weather conditions curtailed its operational schedule, and the Group's crews were in action on only 18 days up to the end of the year with several missions being aborted, all for the loss of 'just' seven aircraft. The Group was moving closer to its 100th mission but like the other three 'Pioneer' Groups it had suffered heavily with over 70 crews missing in action.

In January 1944 the Group gained its second DUC, along with the rest of the 1st Division's Groups, for their operations on the 11th when the Focke-Wulf assembly plants at Oschersleben and Halberstadt were heavily bombed, but at a total cost of 42 aircraft. The 305th went to the latter target, over which far lighter casualties were sustained and its crews survived the torrid mission unscathed. The Group added further to its laurels in the coming months. On 20th February, at the start of the Eighth's 'Big Week', the crews were in action over the Messerschmitt component factory at Mockau airfield in Leipzig. One of its airmen, 1/Lieutenant William R. Lawley Jnr of 364th squadron, who was on his 14th mission, was awarded the Congressional Medal of Honor for bringing back his badly damaged B-17 to make a safe crash-landing at Redhill airfield on a single sound engine. Lawley was suffering from severe injuries, half his crew had been wounded and his co-pilot had been killed. The Medal of Honor had been introduced back in 1861 and was America's supreme award for bravery, equivalent to the British Victoria Cross; only 14 MOHs were awarded to Eighth airmen throughout the war.

Two days after this award one of the Group's B-17s, *Mi Amigo*, found itself in serious difficulties when returning from Denmark. Its pilot, 1/Lieutenant John G. Kreighauser, managed to avoid crashing into houses at Sheffield by making a force-landing in a nearby park but all the crew were killed. There is now a memorial stone at Endcliffe Park, Sheffield to commemorate the sacrifice of the ten American airmen. The pilot was posthumously awarded the British DFC. Sadly, a month later there was another tragic flying accident close to the airfield. On the 24th a PFF B-17 of No 422 squadron, which had only been received four days earlier, was taking off for Deenethorpe with 1/Lieutenant William D. Sellers at the controls, to lead the 401st in an operation to Schweinfurt. The aircraft stalled and fell on a domestic site near the village of Yelden due south of the airfield. A hut was set on fire, as was a nearby house on the edge of the village. Eight airmen in the hut were killed and two young children in the house, occupied by the Phillips family, also died in the fire. The eleven crew members all perished in the dreadful crash. The aircraft was not bombed-up or the circumstances would have been even more catastrophic.

In April another of the Group's pilots, 1/Lieutenant Edward S. Michael, who was serving in the same squadron as Lawley, also received a MOH for nursing his heavily damaged B-17, *Bertie Lee*, back to RAF Waltham despite quite horrendous injuries, loss of blood and extreme exhaustion after an eleven hour flight to Stettin and back. After long spells in hospital both Lawley and Michael recovered from their injuries and returned to the United States, and both remained in the USAAF after the war ended. The award of two MOHs to airmen in the same Group was not unique but was a very rare occurrence.

Despite unfavourable weather conditions at the beginning of the month the Group managed to mount 18 missions in May with the crews going to railway yards, airfields, aircraft factories, U-boat yards, Berlin, oil refineries and V1 rocket sites. This busy month brought its attendant costs in aircraft and crews – 15 went missing. June proved to be even more hectic with many operations in support of the Allied landings in Normandy. But when the crews returned to German targets on the 18th, the 305th suffered its only loss in the month, and sadly the missing B-17 had the Group's CO – Colonel Ernest H. Lawson – on board. He had been in charge since the previous November.

August turned out to be the Group's harshest month of the war. Eighteen crews were lost, two-thirds going missing in just two missions – to Karlsruhe railway yards on the 9th and Merseburg, the fearsome oil target in southern Germany, on the 24th. If a crew could survive this increased rate of operations it could complete its operational tour in about three to four months, despite the fact that the qualifying number had been increased to 30 and would later rise to 35. One lucky Eighth Air Force crew managed to complete its tour in 62 days – an all-time record! From September until the end of the year the Group managed to avoid any heavy casualties on their operations. In October Lieutenant Colonel Henry G. Macdonald was appointed Commander and he remained in charge until 1946. Back in 1943 he had been a squadron commander but had sustained a serious injury whilst flying a target-tower on gunnery practice over the Wash. However, Macdonald returned to operations and was the only combat officer to serve with the 305th throughout the war.

1945 started badly for the Group. On New Year's Day when acting as part of a small screening force (just 13 B-17s) for the Division's main attack on railway yards at Henschel, the crews arrived eight minutes late for the rendezvous with their fighter escorts and the small and isolated force was attacked with relish by a strong force of FW 190s. Five B-17s were shot down, four of which came from Chelveston. A major landmark was reached on 2nd March when oil targets at Bohlen were attacked. It was the Group's 300th mission, and to mark the occasion the 305th was given the honour of leading the Eighth. Sadly,

B-17E Towering Titan *of 305th Bomb Group. (Smithsonian Institution)*

two crews failed to return to Chelveston for the celebrations – only 17 Groups would achieve or exceed this magical figure. On 17th April the Group gained another unenviable record when one of its aircraft, *Towering Titan*, was the last Eighth heavy bomber to fall indirectly to the Luftwaffe, brought down by the wreckage of a Me 262 whilst over Dresden. Eight days later on the Group's final and 337th mission, two aircraft failed to return. One went missing in action and the other crash-landed on the Continent, both victims of flak.

The 305th had conducted a long and arduous war, finally emerging with a most distinguished record which had been achieved at no small cost – 154 aircraft lost in action with more than 780 airmen killed. Unlike many Groups the 305th did not return directly to the United States; towards the end of July it moved to St Trond in Belgium where its crews were engaged in photo-mapping flights over Europe – a project known as 'Casey Jones'. Much of the old airfield has now disappeared but the tower of the church of St John the Baptist of Chelveston-cum-Caldecott bears a memorial inscription to the men of the 305th and it also acknowledges the Group Memorial Association's financial help towards the restoration of the tower.

3
CHIPPING
WARDEN

'Our very first glimpse of the Wellington IIIs squatting heavily in the dispersals ringing the 'drome at Chipping Warden made us sharply aware of the nearer presence of the God of War.' This was the first impression of a young Pilot Officer of the Royal Canadian Air Force, D. Murray Peden, when he arrived at the airfield in May 1943.

There is no doubt that such apprehensions struck most pupil pilots as they moved onto the operational stage of their training. To be faced with what appeared such a massive aircraft, 13 tons fully loaded, after only recently mastering Airspeed Oxfords, a mere three tons, brought home to them the reality that they were now entering the big league and fast approaching the real thing. Peden's time at Chipping Warden is vividly recounted in his book, *A Thousand Shall Fall*, an acknowledged classic account of a wartime Bomber Command pilot. Peden had already had experience of flying from other airfields in the county and his name will crop up again at Croughton and Sywell; he ultimately served with No 214 squadron.

The airfield was situated alongside the A361 road in the far south-west corner of the county, close to the boundary with Oxfordshire. It was just a stone's throw to the north of the village from whence it was named. Most of the communal and living quarters were built in and around the village so perhaps more than most villages in the county, Chipping Warden almost lost its own identity, as well as being inundated by the number of airmen that regularly passed through its gates. To add to the military presence there were Army personnel and Women's Land Army girls also billeted in the village.

The calm of the village was broken in 1940 when the construction teams moved in to build a standard bomber station. Even before it was completed, let alone occupied, it attracted the attention of the Luftwaffe on 10th May 1941 but without any serious damage being caused. An advance party of airmen arrived on 10th July to prepare the RAF station, but it was not officially opened until the following month when it was allocated to No 6 Group of Bomber Command as an operational training airfield, and No 12 OTU moved in from Benson in Oxfordshire. Up until the end of 1940 this Unit had been engaged on training crews for light bombers using mainly Fairey Battles. However, it was now engaged in training heavy bomber crews and had been equipped with Vickers Wellingtons and Avro Ansons.

The Wellington had been designed by Barnes Wallis, of 'bouncing bomb' fame, in response to an Air Ministry specification (B9/32) for a twin-engined medium bomber. Its unique geodetic lattice construction proved to be capable of sustaining considerable punishment and still survive. The aircraft first flew in June 1936 but did not enter the Service until October 1938. Originally named the 'Crecy', this was quickly changed to Wellington in honour of the Iron Duke. It later acquired the nickname 'Wimpy', which was taken from J. Wellington Wimpy Esquire, a popular character in the Popeye cartoons. The aircraft's fame

Wellington IIIs served at Chipping Warden from December 1942 to January 1945. (RAF Museum)

and popularity with the public was ensured with the early and successful propaganda film *Target for Tonight*, in which the aircraft had the starring role.

The aircraft was powered by two Bristol Pegasus XVIII engines, which gave it a top speed of about 235 mph at 15,000 feet, and had a maximum bomb load of 4,500 pounds. There were nose and tail turrets with twin .303 machine guns as well as beam positions for single guns. Wellingtons made the first bombing mission of the war and suffered the first heavy losses in Bomber Command, but in the early years they formed the backbone of the Command's Main Force; in April 1941 they were the first aircraft to drop 4,000 pound bombs. The aircraft became most adaptable with well over 11,000 being built in a variety of marks, the largest total of any RAF bomber. Its use as a crew training aircraft extended right through from 1940 to 1953 – a quite amazing record. The majority of the Command's heavy bomber crews received their operational training on Wellingtons and by mid-1944 all the OTUs in Bomber Command were equipped with Wellingtons – a marvellous testimony for this splendid and well-loved wartime bomber.

Operational Training Units normally comprised four large Flights, which were mainly commanded by Flight Lieutenants, although later Squadron Leaders were sometimes put in charge. During Peden's time at Chipping Warden, Squadron Leader Fadden commanded 'B' Flight, which covered all aspects of operational or applied flying training. The other three Flights were responsible respectively for initial or conversion training, navigation and radio communications, and aerial armament and fighter affiliation. This four Flight system had evoked a certain amount of criticism that trainees had to change their instructors about half-way through the course, but the system remained for almost all OTUs, as it had proved to work well, producing a high standard of aircrews ready for their final stage of training – conversion to the four-engined heavy bombers.

Bomber Command had, in early 1941, opted for the more competent pilots coming straight into operational squadrons rather than having them receive more 'pseudo-operational experience', and the format of the course had to be adjusted to achieve this end. Thus a far greater amount of flying time was given over to pure conversion training, especially at night, with the operational or 'applied' part of the course foreshortened. The ratio on average was about 60% to 40%. To assist the Units in reaching this objective it was decreed that each training airfield would be provided with a satellite airfield, where the majority of the initial training and night-flying would be undertaken.

Chipping Warden's satellite facilities proved to be rather convoluted. When the Unit had been transferred from Benson that airfield's satellite, Mount Farm, had been taken over by No 15 OTU at Harwell and it was not until the following year that Chipping Warden gained its own secondary airfield at Gaydon in Warwickshire. Later in the same year Gaydon was replaced by Turweston, which was (and still is) a grassed airfield near Brackley but just across the boundary into Buckinghamshire. Turweston, despite its distance from Chipping Warden, remained with No 12 OTU until April 1943, when Chipping Warden gained its permanent satellite at Edgehill in Warwickshire. This was about nine miles to the north-west of Banbury, and since October 1941 it had been the satellite for No 21 OTU operating from Moreton-in-Marsh. It is interesting to note that trainee crews frequently landed at Gaydon in mistake for Chipping Warden, especially at night, because the two airfields were only about $2\frac{1}{2}$ minutes flying time apart!

Edgehill ultimately housed two Flights of the Unit under the command of Wing Commander C. N. Scott. Along with the conversion training, the Gunnery and Fighter Affiliation Flight also used the airfield with a mixture of Miles Martinets and a few Hurricanes. The satellite remained in operation until the Unit was disbanded in June 1945. This small and little known airfield had a special claim for a small piece of aviation fame. In February 1942 the Gloster E28/39, W4041, flew some of its experimental trial flights from the airfield, and then exactly a year later the second prototype, W4046, arrived, making its first trial flight on 1st March 1943. The aircraft, after considerable development, would subsequently enter the Service in July 1944 as the Gloster Meteor I – the RAF's first jet fighter.

The intake of crews at OTUs was on a fortnightly basis with anything from eleven to sixteen crews joining depending on whether the Unit had a satellite airfield. The course was planned to last ten weeks though this period tended to be a movable feast depending greatly on the time of the year and weather conditions experienced during the course. Up until mid-1942 each course intake had a greater preponderance of pilots, because of the necessity for a second pilot in heavy bombers. The rest of the intake would comprise an almost equal number of navigators, radio operators, bomb aimers and gunners. Joining an Operational Training Unit was the first time that all the different aircrew categories had come together for training, previously they had been trained at their specialist units or schools. The pilots would have spent the longest time in training, from elementary through to the service schools and then onto a refresher course before they tackled the advanced course. This process could take up to at least twelve months in total. In fact, Murray Peden had been engaged on his flying training for 14 months by the time he arrived at Chipping Warden.

Once the trainees had settled in, they were instructed to form up into crews, and they were given ten days 'to sort themselves out'! Most of the trainees were more than a little surprised that they were given a free choice rather than being officially nominated into crews. As one pilot recalled, 'I didn't know any of them. I needed four of these men to fly with, live with and go to war with.' Although this system appeared to be somewhat haphazard and rather disorganised it had proved to work well, with firm wartime friendships cemented at this stage of the training, and at the end of ten days there were few, if any, remaining airmen to be crewed up officially.

For the rest of the course the training would be concentrated on the five airmen working together as a team, so essential for the efficient operation of the aircraft and their ultimate survival. The pilot was now designated the captain or 'skipper' of the crew regardless of the ranks of the other crew members. From then onwards the airmen would be known collectively as '.......'s crew', and the captain would be responsible for his crew members arriving on time at roll calls, parades, lectures etc.

Any form of flying training was a hazardous business and of course all training units and schools suffered accidents, some more so than others. Generally speaking, No 12 OTU had a below average safety record, and perhaps the location of the airfield and its surrounding high land might have had a bearing on the Unit's performance. During September and October 1941, six Wellingtons were lost in a variety of landing accidents. On 20th October Pilot Officer Kenneth Farnes was killed along with one of his crew when his Wellington crashed onto the village after overshooting the runway. Farnes had only arrived from his advanced flying training in Canada four weeks earlier. He was a famous pre-war Essex fast bowler, who had first played for England in 1934 and was considered the natural successor to Harold Larwood. Four weeks later another Wellington crashed into one of the hangars and burned out, killing one airman and seriously injuring the other four. However, the most serious accident at the airfield occurred on 1st December 1942 when a Wellington crashed into the control tower and the aircraft was set on fire. It hit a civilian car and then landed on one of the hangars. There were 24 casualties, including two civilians, and two of the crew were badly burned. About six weeks later another

LAC Kenneth Farnes, the Essex and England fast bowler, at a pass-out parade in Canada 1941. (Essex County Cricket Club via P. J. Edwards)

Wellington crashed at Woodford Halse killing five of the crew, including Squadron Leader D. M. Foreman, the Commander of 'C' Flight. Only the rear gunner escaped.

One of the most important and essential parts of the course was the bombing practice. The bombing range used by the Unit was at Shotteswell, which was about three miles to the south-east of Edgehill. It was over this range that the $10\frac{1}{2}$ pound practice bombs were dropped, at least when the Unit was allocated practice times over the range. With so many OTUs in the area, time at the bombing ranges was always at a premium and they were usually so crowded that visits had to be arranged well in advance. The bombing runs were carried out in a strict clover-leaf pattern maintaining close radio contact with the ground observers on the high quadrant towers. However, the trainee crews spent far more time carrying out 'simulated' bombing exercises by using a camera, which provided the bomb aimer with some valuable bomb sight practice. It would appear that Banbury Cross, about six miles to the south-west of the airfield, was one of the crews' favourite targets, though others seemed to take a morbid delight in 'bombing' Blenheim Palace!

Some of the trainee crews, during the summer of 1942, were given the opportunity of gaining real live bombing experience. In late May the AOC of Bomber Command, Air Marshal Arthur T. Harris, decided to launch his famous '1,000' bomber raids, and to reach the magical '1,000' figure he called for a maximum effort from his operational squadrons and training units. For the first operation against Cologne on 30th/31st May the two training Groups provided 350 aircraft; many were piloted by the instructors and crewed by trainees, who were in the final weeks of instruction. The Unit sent 22 aircraft, of which one failed to return; it ditched off Harwich and three of the crew were killed. On 1st/2nd June when Essen was targeted, 20 Wellingtons left Chipping Warden and one crew was lost over the target.

The third '1,000' raid (though only 960 aircraft were available) directed at Bremen proved to be a most costly affair for the training units. Another 20 aircraft left the airfield, of which only 16 returned. One of the missing pilots, Sergeant J. T. Shapcott, was aged only 18 years, and became the youngest pilot in Bomber Command to be lost in 1942. Up until the Bremen operation the trainee crews had fared slightly better than the Main Force squadrons. However, in the Bremen raid the training losses exceeded 10%, which was over double the overall loss for the night. One explanation put forward for this high and unacceptable loss was that this operation had involved extra time

No 1517 BAT Flight was equipped with Airspeed Oxfords.

in the air (it was some 200 miles farther), which was thought to have put a greater strain on the older aircraft flown by the OTUs.

The Training Units were again engaged on another major operation on 31st July, this time to Dusseldorf. Thirteen crews left Chipping Warden; all returned safely and into the bargain one of the trainee gunners claimed to have destroyed a Junkers 88. No 92 (Training) Group suffered heavily on the night, losing eleven out of 105 aircraft (10.5%). It was not until September that the Units were called upon again to support the Main Force. Dusseldorf was attacked on 10/11th, followed by Bremen two nights later; in each raid the five crews despatched by the Unit returned safely. But on 16/17th when the Krupps munitions works at Essen was the target, the losses were again heavy – over 10%. Two of the Unit's Wellingtons were shot down over Holland and a third, which was badly damaged, made a crash-landing at Docking in Norfolk. The remaining six crews returned safely. This was the last occasion that trainee crews were used in a major bombing operation.

From November 1942 the Unit shared the airfield with the Airspeed Oxfords of No 1517 BAT Flight, which had moved in from Wattisham in Suffolk. This Flight's function was to instruct crews in the complexities of the Beam Approach System, which the Command had originally considered to be a device to accomplish a blind approach rather than a blind landing. Most Service airfields operated the Standard Beam Approach, which was based on short distance radio beams transmitted from a ground station along the runway approach path up to about 30 miles from the airfield. A receiver in the aircraft indicated to the crew any deviations from the centre line, both visually and aurally. The left-hand beam transmitted Morse dots and the other beam dashes; when the beams locked a steady note was heard and it was by this tone the aircraft was navigated safely down.

The SBA proved to be a most valuable aid to night landings and in unfavourable weather, at least when the cloud base was down to about 50 feet, and virtually blind landings were completed on a fairly regular basis. Strange to say, the system was of German origin; it had been developed by Lorenz A.G. and Telefunken and had been used by Lufthansa since 1935. The British rights to the system had been obtained by Standard Telephones and Cables in 1936. The first BAT Flight had been formed at Wyton as early as December 1940 and ultimately, by 1945, there were more than 40 such Flights in operation mainly attached to Advanced Flying Training Units. Initially these Flights had come under Bomber Command but from 1943 their control was transferred to Flying Training Command.

Throughout 1944 and well into 1945 the Unit continued to train crews for Bomber Command. Twenty-five Wellingtons would be written-off in training accidents and another three would be lost whilst engaged on operational duties – either leaflet dropping or diversionary flights. On 15/16th May 1944 a Wellington X left for a propaganda leaflet mission over Brittany. It never returned; only the pilot survived as a prisoner of war, and amongst the five crewmen killed was Sergeant N. O. Rushton, RCAF, who at the age of 41 years was well above the age normally associated with bomber aircrew. But the Unit's most tragic accident happened on the evening of 25th November 1944. A Wellington had just taken off when at about 300 feet the port engine failed. The aircraft hit a tree and then crashed onto the roof of Manor House at Upper Boddington, a mile or so to the north of the airfield. The aircraft exploded and one of its engines crashed through the house, killing a mother and her two children, who were the family of a RAF airman serving at Chipping Warden. The seven trainee airmen were all killed.

By 1945 there was a gradual slowing down of operational training, though the Luftwaffe was still active over the county. On 4th March a solitary Messerschmitt 410 flew in low and strafed the airfield, but there were no serious injuries. It proved to be the last Luftwaffe attack in Northamptonshire and by the end of June virtually all the training Wellingtons had left the airfield. The last training flight took place on the 1st of the month, with the Unit ceasing to operate three weeks later; the satellite airfield at Edgehill closed down a week earlier. For about three months from August, No 10 Air Navigation School used the

The damaged Manor House at Upper Boddington in November 1944 after the tragic accident. (Northamptonshire Libraries & Information Services)

airfield, until it moved away to Swanton Morley. On 15th September 1945 the airfield was opened to the public on the first Battle of Britain Day.

The last aircraft to use Chipping Warden were the Oxfords of the BAT Flight, but by the end of the year they too had departed. During 1946 the airfield was used for the storage of surplus Horsa gliders, but it was finally closed down at the end of the year, although several years were to pass before the Ministry of Defence decided to sell the site. Today the airfield site is occupied by EPS plc, which provides logistics services for industry.

4

COLLYWESTON

The old First World War training airfield of Easton-on-the-Hill, which had closed in 1919, was speedily resuscitated during the winter of 1939/40 to provide Wittering, about a mile or so away to the east, with a relief landing ground. And yet in less than three years Collyweston, as it was known during the Second World War, would virtually lose its independent identity when Wittering's main grassed runway was extended to join up with the old airfield.

In the early summer of 1940 Hurricanes and Blenheims from Wittering began to use the airfield, which had now been designated 'K3', denoting that it was the third of a clutch of fighter airfields in Sector K of No 12 Group with Wittering as the Sector airfield, although this method of identifying fighter airfields proved to be rather short-lived. From 1st June the Bristol Blenheim Ifs of No 23 squadron used the airfield on a more or less permanent basis. The squadron had been stationed at Wittering since May 1938 and although its crews had spent much of their time on east coast patrols, it was now operating as a night-fighter squadron, just one of a handful in Fighter Command.

The squadron's Blenheims had not yet been equipped with their AI sets, which were still undergoing trials with another Blenheim squadron, so the crews were forced to patrol at night in the vain and almost impossible hope of being able visually to locate the enemy intruders. As Flight Lieutenant R. Myles B. Duke-Woolley, a Flight Commander with No 23, later recalled, 'We hadn't the faintest idea how we were going to find a target, no idea at all!' And yet on the night of 18/19th June, in their first action of the war, the crews managed to

Blenheim If of No 23 squadron.

bag two Heinkel 111s – one of which fell to Duke-Woolley. However, two Blenheims were lost with three airmen killed; Squadron Leader J. S. 'Spike' O'Brien baled out safely, although he would be killed later in action in September 1940 whilst leading No 234 squadron.

Until about the middle of August the Blenheim crews continued their nightly patrols from Collyweston but on the 8th of the month another Blenheim was lost. It crashed near Peterborough killing both crew members; the pilot, Pilot Officer C. F. Cardnell, had only joined the squadron in June. Eight days later the crews moved back to operate from Wittering. During the winter of 1940/1 several Blenheim Ifs from No 29 squadron based at Digby in Lincolnshire were detached to Collyweston mainly to act as night-cover for the defence of Coventry. This squadron had one of the legendary airmen of the war as the Commander of 'A' Flight, Guy Gibson. He had already completed an operational tour on Hampdens with Bomber Command and now the squadron's crews were in the process of converting to Bristol Beaufighters, but there is no evidence that Gibson ever flew from Collyweston. In February (23rd) a couple of bombs fell at Easton-on-the-Hill, possibly jettisoned by an enemy bomber that had failed to locate Hull, which was bombed that night. One person was killed and another two injured.

It was not until the following May that Collyweston accommodated more permanent residents, the Spitfire IIs of No 266 squadron. The squadron had been operating from Wittering for over twelve months, except for the odd spells of detachment at airfields further south. In January 1941 it had been decided that the squadron would be largely made up from Rhodesian airmen. The first Rhodesian ground crews had arrived on the 24th followed about three months later by the first

Rhodesian pilots. Finally in August it became officially known as the 'Rhodesia' squadron.

More than any other single fighter the Supermarine Spitfire epitomised Fighter Command throughout the Second World War, its lasting fame ensured by the Battle of Britain, although in this conflict it had been greatly outnumbered by Hurricanes. The aircraft had originated from an Air Ministry Specification F7/30 (later amended to F37/34) to which R. J. Mitchell, the chief designer with Supermarine Aviation, responded with his first design of a quite revolutionary monoplane – F400. But it was the successful blend of Mitchell's airframe with a Rolls-Royce PV12 engine, later named the Merlin, that ensured the aircraft's amazing and outstanding success. Sadly, Mitchell did not live to see its celebrity as he died in June 1937, but his work was ably continued by Joseph Smith, who had been the chief draughtsman on Mitchell's team. Smith would oversee all the production development of the aircraft over the next eight years.

The first prototype, already christened the 'Spitfire' much to Mitchell's disgust, flew on 6th March 1936 and the aircraft was brought into service in August 1938 with No 19 squadron at Duxford. It was the only Allied fighter in production at the outbreak of the war to remain in continuous manufacture right through to 1945 and beyond; ultimately over 22,000 were produced in all the various marks. The Spitfire was without a shadow of a doubt a thoroughbred, one of the great classic fighters of all time. The aircraft's elegant lines with its sleek and distinctive elliptical wings still excites spectators at air shows today, over 40 years after it was finally withdrawn from operations (June 1954). Indeed, various special air displays were arranged in 1998 to commemorate the 60 years since its introduction into the RAF.

The Mark IIs were essentially the same as the original Spitfires except that they were powered by an improved Merlin XII engine (1,175 hp) and provided with 73 pounds of armour plating for the pilot and nose fuel tanks. As with the first Spitfires, the models that were designated 'a' were armed with eight .303 inch Browning machine guns whereas the 'b' models had two 20mm Hispano cannons in place of four machine guns. Pilots who had flown both versions would describe the machine guns as 'pea shooters' compared with the destructive power of the cannons, which 'really ripped those German aeroplanes to bits'! There was virtually no difference in the performance of the two models. However, in September the squadron began to re-equip with Mark Vbs, which had been provided with a yet more powerful engine – Merlin 45 (1,440hp) – giving it a maximum speed of about 375 mph at

13,000 feet. This mark became the mainstay of Fighter Command over the next twelve months or so, with almost 6,500 being produced, although the aircraft ultimately proved to be inferior in performance to the Luftwaffe's new fighter – the Focke-Wulf 190.

During the squadron's five month spell at the airfield it had three Commanding Officers. The popular New Zealander, Pat G. Jameson, DFC, left in June to become Wing Commander Flying at Wittering, and he was replaced briefly by Squadron Leader T. B. de la P. Beresford, succeeded in October by a Rhodesian airman, Squadron Leader C. L. Green, DFC. The pilots were mainly engaged in fighter sweeps and 'Rhubarbs' over the near Continent. The latter were small-scale fighter operations to targets of opportunity, often trains and troop convoys, and they were frequently mounted in poor weather, which precluded more planned operations. These and other fighter operations proved to be rather costly. By September, Fighter Command had lost over 270 aircraft and the figure would be much higher by the end of the year – a far greater number than the Luftwaffe's losses over the same period.

The squadron was not free from casualties; on 4th June a Spitfire II flown by Wing Commander W. E. Coope was seen to dive into the sea for no apparent reason. It is not clear why Coope was flying with the squadron, he certainly was not a member, so perhaps it was just a matter of 'keeping his eye in'. Coope had entered the Service in 1930 and during the mid-1930s was an Assistant Air Attache in Berlin, and although he flew occasional sorties with No 17 squadron during the Battle of Britain, he was not formally posted to any squadron. Then towards the end of June (27th) two pilots failed to return from a fighter sweep, and six days later another two went missing, both shot down by Me 109s near Dunkirk.

In July one of the most experienced and successful fighter pilots of the war so far joined the squadron as a Flight Commander from No 151 at Wittering. He was Flight Lieutenant Desmond A. P. MacMullen, DFC Bar, who before he left for a training post in November would add a Heinkel 111, a Me 109 and a 110 to his total of 17 victories, most of which had been gained during the Battle of Britain flying with Nos 54 and 222 squadrons. He completed the war with 20 victories to his name.

The squadron was detached to Martlesham Heath in Suffolk for about a week to take part in a large-scale air/land exercise, and it was temporarily replaced by a Hurricane squadron, No 133. This was the RAF's third and last 'Eagle' squadron, so called because it was manned by American volunteer pilots although it was then commanded by a

British airman, Squadron Leader G. A. Brown. The squadron had only been formed at the end of July and it would ultimately be transferred into the Eighth Air Force as the 336th Squadron of the 4th Fighter Group. The American pilots left for Fowlmere in Cambridgeshire on 3rd October when No 266 returned home. It proved to be only a brief sojourn because on the 24th of the month the pilots moved their Spitfires to nearby King's Cliffe, which had just opened as Wittering's second satellite airfield.

The winter of 1941/2 proved to be a relatively quiet time for the airfield. In early April, No 1529 Beam Approach Training Flight moved in from Wittering because the parent station had become rather chaotic with Hurricanes, Havocs, Beaufighters and the odd Mosquito vying for airfield space. The Flight was equipped with Miles Masters and its time at Collyweston was not a particularly happy period. Poor flying weather and servicing problems with its Masters, allied to an acute shortage of instructors, seriously hampered its training programme. Shortly before the Flight was disbanded on 7th November, its misery was compounded when one of its Masters flew into the ground at Marholm, killing the instructor.

Perhaps the RAF's most unusual Flight of the Second World War arrived at Collyweston on 12th April 1943 and it was destined to stay for almost two years. It was No 1426 (Enemy Aircraft) Flight, which had been first formed at Duxford in November 1941. Its main purpose was to study and compare the relative performances of Allied aircraft against captured German aircraft, but it also arranged demonstrations of the captured aircraft to pilots and crews at various RAF and USAAF airfields, as an aid to aircraft recognition and to enlighten the crews on the aircrafts' performances. The Flight's first tour of airfields started in February 1942 and it was considered sufficiently successful that this aspect of its work had continued ever since. Its pilots had also carried out mock dogfights for the benefit of Operational Training Units, as well as putting on special flights for the RAF Film Unit and for Warner Bros, who were making a propaganda film about air gunners, *Combat America*, which will be noted later under Polebrook. The Flight had initially been manned by a small cadre of pilots who were all highly experienced airmen and had previously served as test pilots with Maintenance Units.

The Flight brought to Collyweston its Heinkel 111H, two Junkers 88As, a Messerschmitt 110c and a 109E, but during its time at the airfield other captured aircraft would be added to its stock. For safety and security reasons the Flight was not permitted to fly more than five

Heinkel 111H which arrived with No 1426 (Enemy Aircraft) Flight in April 1943. (via J. Adams)

miles from Collyweston without being provided with a fighter escort. In May it took some of its aircraft to Digby where the Flight was reviewed by HM King George VI and Queen Elizabeth, an official acknowledgement of its contribution to the Service's knowledge of its opponent's equipment.

In the following month the Flight received its first Italian aircraft, a Maachi MC202, which was then considered the best Italian fighter of the war. However, the aircraft proved to be too corroded to warrant a re-build into flying worthiness. At the end of the month a Henschel Hs129B, which bore a striking resemblance to the Westland Lysander, arrived at Collyweston. It took over twelve months to bring this aircraft up to flying standard, which gives some idea of the amount of hard work, effort and dedication that was needed on the part of the Flight's ground crews to maintain these aircraft in an airworthy condition.

Considering the variety of enemy aircraft that its pilots flew, the Flight had a high safety record, which speaks volumes for the skills of its pilots and the technical expertise of its ground crews. But, on 10th November 1943, a serious and tragic accident befell the Flight. The aircraft were returning from a flying demonstration at Goxhill and were coming in to land at the Eighth Air Force base at Polebrook. The Heinkel 111, piloted by Flying Officer Barr, was making its final approach to land on the illuminated duty runway, followed by the Junkers 88, which had turned onto the same runway from the downwind end. Flying Officer Barr saw the Junkers 88 landing so he

Focke-Wulf 190A – PN 999 – flew with No 1426 Flight from November 1943. (via M. Winter)

opened up the throttles to avoid a collision, and made a steep left-hand turn. The Heinkel stalled and spun vertically into the ground from about 100 feet. Seven of the passengers were killed and four survived with injuries; they owed their lives to the bravery and presence of mind of two USAAF officers who had witnessed the crash and managed to drag the men out of the burning wreck. The other aircraft in the Flight managed to land safely. It was a serious blow for the Flight, with almost one quarter of its ground personnel killed. The Air Ministry considered disbanding the Flight, but it was allowed to continue providing the ground crews travelled by road in future.

In February 1944 the Flight took over extra responsibilities when its Me 109G was used for performance trials alongside a Hawker Tempest, Mustang III and Spitfire XIV. These trials were mainly flown and conducted by Flight Lieutenant E. R. Lewendon, the Commanding Officer and one of the Flight's original pilots. He would sadly be killed in a flying accident near the airfield in October when the Focke-Wulf 190 he was flying burst into flames in mid-air.

On 8th May the Flight left for Thorney Island to form part of an 'Air Show Circus', which flew over various Allied units gathered near the south coast in the build-up to D-Day, to provide some visual instruction in aircraft recognition. The captured German aircraft flew alongside 18 different British and American aircraft that would be in action over Normandy. These exercises were not without a number of sad mishaps; on 19th May two aircraft – Junkers 88 and Messerschmitt 109 – were lost in separate landing accidents at Thorney Island but

Messerschmitt BF109-G – a mainstay of the Luftwaffe fighter force. (MAP)

fortunately with no serious injuries. The Flight did not return to Collyweston until after D-Day.

Since January 1944 the Flight had shared the airfield at Collyweston with No 288 squadron, which was engaged in mounting combined training operations with anti-aircraft batteries. It had a mixed bag of aircraft – Hurricanes, Spitfires and Oxfords – although from March the Oxfords were replaced by doughty Beaufighters. Because of the nature of their duties the aircraft were frequently away from Collyweston and temporarily based at other airfields. Much of the squadron's flying was undertaken at night and, of course, poor weather allied with frequent air-raid alarms frustrated many of the squadron's exercises. As the Luftwaffe's night activities began to peter out during late 1944 the Unit's *raison d'être* became far less important and it left the airfield in November.

At the end of January 1945, No 1426 Flight was effectively disbanded, and its seven pilots and over 30 ground personnel were transferred to the Enemy Aircraft Flight of the Central Flying Establishment at Tangmere. Its aircraft would also move to Tangmere, though some were still at Collyweston weeks later; in fact the Flight received its last captured aircraft, Messerschmitt 109G-14, on 14th February. One of its Me 109Gs, which had been captured in November 1942 and had arrived at Collyweston towards the end of 1943, was successfully rebuilt over the 1980s and 1990s and was registered as G-USTV under the ownership of the Imperial War Museum at Duxford.

The Luftwaffe pilots had given the name 'Gustav' to the model 'G', which were built in greater numbers than any other mark and they served with the Luftwaffe from 1942 to 1945. This particular aircraft, in its original Luftwaffe markings, flew at various air shows in the 1990s from Duxford and sadly it crashed there in October 1997; at the time of writing its future is uncertain. Another Me 109, which was acquired by the Flight in April 1942, is now housed in the RAF Museum at Hendon.

The only RAF unit left using the airfield then was the Gunnery Research Unit, which had arrived at Collyweston in the previous April, equipped with a mixture of Wellingtons and Defiants. Until December 1944, when it was written off, it had one of the Service's last surviving Fairey Battles, which brought back memories of their brave but very costly operations over France in the spring of 1940. The Unit had been engaged in trials of the gyro gunsight for RAF fighters. When they left in March 1945 the airfield was silent once again, until in late May about 300 American airmen of 57th Fighter Control Station moved in from the Continent with a large stock of radar and radio vehicles. However, by the end of August the Americans had left for the United States. The airfield was now under the control of No 21 Group of Flying Training Command and had become fully integrated into RAF Wittering, as it is now.

5
CROUGHTON

Today the 'Stars and Stripes' flag can be clearly seen flying over Croughton airfield and the high fences and the strongly guarded gatehouse bear witness to the fact that its present American residents need to maintain a high level of security: Croughton is now occupied by the 422nd Air Base Squadron of the United States Air Force. Over 50 years have gone by since the last RAF aircraft used the grassed airfield and yet during the war it played host to a fair selection of training aircraft including Hampdens, Wellingtons, Ansons, Hectors, Masters, Oxfords and Hotspur gliders.

The airfield was built to the west of the A43 road, about $2\frac{1}{2}$ miles south of Brackley from whence it was first named, although in July 1941 the name was changed to Croughton from the neighbouring village. It was grass surfaced and remained so throughout the war, but George Wimpey & Co Ltd was involved in constructing the infrastructure of the airfield – domestic and technical sites, hangars, control tower and dispersal pads etc. Early in 1940 the rather basic landing ground was used in an emergency by some Whitleys of No 78 squadron, which were a long way from their home base at Dishforth in Yorkshire. By June the airfield was officially allocated as a satellite for No 16 OTU operating from Upper Heyford in Oxfordshire with the intention of providing the Unit with valuable extra airfield space for night-flying training. Although at this stage there was no accommodation yet built, civilian buildings in the near vicinity were commandeered for the Unit's personnel.

No 16 OTU had been formed out of Nos 7 and 76 squadrons, which had acted as No 4 Group's 'pool' or training squadrons. The Unit had been placed in the new No 7 Group of Bomber Command when it was formed on 15th July 1940 with Acting Air Commodore L. H. Cookey in command. The Group was then the smallest of the two Training Groups with just four OTUs. Both of the squadrons would ultimately re-form as operational squadrons; No 7 to introduce the new Short Stirling bomber into operations, and later become a founder member of the Pathfinder Force. The OTU was equipped with Handley Page Hampden 1s and the omnipresent Avro Ansons, without which no training unit would have been complete.

The Hampden was a medium bomber that had been designed back in 1932 in response to an Air Ministry specification which also resulted in the design of the Wellington. The aircraft, known as the HP52, first flew in June 1936 but did not enter the Service until two years later. It was powered by two Bristol Pegasus XVIII engines, which gave it a most respectable speed of 255 mph, but the aircraft proved to be very vulnerable to fighter attacks largely because it was the only bomber in the Command not to be provided with power turrets. Nevertheless, Hampdens operated in many of Bomber Command's early raids, in which two Victoria Crosses were awarded to Hampden crew members. In fact, at this time Hampdens provided a quarter of the Command's strength. They were finally withdrawn from bombing operations in September 1942, although by then they were being used as mine layers and torpedo-bombers with Coastal Command, as well as a crew training aircraft. The aircraft had good handling capabilities with excellent vision for the pilot but its accommodation for the crew was somewhat cramped to say the least, hence its nickname 'The Flying Suitcase'. Over 1,400 Hampdens were produced, with some of them being built in Canada.

A modified Hampden was developed in 1937, which had the same distinctive airframe but was powered with different engines – Napier Dagger VIIIs. Initially the Air Ministry ordered 100 and the first Hereford, as it was named, came into the Service in May 1939. However, the engines proved to be troublesome and unreliable, and although the odd Hereford went into a few operational squadrons, the majority were relegated to training duties with No 16 OTU and No 14 OTU at Cottesmore. The first Hereford was delivered to Upper Heyford in early May 1940.

Despite the Hampden's manoeuvrability, easy and docile controls and good vision, the two Hampden OTUs had a far higher accident rate than either the Blenheim or Wellington Units. For instance, in 1941 no less than 74 Hampdens and Herefords were written off in training accidents. Even within days of 'Brackley' becoming the official satellite of the Unit, a Hampden stalled on its landing approach to the airfield

Handley Page Herefords operated with No 16 OTU.

and crashed into the ground. Another eleven Hampdens would come to grief on or near the airfield whilst the Unit was in residence.

In September 1940 the Air Ministry decided that certain 'landing grounds' were to be designated as 'emergency airfields' to be used by operational aircraft returning damaged or with engine problems. The order went out to the Station Commander at Upper Heyford that 'the flare paths at Brackley would remain open and lighted to afford emergency landing facilities irrespective of enemy activity in the area'. Thus Brackley (or Croughton), along later with Chipping Warden and Silverstone, were used by damaged or 'lost' aircraft returning from operations. Early in October a Hampden of No 44 squadron from Waddington in Lincolnshire made an emergency landing after mine laying off the French coast.

Implicit in the Air Ministry's order was the acceptable high risk that such airfields would attract enemy intruder action, especially as they would remain illuminated at night. Therefore it was no surprise that Croughton and other emergency airfields should be attacked, especially during the first nine months of 1941 when the Luftwaffe's 1/NJG2 – Nacht Jagdgeschwader – began to operate with some effect, mainly with Junkers 88s, from Gilze-Rijen airfield in Holland. A Geschwader was the largest flying unit in the Luftwaffe, usually comprising three Gruppen with maybe a total of 90 aircraft; the 'Nacht Jagd' denoted that it was a night-fighter unit. The Unit had been specially formed to make regular night intruder sorties over eastern and central England. The Luftwaffe, like the RAF, were committed to attacking training airfields, as well as picking off training aircraft engaged in night-flying exercises. Both air forces considered it well worthwhile to attempt to disrupt flying training programmes. It was also an inescapable fact that training airfields were invariably lightly defended with a fair number of aircraft based there and they were therefore thought to be relatively easy targets to attack.

On the night of 12th June 1941 one of the Unit's Hampdens was attacked but the pilot managed to make a reasonably safe landing at Akerman Street Landing Ground in Oxfordshire. Two Ansons were also damaged on the same night but both managed to accomplish a safe landing at Croughton. Two nights later the airfield was attacked once again but little damage was sustained with just a few light casualties. On 31st August another Anson was damaged from an enemy attack; the flying instructor, Flight Sergeant P. C. Maries, brought the damaged aircraft into Croughton but the pupil pilot had been killed and three of the passengers injured. Three weeks later (20th September) both Upper Heyford and Croughton were bombed with the enemy intruder, a Junkers 88C, returning to attack a Hampden as it was landing at Croughton. Witnesses recalled that they 'heard bursts of cannon and machine gun fire before the Hampden caught fire in the air.' The aircraft crashed in flames at Guist near Croughton killing the four-man trainee crew.

Croughton remained the Unit's satellite until July 1942 but during the previous few months the Unit had been re-equipping with Wellingtons; by the end of April it had about half its complement. However, Croughton's immediate future was virtually sealed. No 23 Group of Flying Training Command had been desperately seeking a suitable airfield in the area to rehouse its No 1 Glider Training School, which was then based at Thame in Buckinghamshire, a small airfield that was considered sadly inadequate for glider training. Several other airfields in the near vicinity were considered before Croughton was selected. During July the School started moving in and by the beginning of August the training and ground personnel along with the trainee pilots had settled into their new home.

The whole concept of an 'Airborne Force', a term that was coined by Winston Churchill, was still a relatively new innovation. The Glider Regiment (later Glider Pilot Regiment) had only been formed in November 1941 and was not officially established until 24th February with Major (later Lieutenant Colonel) J. Rock as its first Commandant. Even by April there were just 300 trained glider pilots, and all had been recruited from Army personnel. They had been originally selected for flying training by a joint Army/RAF selection board with the RAF undertaking to provide their flying instruction. The trainee pilots would receive a twelve week basic flying course at an EFTS, before passing on to one of the Gliding Training Schools, which provided instruction on glider techniques over a twelve week period. From there they would pass on (at least from July onwards) to an Operational or Conversion Training Unit on the General Aircraft Horsa, which became the British main operational glider of the war.

Right from the outset it was the objective that all glider pilots would be as highly trained and disciplined as infantry troops, so that when the gliders had landed at the assault areas the pilots would be able to make a positive contribution to the battle pending their recovery. Thus the discipline at Croughton, once the School moved in, reflected this fact and a far stricter regime was enforced than that normally found on an RAF training station. Obviously Wing Commander P. A. Tipping, the School's Commanding Officer, had been specially instructed by the Command to maintain a high standard!

The School was equipped with 18 General Aircraft Hotspur gliders and 14 Hawker Hectors, which operated as the glider towers. The Hotspur had originally been designed as an assault glider capable of carrying six combat troops, but during its early trials with full loads the glider had not really come up to expectations, and it was never used

The Hawker Hector was given a brief new lease of life as a glider tower.

Hotspurs were the standard wartime training gliders. (Museum of Army Flying)

operationally but instead became the standard wartime training glider. The Hotspur was of all wood construction with a plywood skin and over 1,000 were built, mostly by H. Lebus, the furniture manufacturer. Considerable difficulties had been experienced in finding a suitable aircraft to tow the gliders and ultimately the Hawker Hector, an outmoded and obsolescent Army Co-operation bi-plane, was given a brief new lease of life in this role. However, the aircraft never proved to be a really satisfactory solution to the problem, not least because its old Napier Dagger engine gave considerable maintenance and servicing problems. Once satisfactory Service trials had been completed with the Miles Master II, the rather antiquated Hectors were replaced by Masters.

Towards the end of 1942 it was thought that a sufficient number of glider pilots had been trained, at least for the foreseeable future operational needs. Having a large reservoir of trained glider pilots created its own separate problem as they were required to complete a maximum of ten flying hours per month in order to keep their flying skills honed. There had also been a certain amount of inter-Service rivalry between the RAF and the Army Air Force. Some concern had been expressed by Flying Training Command about the number of places at the Elementary Flying Training Schools that were being taken up by the trainee glider pilots. Air Marshal Harris of Bomber Command was also more than a little unhappy with the number of his operational aircraft that were being used for glider towing and parachute troop training exercises. When the last course of glider pilots passed out of Croughton on 24th March 1943 the School closed down. The airfield now became the second satellite of Kidlington in Oxfordshire where No 20 (Pilot) Advanced Flying Unit had been formed – Kidlington had also been engaged in glider pilot training. The first Advanced Flying Unit had been established in November 1942. These Units had been formed to provide refresher courses for pilots who had trained overseas under the British Commonwealth Air Training Scheme. The courses also gave the newly qualified pilots some experience of flying in British weather conditions and handling heavier aircraft than they had hitherto flown. In the case of No 20 AFU these were twin-engined Airspeed Oxfords, which effectively meant that the pilots would ultimately be bound for either Bomber or Coastal Command.

The Oxford was the RAF's first twin-engined monoplane trainer, and perhaps every bomber pilot in the Second World War underwent a spell of training on this small but sturdy aircraft, known to all airmen as an 'Ox-box'. It made its entrance into the Service with the Central Flying School in November 1937. The aircraft's handling qualities were specifically designed to match those of the larger and heavier bombers, and despite its 53 foot wing span it certainly felt like an even heavier aircraft, especially in the landing approach and touch down. The Oxford was powered by two Cheetah engines and flat out it could be nursed to over 185 mph, but cruised at about 140 mph. The aircraft, which had dual controls as standard, became a most reliable advanced trainer, with over 8,500 being produced, and it remained in service at training schools right up to 1954. Murray Peden, our Canadian pilot, (see Chipping Warden) trained with No 20 Unit and used Croughton on occasions. He was most impressed with the Oxford: 'I got to like the old "Ox-box" and soon began to experience a deeper satisfaction with my flying, the sensation that comes with stretching one's powers and mastering a more difficult task.' The Oxford also became the standard trainer for Beam Approach training.

In mid-April 1943 No 1538 Beam Approach Training Flight was formed at Croughton. Prior to that time the Unit's pilots had undertaken their Beam Approach training at Feltwell in Norfolk. Both the Unit and the Flight remained at Croughton until the middle of October 1944 when the airfield was returned to Flying Training Command as it was decided to re-form No 1 Glider Training School.

During the summer of 1944 there had been a number of differences of opinion between the Army and the RAF over glider pilots. In July the Air Ministry had proposed seconding RAF pilots to the Glider Pilot

Regiment as first pilots, largely because for the first time in the war there was a reserve of trained RAF pilots. It should be noted that in late 1943 it had been decided that the Horsa operational gliders would be manned by two pilots, although it was accepted that the second pilot would receive a shorter course of flying instruction. For various reasons the Army was not in favour of the Air Ministry's proposal; a combined Army/RAF force was considered unsatisfactory and the Army still stoutly maintained that glider pilots should also be trained soldiers, with some justification because the Wehrmacht thought the Glider Pilot Regiment to be an 'elite force'. Furthermore the Regiment was beginning to return to full strength as its losses over D-Day had been far lighter than forecast.

The ill-fated Arnhem operation in September drastically changed the position – 460 glider pilots had either been killed or captured, with another 150 wounded. At the end of September the Army reluctantly agreed that RAF pilots should be trained in glider flying to fill the vacancies in the Regiment, and for this reason No 1 GTS was re-formed. It was proposed that the RAF would contribute over 500 glider crews to a planned target figure of 1,000 by April 1945.

The School, now under the command of Group Captain J. A. Glen, began its training courses again but this time with RAF pilots in the preponderance, still using Hotspur gliders and Master IIs as towers. The last major airborne landings of the war – Operation Varsity – resulted in almost a quarter of the Regiment's flying staff being either killed, wounded or missing in action, which meant that the School continued to operate after the end of the war. Indeed, there was also a Glider Instructors' Flight at Croughton, which later moved away to Gaydon in Warwickshire. The School finally closed down in June 1946, when the Hotspurs and Masters were transferred to No 3 GTS at Wellesbourne Mountford, which carried on training until the end of 1947. The airfield was finally left quiet and forlorn, and it was used as an ammunition store. In October 1951 the USAF took over the airfield to set up a communications centre, and it is now completely covered with radio masts.

6
DEENETHORPE

In a lay-by alongside the A427 road from Corby to Oundle and about two miles past Weldon, can be found a most impressive granite memorial. Dedicated to 'The Best Damned Outfit in the USAAF', it commemorates the airmen of the 401st Bomb Group that flew from Deenethorpe airfield from late 1943 until June 1945. It should be said that every American airman thought that his own Bomb or Fighter Group was the best unit in the Eighth, although the veterans of the 401st are the only ones that were prepared to have their belief etched in stone! The memorial stands close to the end of one of the old runways and the airfield lies due north of its namesake village.

This Class A standard airfield was built during 1943 and was one of the last wartime airfields to open in the county. It was handed over to the USAAF by Squadron Leader E. H. G. Watson on 20th December. However, the first American airmen had already arrived on 3rd November and they quickly began the task of preparing their new base for the arrival of the B-17s, which had been temporarily housed at Bassingbourn and Polebrook. The delay had, at least, given the aircrews a breathing space to recover from their rather fraught and harrowing transatlantic crossing via Goose Bay, Meeks Field, Iceland to Prestwick. October was not the most favourable time to fly the northern ferry route especially for such relatively inexperienced airmen.

It was not until the 19th of the month that the first B-17Gs began to move into Deenethorpe. The 401st was the first Group to be almost fully equipped with these latest models of the famous bomber. The main change in the aircraft had been the provision of a Bendix twin-gun 'chin' turret in the nose of the aircraft. This modification had been made by Boeing at the express request of the Eighth Air Force as an attempt to counter the Luftwaffe's head-on frontal attacks to which the

The 401st Bomb Group takes over Deenethorpe on 20th December 1943. (Smithsonian Institution)

B-17Fs were suddenly proving rather vulnerable. The Group had also been assigned 60 aircraft, the first unit to benefit from the increase in the squadron complement from nine to fifteen aircraft, although it would be almost four months before the Group was finally up to a full complement as many of its new B-17Gs and their crews had been transferred to more experienced Groups, especially the 351st at Polebrook. The model 'G' proved to be the most numerous B-17 mark with over 8,600 finally being produced.

The 401st was the last of the county's Eighth Air Force Groups to enter the air war. In theory at least its crews should have been far better prepared for their battle ahead, as they all had passed through the School of Applied Tactics in Florida, where the bitter combat experiences gained by the Eighth in over twelve months of operations were passed on by veteran airmen to the new crews. Even before the Group became operational, two of its officers had received gallantry awards – Captain George Gould and Major Allison Brooks – for their brave actions, whilst stationed at Polebrook, in rescuing nine airmen from that tragic accident noted earlier under Collyweston. Indeed, by the end of the war over 1,000 of the Group's airmen had received awards.

Major Brooks would later become the Group's Executive Officer and gain fame as the leader of the Eighth's first Scouting Force. This Unit was equipped with P-51s, which were flown by bomber pilots who had volunteered for the Force after completing their tours. Flying ahead of the Main Force, they would seek out high cloud formations and the current weather conditions along the planned flight and in the target areas. They would then radio back this information to the formation leaders and maybe advise alternative targets if it was thought necessary.

The ultimate success of the 401st as one of the most efficient and effective Groups in the Eighth Bomber Command owes much to its first Commander, Colonel Harold W. Bowman, who remained in command until December 1944. He had previously been a staff officer in Washington, and under his firm and positive leadership the 401st achieved a fine operational record with the second highest standard of bombing accuracy in the Command. Like the other three Bomb Groups in the county, the 401st was placed in the 1st Bomb Division (it had been upgraded from a Wing in September) and the 92nd Combat Bomb Wing, which would later be renumbered the 94th. The Wing had its headquarters at Polebrook, so the new crews would operate alongside their erstwhile colleagues (351st) at Polebrook, and be joined, in February 1944, by even newer 'greenhorns' – the 457th Group operating from Glatton.

The remnants of the Group's B-17Gs began to arrive at Deenethorpe on 19th November. They carried the Group's special identification code on their tail-planes – a black 'S' within a white triangle – though from August 1944 this would be reversed to a white 'S' in a black triangle with the addition of a yellow diagonal band. Like all Groups in the Eighth, each squadron was given its own individual code – SC, IN, IW and IY for 612th to 615th squadrons respectively. For the next week the crews continued their operational training – assembly skills, navigation exercises, simulated bomb runs, escape procedures and the inevitable close formation flying, remembering the old adage, which would have been emphasised time and time again at the school in Florida – 'the tighter you fly the lower the losses'.

On the 26th of the month the crews were considered ready for their first operation. Twenty left for the port area of Bremen and severe fighter opposition was encountered with 19 aircraft in total destroyed. Despite heavy clouds and enemy smokescreens 16 of the Group's crews claimed to have bombed. On the return flight a B-17 collided with one of the Group's aircraft, named *Fancy Nancy*, which resulted in the ball turret being almost cleanly removed and killing the gunner. With great skill the pilot managed to bring the stricken aircraft back to make an emergency landing at Detling but the B-17 was later declared a write-off.

The problems of operating during a European winter were soon brought home to the crews; on 30th November 21 aircraft left for Solingen but because of heavy cloud formations the mission was aborted by the Division. General Eaker's diktat to his Divisional commanders had always been clear and unequivocal, that if a target had not been effectively bombed, 'you will return again and again until the job is done properly'! Thus it was that on the following day the Division was again in action over Solingen. Almost 300 B-17s, led by six PFF aircraft, attacked this target, which was just to the east of Dusseldorf and sited in the dreaded Ruhr, known to RAF crews as The Happy Valley or The Valley of No Return! It was a severe test for the inexperienced crews. Twenty-four aircraft in total were lost on the mission (8%) but all 15 aircraft returned safely to Deenethorpe and furthermore every single crew claimed to have bombed the target. The foundation was laid of the Group's reputation for the bombing accuracy of its crews, a high standard that was maintained throughout the war.

It was a rather sad fact that during the war almost one in six of the Eighth's heavy bomber losses were due to accidental causes. These accidents were more prevalent on take-off when the heavily loaded aircraft afforded very slim margins of error, be they human or mechanical, and, of course, poor weather conditions only heightened such risks. On 5th December when 20 crews were leaving to attack French airfields around Paris, one B-17, *Zenobia El Elephante*, appeared to lose power on take-off and crashed into a uninhabited cottage at Deenethorpe village. All the crew were miraculously rescued from the blazing aircraft and the villagers were warned before the full load of bombs exploded. Considerable damage was caused to the village but only two airmen were injured. The terrific blast was said to have been felt in Kettering some twelve miles away. It was rather ironic that the subsequent operation had to be abandoned because of adverse weather conditions.

On Christmas Eve 1943, the Eighth launched its first major assault on V1 and V2 rocket sites, which were mainly situated in the Pas de Calais area of northern France. The Allied bombing offensive of these rocket targets was codenamed Operation Crossbow, but these operations soon became known as 'NoBall' missions by the American crews.

B-17 of 613th Bomb Squadron returning from Kiel, 13th December 1943. (Smithsonian Institution)

Although rumours abounded about the nature of these strange targets, most of the crews were unaware of their true purpose. The Group would be engaged over these targets in both January and February but it was not really until the first V1 rocket was launched in June 1944 that their sites were heavily bombed by the Allied Air Forces. The first Eighth operation, which comprised over 700 aircraft, was achieved without a single casualty. But not all of these operations were routine flights, or 'milk-runs' in USAAF slang. Although the crews were only over hostile territory for a relatively short period, quite formidable flak could be encountered, which was often as intense and fierce as that experienced over many German industrial targets.

It was not until the penultimate day of the year that the Group suffered its first loss in action over Ludwigshafen, and the following day's operation proved even more costly. The primary targets were airfields around Bordeaux on the French Atlantic coast, which were being used by the Luftwaffe's long-range bombers to attack and harry the vital Allied shipping convoys. The Group attacked Chateaubernard airfield at Cognac, and the Commander of 614th squadron, Major Wayne Eveland, and his crew were shot down by an enemy fighter. On the return flight another badly damaged B-17 crashed near the Isle of Wight with no survivors. The long eight-hour flight in poor weather conditions resulted in many aircraft running short of fuel and no less than 18 B-17s made crash-landings in the United Kingdom. Two of the Group's aircraft were abandoned by their crews; one crashed near Ware and the other finally came to ground near Kimbolton. During the month the Division had 26 aircraft written-off to add to over 60 aircraft lost in action.

The Cognac mission, difficult though it was, paled into insignificance compared with some of the rugged and torrid operations faced by the crews in the first months of 1944, perhaps none more so than the mission to Oschersleben on 11th January when a fighter assembly factory was the primary target. The Luftwaffe were able to put up their strongest force since the Schweinfurt raid of the previous October. The weather conditions badly deteriorated during the outward flight and the presence of high cloud, at times exceeding 28,000 feet, meant that few of the fighter escorts were able to locate the bomber formations.

The 401st was led by Lieutenant Colonel Allison Brooks and its aircraft had become isolated from the main formations, placing them in a most vulnerable position on which the Luftwaffe was quick to capitalise. The Group's gunners were soon desperately fighting off determined and sustained attacks by about 30 rocket-firing Me 110s, when suddenly out of the blue a solitary P-51 from the 354th Fighter Group of the Ninth Air Force arrived on the scene. The fighter pilot, Major James Howard, began to fight off the enemy aircraft single-handed. It was an amazing and brilliant bravura performance that lasted for about half an hour, which saved the Group from utter decimation. In the process Major Howard probably accounted for six enemy fighters. According to Brooks, 'It was a case of one lone American against what seemed to be the entire Luftwaffe.' Another crewman described it as 'like something out of a Hollywood movie.' It was largely as a result of the crews' reports that Major Howard was awarded the Congressional Medal of Honor, the only American fighter pilot in the European war to receive this highest bravery award. Nevertheless, the Group still lost four aircraft with another crash-landing at RAF Ludham on return, and seven were diverted to Matlaske in Norfolk because of the unfavourable landing conditions at Deenethorpe. One B-17, *Nasty Habit*, overshot the runway and ended up only fit for salvage. Like the other Groups in the 1st Division, the 401st received its first and well-merited Distinguished Unit Citation.

Almost six weeks later the Group received a second Unit Citation for its crews' actions over Leipzig on 20th February when the Erla aircraft assembly factories at Mockau airfield were accurately and heavily bombed causing considerable damage and loss of production. On this day the Group led the formations into southern Germany, with the crews managing to overcome adverse weather, fight through strong Luftwaffe resistance, accurately bomb the target and return to Deenethorpe with the loss of just a single aircraft. This mission was later described by General Williams, the Commander of 1st Division, as 'the most successful operation carried out so far by the Eighth Air Force.' Two days later, again in severe weather, the Division attacked aircraft factories at Bemburg, Halberstadt and Oschersleben, and it was over this latter target that the 401st had two aircraft shot down in the fierce fighter attacks, which on this occasion were estimated to be over 200 strong. The Division lost 38 B-17s (13%) on the mission with another three crashing on return to England. These two operations were just a part of the Eighth's massive assault on the German aircraft industry, which had been codenamed Operation Argument but became better known as the 'Big Week'.

It was not until March 1944 that the Eighth Air Force made their first strike at Berlin or 'Big B' as it was known to the crews. Frustrated by bad weather on three successive days (the 3rd to 5th) the first successful major mission was launched on the 6th, which also happened to be the Eighth's 250th operation of the war. Over 700

B-17F of 613th Bomb Squadron landing at Deenethorpe. (Smithsonian Institution)

bombers and some 800 fighters were engaged in what became a ferocious and sustained air battle, with the bomber crews facing almost 20 miles of heavy flak batteries on their run-in to Berlin. The 1st Division led the attack with the Erkner ball bearing plants as its primary target. The whole operation was conducted on a massive scale and in a grand manner but it proved to be very costly for the Eighth. However, the American press greeted it as a great victory with banner headlines exclaiming '800 US bombers smash at Berlin by day: 68 lost in battles, 123 of the foe shot down . . . 2,000 tons on German Capital . . . Fighters swarm on Nazis'. It was a brave and honest declaration by the USAAF of its true losses, which was quite a rarity considering the disingenuous nature of most wartime propaganda statements. In actual fact, 80 bombers and fighters were missing in action, the heaviest loss of the war for the Eighth, but just one came from Deenethorpe.

Berlin was bombed another three times by the Eighth during the month with the 401st losing only one further aircraft. Subsequently the Group would be in action over Berlin or nearby targets on another 13 occasions and it lost in total 14 crews or 15% of its total losses of the war. Indeed, the German capital and strategic oil targets accounted for a third of the Group's losses although they made up less than one-fifth of its total missions.

Throughout the war each Eighth Bomb Group experienced at least one disastrous day when its losses were well above the tolerable or acceptable level, and the Commanding Officer could only hope that such days were kept to a bare minimum. The 401st had their first really bad day on 28th May when the Ruhland oil plants were bombed by the Eighth for the first time. However, the 94th Wing was engaged over Dessau, some 30 miles due north of Leipzig, with its aircraft factories as the primary target. The Wing came under sustained and intense Luftwaffe attacks and 14 B-17s were shot down. The 401st lost six aircraft with another ditching in the sea but all the crew were saved, also a damaged B-17 was written-off after crash-landing on its return to Deenethorpe. Two days later the crews were back in the same area, this time to Oschersleben, the scene of the award of their first DUC, and another two crews went missing, which brought their total losses in the month to 14. The month of May proved to be a costly time for the Eighth Air Force in general and for the Group in particular.

At half past two on the morning of 6th June the crews at Deenethorpe were briefed for their impending mission. Colonel Bowman said at the briefing, 'Gentlemen remember this day – June 6th 1944. Remember it because your grandchildren probably will ask you about it. This is D-Day.' By five o'clock, 36 aircraft had left the airfield to become part of the Eighth's heavy bomber force – some 1,800 strong – en route for the Normandy beach-heads. The sheer logistics involved in getting such a massive force assembled into formations and safely across southern England and the English Channel were complex in the extreme. Each of the three Divisions had their own designated air corridor to fly along; the 1st Division flew just to the west of London and crossed the coast near Brighton. The crews' specific targets were gun positions and strong points in the Gold 'area', which was one of the British forces' landing points. A second but much smaller mission left the bases about three hours later but only six crews from Deenethorpe were in action on this second wave. On that fateful and historic morning over 2,300 Allied heavy bombers were airborne with just a single aircraft lost to enemy action.

During this time there was a B-17G operating with the Group that was to gain lasting post-war fame in a somewhat indirect manner. The aircraft had been allocated to the 615th squadron and was named *Mary Alice* by its original pilot, Lieutenant Dan Knight, in honour of his mother. The aircraft received more major repair work and was patched up more frequently than most B-17s. One pilot commented that, 'She was put together like a jigsaw puzzle!' During its operational life two of its crew members were awarded the Distinguished Service Cross and the Silver Star – the second and third highest gallantry awards. On three occasions *Mary Alice* returned so badly damaged that emergency landings had to be made at Beccles, Boxted and the 'crashdrome' at Carnaby. Indeed at times *Mary Alice* appeared to be indestructible, perhaps an extreme example of the solidity and durability of the B-17.

Mary Alice flew its last and 98th mission on 19th April 1945. Despite all its history of damage the aircraft was still thought sufficiently airworthy to be ferried across the Atlantic after the end of the war and it finished its days, like hundreds of other B-17s, in the Arizona desert. Its post-war fame springs from the splendidly restored B-17G on display at the American Air Museum at Duxford. This aircraft was built in 1945 and delivered to the Eighth Air Force too late to see war service. It was subsequently acquired from France in the 1970s, and is now resplendent in the original colours and markings of *Mary Alice* – 231983 IY-G of 615th Bomb Squadron — a fine and lasting reminder of probably the most battered and damaged B-17 to survive the Second World War.

During July the 401st was in action on 17 days, mounting two separate missions to V1 rocket sites in the Pas de Calais on one day

Mary Alice *on display at the American Air Museum at Duxford.*

(6th). These were just short hops compared with most of the other operations in the month – Munich, Leipzig, Merseburg, Augsburg and Peenemunde – with Munich being visited on five separate occasions. However, on the 24th and 25th of the month the crews, like the rest of the Eighth Bomber Command, were detailed to bomb the Wehrmacht's strongly fortified positions in the area of Periers and St Lô in Normandy, which were blocking the US 1st Army's attempts to break out of Normandy. On the first operation over 1,500 heavy bombers were despatched but because of a persistent ground haze, only about a quarter actually bombed, and despite every care being taken 20 American troops were killed and another 60 wounded. Just three aircraft were lost. A damaged B-17 from Deenethorpe ditched in the Channel and eight of the crew were rescued. The following day there was a greater force in action, of which over 1,500 managed to bomb, but sadly American casualties on the ground were even higher than the previous day, almost 500, of whom 102 were killed. These two operations were the only serious blemishes in the Eighth's long bombing offensive.

On 5th December Colonel Bowman left the Group to become General Spaatz's right-hand man, but he was replaced by an equally able Commander – Colonel William T. Seawell. Both men would reach the rank of Brigadier General in the post-war USAF, and Seawell later went on to become the Chairman of Pan American Airways.

The 401st was passing through what could only be described as a 'purple patch'; since 6th November not a single aircraft had been lost in action, and the Group would ultimately complete 37 missions unscathed. This fine record came to an end on 3rd February 1945 over the Templehof railway yards at Berlin. One of its damaged aircraft force-landed in Poland though the crew was able to fly it back to England later in the month. It was during this period that the 401st passed its 200th mission mark and from early February onwards until the end of the war only eight B-17s went missing in action, three of these in one mission to oil targets in central Germany on the 16th of the month.

The heavy flak batteries that surrounded Berlin were still taking a toll of the Eighth Air Force even at this late stage of the war. The Group lost three aircraft over the German capital during this period, including one over Brandenburg, about 30 miles west of Berlin, on its 254th and last mission, which left Deenethorpe on 20th April. This was the 95th and last aircraft to be lost in action, a total which gave the Group the second lowest loss ratio of all B-17 Groups in the Eighth.

By the end of June all the B-17s had left and the ground crews had departed for the States on the *Queen Elizabeth* having originally arrived on the *Queen Mary*; not many American airmen could claim to have

Memorial to 'The Best Damned Outfit in the USAAF'.

travelled on both the 'Queens'! The airfield was handed back to the RAF and Technical Training Command took it over, placing No 11 Recruit Centre there, who remained for about twelve months.

The main runway was restored during the 1960s by British Steel and used for the arrival and departure of VIPs visiting its steelworks at nearby Corby. The old control tower bearing the lettering 'Flying Control' survived until the early 1990s but sadly it has since been demolished. However, at the time of writing, the airfield is still used for private flying by C-10 Air Sport and the appropriately named Fortress Flying Club. As well as the fine memorial stone there is a stained-glass window in the church of St Mary the Virgin at Weldon, containing panels from the chapel of US Station No 128 – Deenethorpe – in memory of those men of 'The Best Damned Outfit in the USAAF'.

7
DENTON

During the summer of 1940 a considerable number of relief landing grounds were hastily brought into Service use, either to provide extra valuable airfield space for the dispersal of operational aircraft, both fighter and bomber, or perhaps more numerously for Elementary and Service Flying Training Schools to add to their training facilities. Denton, which was situated to the south of the A428 road and between the villages of Brafield-on-the-Green and Denton, became the relief landing ground for No 6 Elementary Flying Training School at Sywell about eight miles away farther north.

These landing grounds were not really considered by the Air Ministry to be aerodromes in the true sense. Largely because of the urgent need for airfields and their planned ultimate use, only very basic preparatory work was undertaken at the sites. Trees and hedges were removed, ditches were filled in and levelled, and a rudimentary drainage system installed, if it was thought necessary. Perhaps only a handful of service units were erected, just sufficient for the Flight commander, a crew room, time-keeping room, maybe a couple of huts for the defence guards and certainly a small fuel tank. By 1941 facilities at Denton had improved somewhat with extra accommodation huts being erected, and ultimately ten Blister hangars, mostly of the standard type, had been provided and were sited along the perimeters of the airfield.

It was an Air Ministry directive that the training satellite airfields should be used mainly for the Schools' night-flying commitment, largely in order that the main training airfields could remain unlighted at night. Such a decision resulted in many of these small airfields attracting the attention of the Luftwaffe, really out of all proportion to their importance. However, in this respect it must be said Denton escaped relatively lightly, although on 17/18th July 1941 its lights

Tiger Moths of No 6 EFTS used Denton from the summer of 1940.

attracted a solitary enemy intruder and eight bombs were dropped. Most fell round the edge of the airfield and caused minimal damage.

The only aircraft to use the airfield throughout its existence were de Havilland Tiger Moths. These rather graceful and delicate looking bi-planes became the most famous and successful training aircraft of all time. Virtually all the pilots that served in the Second World War received their initial flying training on these excellent and very forgiving training aircraft, which were universally admired and known familiarly as 'Tiggies'. The Tiger Moth was a direct development of the company's very successful civil aircraft, the Gipsy Moth, which had gained so much fame with the various exciting long-distance flights undertaken in them during the late 1920s. The Tiger Moth first flew in October 1931 and two months later the first Moths were delivered to No 3 Flying Training School.

The company decided to develop an improved version with a 130 hp Gipsy Moth engine, a plywood rear fuselage in place of the fabric coating, and with a fitted hood, which could be pulled over the rear cockpit for instrument flying training. This aircraft was designated the DH 82A but became better known as a Tiger Moth II. It had a maximum speed of 109 mph at 1,000 feet but it cruised at about 90 mph. Despite its fragile appearance the Moth was a sturdy and very reliable aircraft, which was able to survive the rough handling it received at the hands of trainee pilots. Over 7,000 Tiger Moths were built and they remained in service with the RAF until 1951.

At the height of Sywell's training commitments the small airfield at Denton could cope with three Flights and it became very involved in the Grading Courses that were such an integral feature of the School from 1942 onwards. The trainee pilots were transported into Denton by buses on a daily basis, either from Sywell or directly from their lodgings in Northampton. Several trainee pilots swore that they were in greater danger travelling along the winding country roads in the old buses than they ever were in the air! Although some living quarters had been provided at Denton, these were, by 1942, occupied by a Flight of the RAF Regiment, which was responsible for the defence of both Sywell and Denton airfields.

The RAF Regiment had been first formed on 1st February 1942 with Major General Sir Claud Liardet, CBE, DSO, being loaned from the Army to become its first Commandant. The nucleus of the Regiment had been provided by the 'ground gunners', who really dated from the summer of 1940 when the responsibility for the defence of RAF airfields was firmly placed with each station commander. They were expected to organise and train station ground personnel for this task. By 1942 these airfield defence forces had increased to about 65,000 throughout the country. The members of the Regiment were dressed in khaki battledress with RAF blue berets and blue 'RAF Regiment' shoulder patches; their now familiar blue battledress did not appear until 1950. The contingent at Denton did get engaged in some ground training exercises at Sywell when units of the Northampton Home Guard acted as enemy attackers.

The airfield at Denton had its fair share of accidents but really they were far less numerous than would have been expected considering the amount of night-flying that took place at the airfield. The most serious accident occurred on 5th December 1941 when a Tiger Moth was completing a night circuit of the airfield and it collided with a Wellington from No 15 OTU from Harwell. The instructor, Flight Lieutenant E. M. Frisby, and his pupil were killed in the crash. On two successive days in July 1944 (25th and 26th) two very early Tiger Moths were written-off in accidents. The first, with the School since before the war, hit some power cables near Turvey in Bedfordshire killing the two airmen. The second hit a hedge near the airfield whilst the pilot was making an unauthorised forced landing; this Moth had successfully survived the ministrations of hundreds of trainee pilots since October 1939.

Denton continued to be used by No 6 EFTS well into the spring of 1945 but it was finally closed down on 9th July, although the School still continued to operate from Sywell. The site quickly returned to its original use – farming – and little evidence remains of this small wartime airfield. Denton was like so many other small airfields dotted around the countryside. They made a valuable contribution to the RAF's massive training programme but, sadly, this has now been largely forgotten and their presence has passed without any permanent reminder of their brief wartime existence.

8
DESBOROUGH

Of all that are left of the wartime airfields in the county, Desborough proved to be the most difficult to locate and identify. At least, that was my experience as an outsider to the area. The actual airfield was situated closer to Stoke Albany and Wilbarston than to the town from which it gained its name. Most of the technical and domestic sites were placed to the south-west of the airfield along and adjacent to the B669 road from Wilbarston to Desborough; several of these buildings have survived and are still being used for a variety of purposes.

The airfield was first allocated to the Eighth Air Force as a heavy bomber base in June 1942, but this decision was rescinded two months later, for whatever reasons, and Desborough airfield was never occupied by the USAAF, although, of course, its satellite at Harrington was. The development of the site into a Class A standard airfield was undertaken by Tarmac Ltd in late 1942, and was completed by the following summer. The airfield was placed under the control of No 92 Group (Training), which was then commanded by Air Vice Marshal H. K. Thorold, CBE, DSO, DFC, AFC, and was allocated to a newly formed Operational Training Unit, which would inevitably be equipped with Vickers Wellingtons.

The new Unit – No 84 OTU – came on stream on 1st September 1943 when the airfield was formally opened. It was the third and last OTU in Bomber Command to be formed in the year; the other two, Nos 82 and 83, had been activated in June and July respectively in Nottingham-shire and Shropshire. Now there were 23 OTUs in operation and all but two were equipped with Wellingtons. Although the Command considered that the number of OTUs was actually equivalent to $22\frac{1}{2}$, on the principle that if a Unit was not provided with a satellite airfield it just counted as $\frac{3}{4}$ but if a Unit operated two satellites it was then

Three Wellingtons of No 84 OTU left Desborough for a ceremonial fly-past at the opening of Harrington.

equivalent to $1\frac{1}{2}$ Units! So until Desborough's satellite at Harrington was ready for occupation in early November it was merely considered to be a $\frac{3}{4}$ OTU with its complement of training Wellingtons set accordingly.

The Unit's Commander, Group Captain G. Lowe, was appointed on 1st September 1943, and he would remain in charge of the Unit for the whole of its existence. It fell to the Group Captain to make all the arrangements for the formal opening of Harrington on 6th November when there was a fair amount of 'scrambled egg' on view: RAF slang for officers of Group Captain and above, it referred to the gold trimming on their peaked caps. The opening of the satellite, which will be described under Harrington, was marked by a fly-past of three Wellingtons from Desborough. Like all RAF operational squadrons, the Unit's aircraft carried its unique identification codes, and in the case of No 84 OTU they were CO, 1F and CZ.

The number of flying hours that trainee pilots were expected to complete at the OTUs varied quite considerably during the progress of the war. At the outset of OTUs (May 1940) they were scheduled to complete a minimum of 55 hours, of which at least 22 were required to be flown at night, but within a matter of months these totals were reduced. In 1941, largely because of an increase in Bomber Command's operations and the resultant growing aircrew losses, allied to the formation of new squadrons, the courses at OTUs were further reduced in length and about 30 hours became the average number of flying hours completed at the operational stage. However, there were many instances of pilots only completing half this total because of poor weather conditions and the urgent need for replacement crews as Bomber Command's operational losses began to escalate. The reduction of time spent at the operational or 'applied' stage proved to be rather self-defeating, because many of the Command's crews were lost in their first few operations. Early in 1942 it was decided that 45 hours should be the minimum, but by May 1944 largely as a result of the greater number of OTUs this figure had increased to an average of 80 hours – thus the operational flying training programme had almost doubled in two years. It is interesting to note that Murray Peden in mid-1943 managed to total 84 flying hours whilst training with No 12 OTU at Chipping Warden.

In order to achieve the requisite number of flying hours, all Units imposed a strict regime during the ten week course, which was adhered to in case poor weather and the threat of enemy action seriously affected the flying training programme, especially night-flights and exercises. Another factor, which could seriously impact on the completion of the courses within the time scale, was the serviceability of the aircraft. The normal complement of a full Unit was 54 Wellingtons, which meant that on average only about 60% were available for flying training at any given time. As one pilot later recalled: 'Flying weather and serviceable aircraft were priceless commodities in the eyes of the vigilant and harassed OTU Flight Commanders, and a trainee crew could commit no greater sin than damage an aircraft unnecessarily, or waste valuable air time when performing an assignment.' Landing at another airfield at night was considered a heinous crime and was certain to incur the displeasure of Flight Commanders because of the loss of precious flying time in retrieving and returning the aircraft back to base.

The flying day usually started at 08.00 hours, or half-an-hour or so earlier in the summer months, with an hour's break for lunch, and it ceased at dusk. Night-flying, which was perhaps the most important and vital part of the flying training, usually commenced late in the evening depending on whether meteorological clearance for the flight had been obtained, and flying training continued well into the early hours of the morning. It was surprising the number of training

Wellington X – CO-O – of No 84 OTU. (RAF Museum)

accidents that occurred in the early hours of the morning. The various night-exercises and practices – circuits, landings and long-distance flights – were further complicated by having to move the aircraft from their dispersal points sited around the airfield, which invariably was poorly lit and there were frequent taxiing accidents, which were the bane of the harassed Flight Commanders!

The ultimate target for bomber pilots, certainly by late 1943, was that they should have completed a total of about 430 flying hours before being finally transferred to an operational squadron. During 1943 No 92 Group trained over 2,160 crews and had flown 23,000 hours, which averaged out at 310 crews for each of the Command's Operational Training Units.

As probably could be expected, there was always a fairly high frequency of accidents at OTUs. Many of these could be directly attributed to human error brought about by the increased weight, size and complexity of the aircraft and the lack of experience of the pilots in coping with sudden emergencies such as mechanical and engine failures, let alone the odd enemy attacks. In some measure the aircraft themselves were at fault, because up until mid-1943 the training Wellingtons were mostly tired and war-weary aircraft that had been transferred out of operational squadrons and were thus more prone to engine failures and other defects. It was rumoured that the trainee pilots were forbidden to use full throttle on their Wellingtons because this could put too much strain on their old engines!

Many of the accidents happened in poor flying conditions, as the pressure on OTUs and their tight training schedules were such that night-flying had to be conducted in weather conditions that would have grounded operational squadrons. This only imposed added pressures and complications for the trainee crews. During 1943 No 92 Group suffered one accident for every 440 hours flown, which although this figure was almost a 100% improvement on the previous year, was still considered by the Command's chiefs to be 'far too high'. A Group directive was issued to all Unit Commanders to 'do all within your powers to reduce the number of these needless and costly accidents', but it was not made clear just how they should achieve this objective!

In theory, at least, No 84 Unit's safety performance should have been better than most, as it was equipped with a fair percentage of Wellington Xs, the last bomber variant and indeed the most numerous with over 3,800 being produced. The last production Wellington was a Mark X delivered in October 1945. The Wellingtons had been removed from the Main Force's bombing operations in early October 1943, although they would continue to be used for mine laying until March 1944. Therefore most of the Wellingtons coming off the production lines were supplied to OTUs. Indeed by 1944 most Units had the luxury of being equipped with new Mark Xs. This mark was based on the Wellington III but had been provided with the more powerful Hercules VI or XVI engines, and the Wellington, through long experience of operational and training flying, had developed into a most reliable and versatile aircraft. They performed in a diversity of roles unequalled by any other bomber of the Second World War, and furthermore, had been instrumental in the training of the majority of Bomber Command's aircrews.

On the day the airfield opened, a Wellington of No 22 OTU based at Wellesbourne Mountford in Warwickshire crash-landed at the airfield. Fortunately there were no serious casualties but it did not augur well for the new Unit. The rest of 1943 proved to be accident free but in January matters changed dramatically. On the 21st a Wellington crashed at Geddington Chase Wood, about five miles to the north of Kettering, killing three of the crew and injuring the other four. Six days later (27th) there were two more fatal accidents, one at Molesworth and another, about three hours later, at Arthingworth not far from the airfield. During the rest of the year another nine Wellingtons were lost,

114

which was the third lowest accident rate of the Wellington Units, although on 18th November 1944 a pilot was killed when his Wellington landed too quickly and collided with another on the ground. The final Wellington mishap at the airfield came on 12th April 1945 just days before the final course was mounted, when an aircraft made a belly-landing and burst into flames.

The training of air gunners was undertaken by the Armament Flight and for this purpose a number of target-towing aircraft were operated by each Unit. For many years the RAF had used obsolete aircraft that had been specially adapted for the purpose. The odd Wellingtons were used to tow the target drogues and some of the Units were supplied with Westland Lysanders, but by the time No 84 OTU was formed the Command was using mainly Miles Martinets for this task.

In 1941 F. G. Miles had been asked by the Air Ministry to design an aircraft specially for target-towing under Specification 12/41. The aircraft, known as M25, first flew in April 1942 and it was largely based on the Master II, the company's most successful trainer, but it had a longer nose section designed to compensate for the weight of the target-towing equipment. It was a two-seater aircraft and was powered by a single Bristol Mercury XX or XXX engine, which gave it a maximum speed of 240 mph, although its cruising speed was 195 mph at about 5,000 feet. Like all of the company's aircraft the Martinet was of wooden construction and covered with plywood. The winch for the target equipment could either be wind driven or motorised and the aircraft had stowage space for six flags or sleeve drogues. Over 1,700 Martinets were built and from 1942 onwards they became very familiar sights at all training airfields. The pilots that flew these Martinets, or

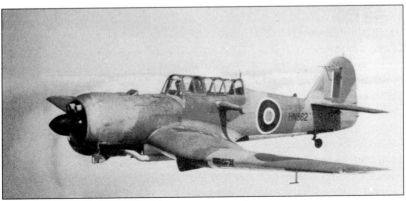

Miles Martinet – the RAF's first specially designed target-tug.

115

Some of the wartime buildings at Desborough have survived.

indeed any other target-towers, were thought to be more than a little intrepid; as one trainee pilot said, 'you wouldn't get me up in one of those when I think of the shooting accuracy of some of the gunners on our course!' Although having said that, only one Martinet was written-off at Desborough on 1st March 1944, and this accident was due to engine failure rather than any inaccurate or stray firing!

When Harrington was handed over to the Eighth Air Force towards the end of March 1944, No 84 became a $\frac{3}{4}$ OTU and its complement of aircraft was reduced to 40 Wellingtons, then mostly Mark Xs, but crew training continued from Desborough until mid-1945. The 38th and last course commenced in April and when the crews finally completed their training in the middle of June, the Unit was disbanded with the Wellingtons being ferried away to various Maintenance Units. Over 410 crews had been trained by the Unit in less than two years.

During the summer of 1945 RAF Transport Command took an interest in the airfield and some repairs were made to the runways before C-47s or Dakotas of No 107 OTU, then based at Leicester East, used the airfield for practice circuits and landings. At the beginning of November No 1381 (Transport) Flight, also equipped with Dakotas, arrived from Bramcote. The Flight was a Conversion Unit, which was the next and final step for crews before they were posted to operational squadrons in Transport Command. For almost twelve months the Flight used the airfield, but by the end of 1946 it stood empty and forlorn. It was ultimately de-requisitioned and the land returned to farming.

9
GRAFTON
UNDERWOOD

Grafton Underwood holds a special place in the annals of the United States Air Force. It was from this airfield that the Eighth Air Force began its heavy bombing operations and moreover it fell to the crew of a B-17 operating from the airfield to drop the final bombs of the Eighth's bitter campaign. Thus right from the outset until the conclusion, apart from a few months in 1943, B-17s flying from Grafton Underwood were deeply engaged in the American air war. Well over 300 operations were mounted from this airfield, making it really a microcosm of the Eighth Bomber Command. Also no less than four different Bomb Groups operated from here – a quite unique claim to fame.

The airfield, which was built during 1941 by George Wimpey & Co Ltd, was sited to the north of the village and on land owned by the Duke of Buccleuch. As the village's name suggests, the surrounding countryside was well wooded, and the airfield was bounded in the north by Old Head Wood, where the bomb dumps were placed, and in the east by Grafton Park Wood. It was originally planned as a satellite airfield for RAF Polebrook, which had, by early 1942, become engaged in the conversion flying training of crews for RAF Liberators or B-24s.

The first American airmen to appear in the county arrived at Grafton Underwood on 14th May 1942, having arrived at Newport docks the previous day. The journey across the Atlantic had taken almost three weeks. The 500 or so airmen were serving with No 15 Bomb Squadron (Light) under the command of Major J. L. Griffith, and they had been transferred to the European Theater to train as a night-fighter unit with Turbinlite Havocs. The RAF had already decided that the Turbinlite

Control Tower at Grafton Underwood. Note '30' shows runway in use. (USAF)

experiment, which had not been very successful, would be phased out, so the American crews would instead be trained for low-level bombing operations and equipped with Boston IIIs or DB-7Bs, as they were known in American circles. These twin-engined Douglas light bombers had been introduced into the RAF as replacements for Blenheim IVs. The 15th squadron was not yet equipped with their own aircraft (they did not arrive until August) so in the meantime they commenced training on Bostons borrowed from the RAF and under the Service's guidance and instruction. Because the airfield was needed as a satellite for a Heavy Bomb Group, the squadron left for Molesworth in early June.

The ground personnel of 97th Bomb Group (Heavy) arrived on 13th June at both Polebrook and Grafton Underwood, with just two squadrons, 342nd and 414th, occupying the latter airfield. It was then the USAAF's policy that each Bomb Group, because of the number of aircraft allocated, would occupy two airfields. The operational problems as a result of split Groups, along with the pressure of finding sufficient airfields in eastern England, eventually forced the USAAF to reverse this policy, with the result that just a single airfield was allocated to each Group.

119

The 97th was the first Heavy Bomb Group to be assigned to the Eighth and its crews were the only ones to fly their B-17Es across the Atlantic. The model 'E' was the first B-17 to be provided with an enlarged vertical tail surface and tail gun positions and first flew on 5th September 1941. Just over 500 were produced as they were quickly superseded by the much improved 'F' models. The first Eighth Air Force B-17 to land in the United Kingdom touched down at Prestwick on 1st July, and over the next three weeks or so B-17Es arrived at the two airfields at regular intervals. By the end of July the crews had started an intensive training programme under the direction of a new Commanding Officer, Colonel Frank Armstrong, who had come over to England with General Eaker in February. On 1st August a B-17E, *King Kondor*, overshot the runway at Grafton Underwood and hit a lorry passing through the base, killing its civilian driver – this was the first Eighth Air Force B-17 to be written-off due to accidental causes.

The big day for just twelve crews arrived on 17th August when eleven aircraft of 342nd and 414th squadrons were prepared for the first bombing operation. One aircraft, *Butcher Shop*, from 340th squadron flew across from Polebrook to join the Eighth's first operation. It was flown by Major Paul L. Tibbets, who as a Lieutenant Colonel would pilot the B-29, *Enola Gay*, that dropped the first atomic bomb on Hiroshima. Tibbets had Colonel Armstrong alongside him as

B-17E Peggy D *of 97th Bomb Group went on the Eighth's first heavy bombing mission on 17th August 1942. (Smithsonian Institution)*

co-pilot on this historic mission. The aircraft left in two flights of six, the second of which was led by *Yankee Doodle* piloted by Lieutenant John P. Dowsell and with General Eaker on board. The Sotteville marshalling yards at Rouen were the target, and only 18 tons of bombs were dropped from about 23,000 feet and some moderate but accurate flak encountered. A small number of FW 190s appeared but they were adequately dealt with by the large escort of RAF Spitfires. All the aircraft returned safely with only two slightly damaged. The bombing had been light and not particularly accurate but at least the Eighth Air Force had opened its score.

On 8th September the two squadrons operating from Grafton Underwood moved away to join their colleagues at Polebrook, but within days they were replaced by yet more American airmen, who were the ground crews and support personnel of the 305th Bomb Group. They would have plenty of time to get settled in before their charges – B-17Fs – arrived, as the aircrews were still receiving six weeks additional advanced operational training in the United States, and they did not begin to fly in until the third week of October. The Group was commanded by Colonel Curtis LeMay, who was not particularly impressed with the airfield or its facilities. Amongst his many complaints he considered that 'the runways are all wrong'! Nevertheless, on 17th November ten crews were sent out an a 'diversionary flight', which as its name suggests was an attempt to draw the Luftwaffe away from the Main Force. No bombs were carried so the crews were not credited with a mission!

After an aborted mission on the 22nd because of heavy cloud formations, it was on the following day that the crews were in action for the first time over St Nazaire; this target would become the most heavily defended area outside Germany. Twenty aircraft left Grafton Underwood and 14 crews claimed to have bombed the U-boat pens, but how effectively was another matter. Almost two weeks passed before the Group was operational again, this time over targets at Lille in northern France, but only four of the crews were effective. No doubt much to Colonel LeMay's relief the Group moved away to Chelveston, which would be its permanent base for the rest of the war.

The decision was now taken to improve the airfield. The three runways were extended and extra hard-standings were put down, the construction work carrying on through the winter of 1942/3 as and when weather conditions would allow. Although the airfield was undoubtedly 'improved' and enlarged, the inevitable problem of mud was never really solved. The same complaint could be levelled at many wartime airfields but Grafton Underwood seemed to have more drainage problems than most, and its permanent American residents somewhat fondly dubbed it 'Grafton Undermud'. The airfield was still technically the property of the RAF and was not officially handed over to the USAAF until July 1943, but by this time its third American Bomb Group had come and gone!

The 96th Bomb Group arrived on 16th April, but only the air crews appeared. The rest of the Group had been directed to a newly constructed airfield in Essex – Andrews Field – which was the first to be built solely by American Aviation Engineers (it was also the only airfield in the United Kingdom to be named after an individual – Lieutenant General Frank M. Andrews, one of America's most celebrated airmen). The Group was allocated to the new 4th Bomb Wing (later the 3rd Bomb Division), which would control the many Bomb Groups operating from Norfolk and Suffolk airfields, so the Group's stay at Grafton Underwood would necessarily be of a fairly temporary nature. Key ground personnel were temporarily drafted in from Chelveston and Molesworth in order to get the 96th operational. Considering the lack of support staff it was quite amazing that the Group's Commanding Officer, Colonel Archie J. Old Jr, managed to get his aircrews to operational readiness in under a month.

The first mission from Grafton Underwood on 13th May turned out to be rather a disaster. Twenty crews were briefed for the Wing's first mission to the Luftwaffe airfield of Longuenesse at St Omer, joining two other 'greenhorn' Groups. The operation got off to a bad start when, shortly after take-off, a waist machine gun was accidentally discharged whilst being stowed, damaging the control cables as well as injuring two gunners. The pilot was unable to land the aircraft so he ordered the crew to bale out. He jettisoned the bombs over the Wash before he and the co-pilot baled out. The co-pilot was rescued but when the pilot was eventually located he was found to be dead. The rest of the crews had experienced great difficulty in assembling and remaining in formation, so the leader abandoned the mission over the English Channel.

The following day the Group joined the 351st (at Polebrook) for an attack on the air depôt at Courtrai in Belgium, and they were escorted by a large force of RAF Spitfires. This time all 21 crews bombed the target. The port of Emden was attacked the following day, and two days later (17th) the Group lost an aircraft whilst bombing the power station at Lorient. Another crew went missing in action over Emden, with another damaged aircraft crash-landing on its return to the airfield. The aircraft started to leave for Andrews Field on 27th May, though within a couple of weeks they would have moved again, this time to their permanent base at Snetterton Heath in Norfolk. The 96th Group would ultimately sustain the second highest losses in the whole of the Eighth Air Force, whilst completing over 320 missions.

As the Group's aircraft were leaving Grafton Underwood, they were replaced by the first B-17Fs of 384th Bomb Group, which somewhat unusually arrived before their ground crews. The Group had been placed in 103rd Provisional Combat Bomb Wing and its Commanding Officer, Colonel Budd J. Peaslee, was eager 'to get the show on the road'. In fact, the Group adopted 'Keep the Show on the Road' as the motto on its badge, but little did they realise just how difficult it would be to live up to this in the months ahead, when the 384th sustained

The Badge of the 384th Bomb Group.

some heavy operational losses. On 11th June a few of its crews went over to Molesworth to fly a mission with one of the pioneer Groups – 303rd – to gain some operational experience. Unfortunately, on the following day, the Group's first B-17 was lost in a collision with another B-17 making its final approach, which killed all five of the crew.

Ten days later (on the 22nd) 20 crews joined other newcomers of the 381st at Ridgewell in a joint attack on the Ford Motor works at Antwerp. The operation was really intended as a feint for the Main Force, which was attacking synthetic rubber targets at Huls. Largely due to inexperience the crews failed to make the rendezvous with their fighter escorts, P-47s, and were made to pay dearly for their errors. The formations were heavily attacked by FW 190s and each Group lost two aircraft. It was not a particularly auspicious start for either Group, both of which were destined to suffer heavy losses during their first year of operations. By the end of the month the 384th had completed another four missions for the loss of eight aircraft. In a matter of eight days 100 airmen had been lost in action – a really harsh introduction into the air war.

July turned out to be even more costly for the Group as twelve aircraft were lost (7%), of which seven crews failed to return from bombing diesel engine works at Hamburg. This was the highest monthly loss in the 1st Bomb Wing. On the 30th of the month the Group had only 13 serviceable B-17s on hand and these were despatched to the Fieseler works at Kassel, which made component parts for FW 190s. Two aircraft returned early because of mechanical faults, and one of the remaining aircraft was badly damaged by flak and fighter action. With six wounded crewmen on board, the pilot, 2nd Lieutenant William R. Harry (himself wounded) and his co-pilot, Lieutenant Ivan Rice, managed to land the stricken B-17 at Boxted airfield in Essex. The aircraft was said to have had 'about 1,000 holes in it' and was written-off; it had acquired the name *Patches* because of the amount of battle damage it had sustained since the Group's first operation. After a short spell in hospital Harry returned to operations with his co-pilot, only to be shot down over Schweinfurt in October. He survived as a POW but Lieutenant Rice was killed.

There was a blessed lull in operations for all of twelve days, a time to allow aircraft to be repaired, replacement crews to be trained and the veterans of 13 missions to relax a little and perhaps reflect on what had happened in less than three months. However, there were rumours circulating around the bases about 'a big and major operation' that was

124

in the offing. It all sounded rather ominous to the crews, who were still coping with the stresses of combat flying. The Eighth returned to operations on 12th August when the 1st Bomb Wing was given oil targets at Gelsenkirchen. However, the formations became separated on the bomb run and other targets were bombed instead. Twenty-three aircraft were lost, five of which came from Grafton Underwood. The Group's bad luck still seemed to be dogging them.

Five days later the crews were briefed for the most ambitious operation yet to be undertaken by the Eighth – a two-pronged strike on the ball bearing plants at Schweinfurt and the Me 109 factories at Regensburg. The views of the crews after their briefing were perhaps summed up by one bombardier at Grafton Underwood: '... too deep, so many miles without fighter protection. It was sheer fear that gripped us all ...' The Wing's Commanding Officer, Brigadier General Robert B. Williams, would lead the two task forces heading for Schweinfurt, which were timed to be flying about twelve minutes apart. The European weather interfered with the execution of this carefully planned and massive operation.

The original plan had allowed for only a short interval of time between the departure of Regensburg and Schweinfurt formations, but the bad weather completely altered that, with the result that the Schweinfurt force finally left about three and a half hours after the 4th Bomb Wing's Groups were airborne for Regensburg and beyond. Unfortunately this serious and lengthy time delay turned out to be critical and indeed proved fatal for so many crews; it allowed the Luftwaffe fighters sufficient time to land, regroup and refuel and be ready and waiting for the second force bound for Schweinfurt. In direct contrast the Allied fighter escorts, P-47s and RAF Spitfires, did not have sufficient time to return to their bases to refuel and in any case their operational range only barely reached the German border. With the benefit of hindsight the changed plan appeared to be a blueprint for disaster, which of course it turned out to be.

The 384th could only provide 18 aircraft, the lowest Group total in the whole of the Eighth, although one crew from Grafton Underwood flew with the 303rd. Of the 36 B-17s lost by 1st Bomb Wing, five came from the 384th (27%). One damaged aircraft crash landed near Rheims after a hair-raising low-level flight across southern Germany and France, and four of its crew managed to evade capture and return to England. Another made a spectacular crash-landing at the airfield. One of the pilots said that he would never forget that day as long as he lived, he had seen 'things that will live with me for the rest of my life.'

When the Eighth returned to the same target in October, another six aircraft were lost by the Group mainly to the fearsome yellow-nosed FW 190s, which had been dubbed the 'Abbeville Kids'. Three damaged B-17s were abandoned by their crews over England, at Blaydon, Wakerley and Chetwode; only seven crews returned to Grafton Underwood – an effective 56% loss rate. And yet the Group's ordeals over the dreaded Schweinfurt were not quite over, because when the Eighth bombed this target again on 13th April 1944 the 384th would lose nine aircraft out the Division's total of 14 – the Group's single heaviest loss of the war! It was on this operation that the formation leader, Colonel Maurice Preston of the 379th Group, considered that the Luftwaffe's attacks were the most severe and sustained that he had ever encountered. The Group had taken the brunt of a mass frontal fighter assault, a tactic that the Luftwaffe was now perfecting with quite devastating results.

By the end of 1943 over 60 aircraft had been lost in action along with over 530 airmen and the Group had not yet completed 50 missions. In barely six months it had been led by three Commanding Officers, with Colonel Dale R. Smith now in charge; he proved to be most able and would remain in command until October 1944. Without a shadow of doubt it had been a traumatic time for the Group, and everybody at Grafton Underwood – veterans and newcomers alike – hoped for a better New Year.

Although the Group lost four crews in the first week of January, it managed to return from Halberstadt on the 11th without loss and gained its first Distinguished Unit Citation, along with other Groups in the Division. In February (22nd) when the Junkers 88 components factory at Aschersleben was attacked, the Division suffered heavy losses – 38 in action and another four in crashes (14.5%) The 384th lost four crews, but it had already lost another aircraft in a collision whilst assembling with a total of 18 airmen killed. The assembly of heavily loaded aircraft first into squadrons, then groups and finally into combat formations was always fraught with danger. The procedure required accurate timing and precise flying with little margin for human error, and poor weather conditions only heightened the risk of collision. In the next six months another five of the Group's aircraft would come to grief during assembly. During the course of a thousand days of operations the Eighth Air Force lost over 1,000 aircraft in collisions with friendly aircraft – a very high price to pay for their close and complex formation flying.

B-17 Ruthless *of 547th Bomb Squadron, 384th Bomb Group. (Smithsonian Institution)*

Another German target became the Group's *bête noir* during the next two months – the Dornier factories at Oberpfaffenhofen, which was about 15 miles to the south-west of Munich. It was first targeted on 18th March and on this mission two of the Group's aircraft failed to return. Both had landed with battle damage in Switzerland, where they were joined by another 14 B-17s and B-24s, and all the crews were interned. As the Eighth struck increasingly at vital targets in southern Germany the number of damaged bombers that were forced to seek refuge in this neutral country grew steadily. Over a month later (24th April) the crews returned to the same target, but this time it was an even more torrid mission. On this operation the 41st Bomb Wing (as the 103rd had become in September 1943) came under heavy attack from Me 109s and FW 190s for well over an hour, and according to the crews' reports, '... they repeatedly came in waves head-on into the formations in elements of ten abreast ...'. The 384th bore the brunt of these ferocious attacks and lost seven aircraft. A badly damaged B-17 made for Switzerland but it was shot down by a Swiss fighter and crashed into a lake, killing five of the crew. For this operation the 384th was awarded its second and thoroughly deserved DUC.

Compared with the heavy losses suffered in April when 20 crews were lost in action, the two following months passed tolerably well considering the number of missions that were mounted during the period. On 8th May some crews went out to Berlin and were fortunate to return to Grafton Underwood intact as 25 B-17s were lost on this early morning operation. Then in the afternoon the 41st Wing sent a force to a large V1 rocket site at Sottevast, about eight miles south of Cherbourg; three crews were lost, one ditched about 60 miles from Thorney Island and only two of the crew were rescued. On return a badly damaged aircraft crashed heavily at the airfield and it was ultimately scrapped – so much for these missions being 'milk-runs'!

In July a number of strategic oil targets and aircraft factories in southern Germany would test to the limit the determination and strength of the Eighth. Many crews felt, with some justification, that such missions should count as double at least when compared with the short trips to V1 rocket sites in northern France. These deep penetration raids involved long flights across hostile skies and were fraught with great danger. Often unfavourable weather conditions were encountered, certainly heavy flak had to be faced, there was also the ever present threat of enemy fighters and if the crews survived all these dangers, there was the possibility of running short of fuel on the long trip home with the risk of ditching or a forced landing.

The Group was active on 18 days in July and ten of these operations were to Leipzig, Augsburg, Merseburg, Dessau, Ludwigshafen and Munich, with the latter target being attacked on five occasions. Just purely on the law of averages a Group would be fortunate indeed not to suffer one costly mission, perhaps a day when one of its squadrons just happened to be in the wrong place at the wrong time. For a change the 384th emerged from these long and dangerous raids with relatively light losses in the circumstances, 'only' six crews went missing in action during the month. From now on until the end of the war the Group's losses remained at a tolerable level, in fact they averaged out at three aircraft per month. Nevertheless on seven separate operations the Group suffered the only loss in the 1st Division, so perhaps it could be said that 'Lady Luck' or 'Dame Fortune' still seemed to elude the crews of the 384th.

The 300th milestone was passed at the beginning of April 1945 and the European air war was drawing to a blessed conclusion. But on the 6th of the month when the Division sent a force of 230 aircraft to the railway station at Leipzig, it turned out to be a sad day for the Group. Shortly after take-off one of its B-17s caught fire and all the crew were killed; this proved to be the last fatal accident to befall the Eighth Air

Memorial at Grafton Underwood.

Force in the county. Then over the target area two of the Group's aircraft were involved in separate collisions. Just 19 days later the last B-17s to leave Grafton Underwood in anger attacked the Skoda armaments works at Pilsen. Either by design or by luck the 384th was the final Group to arrive over the target and it broke up into individual squadrons for the bombing run. Thus the last bombs dropped by an

Eighth heavy bomber crew fell to *Swamp Angel* and to its bombardier, 1/Lieutenant Earl Fisher. On this final mission six B-17s were destroyed by enemy flak, one of which came from the 384th. Throughout the war and more particularly during 1944 enemy flak accounted for more of the Eighth's heavy bombers than the much vaunted Luftwaffe fighters.

The Group had paid a high price for its part in the Eighth's bombing offensive – 154 aircraft and over 1,500 airmen lost or missing in action. This was the fourth heaviest loss in the 1st Division, and the other three Groups had all operated at least nine months longer. During June 1945 the 384th left for Istres in France and the RAF occupied the airfield until February 1959, when the site was handed back to the estate of the Duke of Buccleuch.

There is a particularly fine stained-glass window in the church of St James the Apostle at Grafton Underwood, which portrays a B-17 and has a plaque below inscribed with the simple words 'Coming Home'. The memorial stone, which stands on what was part of the main runway records the fact that 'The First and Last Bombs dropped by the 8th Air Force were from airplanes flying from Grafton Underwood.'

10
HARRINGTON

On 6th November 1943 there was a rather select gathering of top brass at the new airfield at Harrington, which was situated about $5\frac{1}{2}$ miles due west of Kettering. The most notable officers were Lieutenant General Ira C. Eaker and Air Chief Marshal Sir Arthur T. Harris, the respective heads of the Eighth Air Force and RAF Bomber Command. They were supported by Major General O. H. Lees and Air Vice-Marshal H. K. Thorold along with other senior officers of both air forces. The two commanders had managed to escape briefly from the daily pressures of their desks and commands because rather unusually neither air force had any major operations planned for the day or the coming night.

The special occasion that had brought them together was the formal hand-over of the new airfield to the RAF. It had been built by American Aviation Engineers, the 826th and 852nd Battalions, and was the only wartime airfield to be built by American engineers for the RAF, hence the special ceremony and formalities, which were closed by a fly-past of three RAF Wellingtons from Desborough. The airfield at Harrington was unusual in two other respects; it ultimately became the most westerly operational base used by the Eighth Air Force, and as it was situated at over 530 feet above sea level it was also the highest airfield used by them.

After all the excitement of the big day, construction work still continued on the airfield and it was not completely finished until well into the New Year. However, the first RAF personnel arrived at Harrington to prepare the satellite station for members of No 84 Operational Training Unit, which had its main base at Desborough.

Formal opening of Harrington – 6th November 1943 – Air Chief Marshal Sir Arthur Harris, Lieutenant General Ira C. Eaker, Air Vice-Marshal H. K. Thorold and Major General O. H. Lees, from left to right. (National Archives & Records Administration)

Ground training commenced almost immediately with the first flying training from the airfield not starting until January. The Unit's Wellingtons would not use Harrington for very long because operational training in Bomber Command was well up to requirements and some Units were being reduced in size, while the airfield was required for USAAF use. By 1st April the RAF had vacated Harrington and it was taken over by the Eighth Air Force, though the airfield was not officially handed back until 1st May, again with due ceremony, only on this occasion the RAF was represented by just a Squadron Leader.

The American unit that was to occupy Harrington was No 801 (Provisional) Bomb Group, which had been formed on 28th March by the merging of the 36th and 406th squadrons. They were two special squadrons that had been formed to deliver supplies, and later secret agents, to the various groups of Resistance forces in occupied Europe. They operated on behalf of the Office of Strategic Services (OSS), which was the American counterpart of the British Special Operations

Colonel Clifford J. Heflin, Group Commander at Harrington. (National Archives & Records Administration)

Executive (SOE). These operations were all part of a grand Allied plan, which was co-ordinated with the SOE. The Americans, as was their wont, codenamed their special missions 'Carpetbagger' – a name that was redolent of post Civil War days and its opportunist travelling salesmen. The nucleus of this special force had been formed from the two squadrons, Nos 4 and 22, of the disbanded No 479 Anti-Submarine Group, mainly because its crews had gained valuable experience of long navigational patrols at night operating from an airfield in Devon.

The 22nd squadron, under the command of Lieutenant Colonel Clifford Heflin, had moved into Alconbury in October 1943 and was redesignated the 406th Bomb squadron. The first American Carpet-bagger operations had been mounted from RAF Tempsford in Bedfordshire, where the two RAF squadrons – Nos 138 and 161 – had already acquired considerable experience and expertise in mounting such clandestine operations. During November and December each American pilot, navigator and bombardier made at least two operational flights with the RAF crews, normally in Halifaxes, before their squadrons went 'live'. They first operated from Alconbury and later moved to Watton in Norfolk before finally transferring to Harrington in late March; by this time their crews had completed 63 sorties delivering over 150 tons of supplies. The supply packs contained radio equipment, specialised tools, money, forged documents, foodstuffs and clothing; munitions, arms and explosive were dropped separately. Harrington was conveniently close to the central packing and storage centre at Holme, about 35 miles away, which supplied both the British and American squadrons.

The two American squadrons were equipped with Consolidated B-24Ds and Hs, and later with some C-47s (Skytrains). The B-24 was the second heavy bomber to be used by the Eighth Air Force. It had been designed in 1939 to have a superior performance to the B-17, but had not entered the US Army Air Corps until late 1941, the model 'D' being the first version to be mass produced. It was powered by four Pratt & Whitney R-1830-65 engines, which gave it a top speed of 270 mph, and B-24s were in greater numbers than any other American wartime aircraft – well over 18,000! B-24s operated most successfully as heavy bombers with 14 Groups of the 2nd Division of the Eighth from bases in Norfolk and Suffolk, and in their various models served in 15 Allied air forces and in every theatre of war, but perhaps notably and most effectively in the Pacific. The RAF operated 42 squadrons of B-24s or Liberators as they were known in the Service.

The aircraft's name had originated as a result of a competition held in the manufacturer's works in San Diego (originally the company had tentatively suggested that 'Eagle' would be an appropriate name). The B-24 proved to be a highly versatile aircraft, and its long operational range (2,000 miles) made it ideal for use as a maritime patrol aircraft. Not even its most devoted admirer, and of these there were many, could describe the B-24 as a particularly attractive aircraft, its twin tails and slab-like appearance making it appear somewhat cumbersome. Indeed, B-17 crews dismissed it as 'the crate our aircraft came across in'! Nevertheless, the B-24 proved to be one of the most durable and successful aircraft of the Second World War.

The squadrons' aircraft had been specially adapted for their new clandestine role, the modification work undertaken mainly at the Eighth's Air Depôts at Burtonwood in Lancashire and Watton in Norfolk. The B-24Ds were considered the best model for such work, as they had a superior outlook from the nose and were considered to have far better handling qualities. The aircraft were painted overall in non-glare black, although later this was changed to gloss black as its reflective qualities were thought to have a greater chance of evading the searchlight batteries. The nose and waist guns were removed, as well as the ball turret, and this left an opening for a cargo hatch and an exit for parachutists, which became known as a 'Joe Hole' – 'Joe' was the American slang for a secret agent. The waist windows were blacked-out and teardrop perspex blisters were added to both cockpit windows to afford the pilots better visibility. The oxygen equipment was removed, extra room was provided internally for the crews and the fuselage was fitted with plywood flooring to aid movement of supplies.

Each aircraft was provided with 'Gee', the British navigational aid, which was later replaced by 'Loran', the American-built version. Special radio equipment was installed, 'S-phone', which was a two-way ultra-high frequency radio/telephone powered by batteries, enabling the crew to communicate with the people on the ground and vice versa. An airborne air/ground homing device known as 'Rebecca' was also installed, which could receive radar impulses from a ground set ('Eureka'), and the equipment greatly aided navigators to locate the precise dropping points, although the Eureka sets were disliked by the agents as they were heavy and cumbersome and difficult to secrete. During the night flights the aircraft would be completely blacked-out save for a small light in the navigator's compartment. Over the dropping zone the aircraft would be flown to within 400 to 600 feet of the ground at a speed of about 130 mph or less. As the RAF crews had found to their cost these special missions were full of risks and dangers, and already three American crews had been lost since their first Carpetbagger operation left RAF Tempsford on 4/5th January. This operation had been led by Colonel Clifford J. Heflin, who had now been given the command of the new No 801st Group, with Major Robert W. Fish, the ex-Commanding Officer of the 36th squadron, as his deputy.

The first Carpetbagger operation to be mounted from Harrington left on 5/6th April. Of the 17 B-24s taking part only one, piloted by Lieutenant William W. Nicholl, failed to return; because of the nature of the operations the circumstances of the missing aircraft were only known on rare occasions. Their first month at Harrington was quite busy with the crews operating on twelve nights making 180 sorties, and another B-24, named *Worry Bird* of the 36th squadron, went missing on 27/28th, though the other 20 crews operating that night arrived back safely.

It was during April that the Group began parachuting special agents and 'Jedburgh' teams, known as 'Jeds'. These three-man teams usually comprised a British or American and French or Dutch serving officer along with a radio operator, and were mostly dropped in full military uniform. They would help to train Resistance groups in the use of weapons and explosives, as well as plan and take part in sabotage operations. The Jedburgh teams were trained at Milton Hall near Peterborough. Each team was given a male Christian name as a code, and 93 were dropped into France, of which 27 men were killed or taken prisoner.

In May the crews were in action on 16 nights with the number of successful sorties exceeding 200 for the first time, although three B-24s were lost in action. One went missing on the night of 5/6th, when it was shot down by enemy flak from a troop train travelling through northern France.

The pace of these special operations had so increased, because of the impending invasion of Europe, that the Group found great difficulty in meeting the demands of the OSS. However, some welcome reinforcements for the Group were forthcoming when Major John Dickerson with his 850th squadron flew in directly from the United States to join the Group. Another squadron, the 788th, was transferred in from the 467th Bomb Group based at Rackheath in Norfolk, and both squadrons moved into Cheddington for a spell of training. These new additions to the Group almost doubled its complement of B-24s at Harrington to over 40. By mid-June this figure would increase to 54 and ultimately some 80 B-24Ds and Hs had been modified for Carpetbagger duties.

During June the first C-47s were allocated to the Group, and Colonel Heflin was the first pilot to make a night-landing with this aircraft. They would be used to land valuable cargo and passengers, as well as returning with passengers. The month saw a further increase in the number of sorties flown, still mostly to France although seven were made to Belgium, with one B-24 failing to return. During the month over 400 sorties had been mounted, of which over a half had been successful, compared with just 18 back in January. Unfortunately a B-24 was shot down by an enemy intruder whilst on a training flight on 28th June; the aircraft crashed at Eaton Socon killing three of the crew.

The Group's Carpetbagger activities over France reached a peak in July with the crews in action on 27 nights. Nearly 540 successful sorties were despatched with over 100 agents dropped. On the night of 4/5th, 36 crews were in action; three were lost with a fourth aircraft crash-landing at Ford airfield in Sussex although four of the crew had already baled out over enemy territory. This was the Group's heaviest loss on a single night.

Two nights later Colonel Heflin, with Captain W. Stapel as co-pilot, made the first C-47 landing at a secret airstrip at Izernore near Nantua, which was about 45 miles north-east of Lyons. The operation was coded 'Mixer I' and eleven passengers were carried, including a Major G. E. Parker (RAMC) who was bound for an emergency hospital at Nantua, where many of the French Maquis casualties were treated. The aircraft returned on 9/10th, after a round trip of 1,000 miles, with ten passengers including Richard Heslop or 'Xavier', one of the SOE's most successful British agents; his circuit – 'Landsman' – had survived in eastern France since 1942. Later in the month (18/19th) a B-24 collided with an RAF Halifax of No 138 squadron on a similar operation. Both aircraft crashed near Malgny-l'Eglise in France; all 15 airmen were killed in this tragic accident. The Group had five crews missing in action, compared with six RAF aircraft lost whilst employed on SOE operations.

There were changes afoot in August, when the Group was redesignated the 492nd, thus inheriting the identity of the Eighth's most unfortunate Heavy Bomb Group: it had lost over 50 B-24s in less than three months of operations from North Pickenham in Norfolk and had been disbanded on 12th August. The Group's squadrons operating on special duties were also renumbered – 36th, 850th, 406th and 788th becoming 856th to 859th respectively. Colonel Heflin left Harrington on the 25th of the month, when he was transferred back to the States to command a B-29 training centre at Wendover in Utah. He was replaced by his very able and popular deputy, Lieutenant Colonel Robert W. Fish, who would remain in charge to almost the end of the year. It had been a record month for the Carpetbaggers – over 340 successful sorties with 700 tons of supplies dropped, along with 227 agents.

Carpetbagger operations to France ceased in the middle of September but nevertheless over 350 sorties were mounted. On the 16/17th a B-24 from 858th squadron flown by Lieutenant James M. McLaughlin, who was on his 35th and final mission, was shot down over Chartres by American anti-aircraft guns; four of the crew were killed but McLaughlin survived and was rescued by American troops. On the same night another 31 B-24s and C-47s had made successful drops. Only one squadron, the 856th, was retained for a limited number of special operations to be conducted over Holland, Belgium and Denmark, and it was now placed under the direct control of the Eighth Air Force headquarters with the small detachment of OSS personnel leaving Harrington.

From 21st September the crews became engaged, along with crews from many B-24 Bomb Groups, in 'trucking', which was the transport of urgent and essential petrol supplies for the Allied land forces. The Group had been given a delivery target of 115,000 gallons per day and their aircraft had been swiftly modified to carry as much fuel in five gallon cans as possible. The trucking operations continued until the end of the month when over 800,000 gallons had been delivered by the Group for the loss of a single B-24.

In December the 859th squadron was sent on detachment to Brindisi in Italy to undertake Carpetbagger missions over northern Italy and the Balkans, and the squadron never returned to Harrington, remaining with the Fifteenth Air Force. On 17th December a new Commanding Officer was appointed, Colonel Hudson H. Upham, who was a graduate of the West Point Academy and had no previous combat experience, although he was later described as 'a quiet, effective administrator and a good flyer.' Upham would later command the 306th Bomb Group and was killed in a flying accident in July 1946. His immediate task was to organise his two remaining squadrons to commence night-bombing operations in co-operation with No 100 (SD) Group of Bomber Command. On Christmas Eve twelve B-24s attacked La Pallice coastal batteries around Bordeaux, and the crews returned to the same area on the nights of 28/29th December and 4/5th January. In three nights a total of 40 sorties were despatched, of which 27 were effective but only 56 tons of bombs were dropped. The crews would now be engaged in night-training for future bombing operations.

The Group was effectively reduced to just one squadron when the crews and aircraft of the 857th squadron were absorbed into other units of the Eighth and, in March 1945, the squadron became formally established as 1st Scouting Force. During the last two weeks of February 1945 Carpetbagger operations recommenced with 15 crews active on three nights. Bombing missions were also mounted during the same period, with an average of 26 crews active each night over railway yards and oil and gas targets at Neustadt, Duisburg, Wilhelmshafen and Freiburg. Two B-24s were lost on the 21st/22nd whilst bombing the power and gas stations at Duisburg. From a relatively quiet winter period Harrington would become a most active airfield during the last two complete months of the war. Bombing operations continued until mid-April along with a variety of Carpetbagger operations over Holland, Denmark and Norway and special flights over Germany would also be mounted throughout March and April.

During March two new aircraft appeared at Harrington and both would be employed on special duties. The first to arrive was the Douglas A-26 or Invader. This twin-engined light bomber had been designed in 1940 as the replacement for the A-20 (Havoc) and ultimately the B-26 (Marauder). It had first flown in July 1942 and was the last American attack aircraft to be developed during the Second World War. With a maximum speed of 355 mph, it was the fastest American wartime bomber. The A-26Bs began to enter the USAAF during mid-1944 and were first allocated to the Ninth Air Force. However, it was thought that the Invaders would be particularly suited for special duties, especially to drop agents over Germany, and on 2nd March one A-26C operating from Watton managed to drop two agents close to Berlin. The aircraft were painted overall in black and on these special missions they operated with two navigators to pin-point the dropping zone. By the middle of March the Group had five A-26Cs at their disposal at Harrington.

The other aircraft that was new to Harrington was the de Havilland Mosquito PRXVI, which had first entered into service with the USAAF in April 1944 equipping the 25th Bomb Group. They were mainly flown by ex-P-38 fighter pilots. The PRXVI was the high-altitude and long-range model of this legendary aircraft which had been specially developed for high-altitude photo-reconnaissance duties. The aircraft had been provided with a special pressurised cabin, and just over 430 of this PR Mark were finally produced. The Mosquitos were engaged on special operations that were given the code 'Red Stocking' – the receiving and recording of signals transmitted by Allied agents operating in enemy occupied territories and in Germany. This equipment was known as 'Joan-Eleanor', from a Major in the Women's Army Corps and the wife of the US research engineer who had developed the new device. The Mosquito's bomb bay had been converted to accommodate an oxygen system and the special phone and recording apparatus (an early form of a tape recorder) necessary to pick up the agents' UHF transmissions. By the 20th the Group had three Mosquito PRXVIs at Harrington and by the end of the month another two had been received.

In January the Group had established a forward air base at Bron Field near Lyons to operate missions over southern Germany, but because of severe weather conditions not many sorties were flown. During March the Group had also sent a detachment of crews to operate from a forward base near Dijon in France, specifically to drop agents and supplies into Germany. The crews made their first successful sorties from Dijon on 16th March, and they ultimately

B-24s lining up for a bombing mission, March 1945. (Smithsonian Institution)

managed to make 54 successful sorties and parachute over 80 agents into Germany and Austria.

The pace and tempo of operations from Harrington really began to accelerate from the night of 2nd/3rd March when four B-24s were engaged on Carpetbagger operations, and by the end of the month over 80 successful sorties had been made with just a single B-24 lost in action; it had crashed in the Orkneys whilst returning from Norway. Six bombing operations were also mounted to Wiesbaden, Dortmund, and Munster, and all the crews returned safely to Harrington. On the 14th of the month the 856th squadron returned to the Group's control, and No 406, the Night Leaflet Squadron, arrived from Cheddington.

There had been several changes in the squadron since its days at Chelveston. The crews were now mainly operating with B-24s, and in fact back in November 1944 the squadron had been augmented with aircraft and crews from the 492nd Bomb Group. Sadly their most experienced Commanding Officer, Lieutenant Colonel Earle J. Aber, was no longer with the squadron. He had been shot down by 'friendly' anti-aircraft fire at Harwich on 5th March when returning from Germany in one of the squadron's last remaining B-17s; this had been the Colonel's 51st mission. The squadron recommenced their operations from 16th March and continued almost nightly dropping leaflets and newspapers over France, Holland and Germany.

The first A-26 operation from Harrington was mounted on 19th/20th March over Hamm but unfortunately one of the two aircraft failed to return. The previous night the first Mosquito Red Stocking mission had been despatched, with another seven leaving Harrington during the

A-26 (Invader) of 386th Bomb Group. Some A-26s operated from Harrington. (USAF)

month. April continued in much the same vein, with over 120
Carpetbagging sorties despatched, mainly to Norway and Denmark,
with the loss of five crews. Four bombing operations were also
mounted, the last leaving on the night of the 13/14th when the rail
junction at Beizenburg was attacked. Although on the two following
nights two bombing missions were despatched, both were unsuccessful. On most nights at least one Mosquito crew left on a Red Stocking
operation, although many of the sorties were unsuccessful, and the first
and only Mosquito lost as a result of enemy action crashed at
Winchfield on return.

The Group's last Carpetbagging missions left the airfield on the night
of 26/27th April for Norway; over 2,800 sorties had been made with
over 1,040 persons delivered behind enemy lines. During these
operations 25 B-24s were lost in action and another eight written-off
in operational accidents with 208 airmen killed in action. Even after VE
Day the airfield was certainly not completely idle, with the Night
Leaflet Squadron active until the end of May, by which time it had
dropped almost $1\frac{1}{2}$ billion leaflets in well over 300 operations!

In June No 492 Group returned to the United States and the Night
Leaflet Squadron departed for Wiesbaden in Germany on 4th July. The
airfield was finally returned to the RAF on 9th October 1945, and was
used for the storage of motor vehicles. From late 1959 until August
1963 it became a site for Thor Intermediate Range missiles.

Somewhat belatedly the Group was awarded a Distinguished Unit

Memorial to the 'Carpetbaggers' at Harrington.

Citation in March 1947 for its operations during 20th March to 26th April 1945; the citation highlighted '... the perilous flying conditions and opposition from the close range enemy ground defences ... the 492nd B.G. continued to distinguish itself in special operations involving long flights into enemy territory ...'. The splendid memorial to the 801st/492nd 'Carpetbaggers' stands on the east side of the B576 road from Lamport to Rothwell, and it depicts a B-24 taking-off from the airfield, replicating a famous wartime photograph.

11
HINTON-IN-
THE-HEDGES

Hinton-in-the-Hedges, along with Bog's O'Mayne, Findo Gask, Half-penny Green, Hell's Mouth, Moreton-in-Marsh and Needs Oar Point, is one of the more unusual names of RAF wartime airfields; making 'Much-Binding-in-the-Marsh' of wartime radio fame almost seem normal! Although the name evokes an image of a pleasant and tranquil rural retreat, it was in reality a far cry from that. The noise, bustle and activity of a wartime airfield, and especially one that was devoted to operational training for much of its existence, where heavy aircraft would take-off and land far more frequently than at operational airfields and at all hours of the day and night, ensured that Hinton-in-the-Hedges was anything but a serene and peaceful place!

Perhaps in one respect the airfield's name was quite apt. Although it is only about $2\frac{1}{2}$ miles to the west of Brackley, the airfield could be considered as being rather remote, and is now reached by a long and narrow country road from the A422 Banbury to Brackley road from where it is signposted. In the summer of 1940 it was built around Walltree Farm as a grassed airfield. The concrete runways, some stretches of which have survived, were put down later in 1943. Hinton-in-the-Hedges was intended to act purely as a satellite airfield for No 13 OTU at Bicester and ultimately it became one of a clutch of wartime airfields – including Turweston, Croughton and Finmere – that surrounded Brackley, although only two were situated in North-amptonshire.

Even in 1940 the concept of satellite airfields was a fairly recent innovation. The first trial 'satellite landing ground' was established at Alconbury in May 1938 and used as a relief airfield for Upwood. The original intention was that the aircrews would be transported there daily and the aircraft would return to the permanent station for refuelling, maintenance and repair, as at that time there were no plans to provide other than basic facilities at these grassed airfields. However, the exigencies of war and the pressure on airfield space quickly changed that idea, facilities were improved and later many satellite airfields became independent stations in their own right. Fighter Command were the first to use satellites during the summer of 1940 followed by training satellites and, by February 1941, most of the OTUs had a satellite airfield, which ideally should not be more than 15 miles distant from its parent station. It was anticipated that these training satellite airfields would be staffed by some 200 officers and airmen, and would normally house one of the Unit's flights. Later, when facilities at these airfields were improved, it was normal for a second Flight to be based there.

The two original 'Pool' or training squadrons of No 2 Group of Bomber Command – Nos 104 and 108 – had operated from Bicester since shortly before the outbreak of the war. They had been moved from Bassingbourn to Bicester under what was known as the Group's Scatter Plan, which was mainly designed to remove flying training farther inland for safety reasons, as well as freeing more forward airfields for the use of operational squadrons. Both squadrons had been re-equipped with Bristol Blenheim Is early in 1939 and they merged to form No 13 OTU in the spring of 1940. It was one of just two Units training crews for the light bomber squadrons of No 2 Group of Bomber Command, as well as for service in the Middle East.

The satellite airfield officially opened in late November 1940, which was not a particularly propitious time as the autumn had been plagued with very heavy rainfall. This caused endless problems at most of the grassed airfields, with many remaining waterlogged and unserviceable for long periods during the following winter. Although the Blenheims were not especially heavy – about $4\frac{1}{4}$ tons unladen weight – they could still cause considerable havoc with grassed runs. In fact after about two months of training the airfield was effectively put out of commission until the following May when 'D' Flight moved in with its Avro Ansons, followed a few months later by Blenheims of 'A' Flight.

It is interesting to note, in the light of the Air Ministry's view of concrete runways, that during 1940 the provision of 'firm' runways for all flying training airfields was seriously considered. However, Flying Training Command were not particularly enthusiastic, nor greatly in favour of the idea. It was considered that the necessary construction

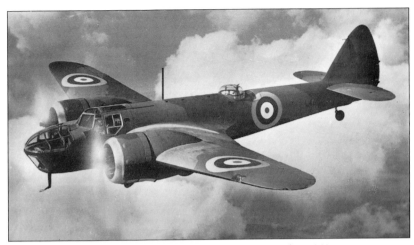

Blenheim IVs of No 13 OTU used the airfield from November 1940.

work would have to be undertaken mainly during the summer months, which would mean that the airfields would become unserviceable during the most valuable training period of the year and furthermore the Command was very conscious that it was under considerable pressure to maintain its training targets. It also put forward the considered opinion that the standard 50 yard wide concrete runways were 'dangerous for night-flying because there was far greater risk of trainee pilots running off the runways and crashing on reaching the grass surfaces'! Subsequently all OTUs were based at airfields that were already provided with concrete runways, at least whenever it was possible.

The Unit was equipped with both versions of the Bristol Blenheim, Marks I and IV; the latter mark had been developed during 1938 and was distinguished by its longer nose section and conventional stepped windscreen. The aircraft was powered by two Bristol Mercury XV engines, which gave it a maximum speed in excess of 260 mph and enabled it to carry 1,000 pounds of bombs. The Blenheim IV proved to be a most reliable, tough and pugnacious light bomber, and its squadrons spearheaded Bomber Command's day-bombing offensive until the aircraft was withdrawn from the fray in August 1942. By then Blenheim crews had pioneered and perfected many of the low-level bombing tactics that were later used so effectively by the Mosquito squadrons. The brave and valiant exploits of these crews during the early war years have become legendary, certainly the aircrew losses that were sustained by the Blenheim squadrons over this period were truly horrendous.

The most ubiquitous aircraft at any RAF wartime airfield were the Avro Ansons, and especially at OTUs where they were used for a variety of training purposes. The Anson was probably the most beloved RAF aircraft of the war and was affectionately known to its pilots and crews as 'The Faithful Annie'. It had been designed in 1933 by Roy Chadwick of A. V. Roe Ltd, who was also responsible for the design of the Lancaster. The aircraft owed much to Avro's successful six-seater commercial aircraft, the Avro 652, which had been built at the behest of Imperial Airways. The prototype Anson first flew in March 1935, and entered the Service exactly a year later as the RAF's first monoplane, which also was the first to be provided with a retractable undercarriage. Ansons ultimately operated as trainers, general transport and communications aircraft as well as air ambulances, and were used operationally by Coastal Command. Indeed, on 5th September 1939 they made the first RAF attack on a German U-boat. They flew very successfully with the Command on coastal reconnaissance and search and rescue duties. In all 21 squadrons were equipped with Ansons until they were replaced by Lockheed Hudsons. Rather famously, on 1st June 1940 an Anson of No 500 squadron, piloted by Pilot Officer P. W. Peters, shot down two Me 109s over Dunkirk. Peters was awarded an immediate DFC for this most improbable combat victory of the war; he died in 1997 aged 81 years.

Nevertheless, the Anson's wartime fame stemmed from its universal use as a training aircraft for pilots, navigators, radio operators and air gunners and it was the standard trainer used by the Empire Air Training Scheme. Its array of cabin windows provided excellent vision for its trainee airmen, and gained the aircraft the name of 'The Flying Greenhouse'! The aircraft's two Armstrong Siddeley Cheetah IX engines gave it a maximum speed of 188 mph with a rate of climb of 750 feet per minute. The Anson was considered a most reliable and sturdy aircraft, and once was famously described as 'a well mannered and forgiving old lady'! Some 11,000 Ansons in a variety of marks were produced right up to 1952, one of the longest production runs of any British aircraft. They finally left the RAF in June 1968 after 32 years of long and faithful service.

The Unit's training flights from the airfield seemed to be blessed with few accidents, with just one in 1941 and four in the following year. The last Blenheim accident occurred on 24th July only weeks before 'A'

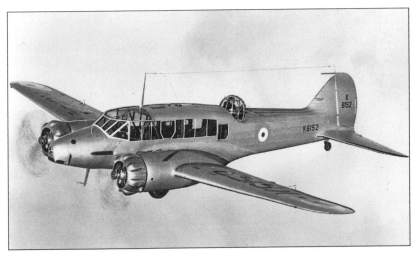

Avro Anson or 'The Faithful Annie'.

Flight departed for Finmere, which had now been appointed Bicester's new satellite airfield. The Blenheims were quickly replaced by Wellingtons of 'A' Flight of No 16 OTU, which was based at Upper Heyford. The Flight had hitherto been operating from nearby Croughton. No 16 Unit had, until May 1942, been equipped with Hampdens and Herefords, and Hinton-in-the-Hedges was used by the Unit until the beginning of April 1943 when the Flight moved away to Barford St John in Oxfordshire, which had been serving as the Unit's second satellite since the close of 1942.

Early in April 1943 Hinton-in-the-Hedges was transferred into No 26 (Signals) Group. This Group had been moved into Bomber Command from Technical Training Command in February 1942 under the command of Air Vice Marshal O. G. W. Lynwood, CB, CBE. It had been denuded of its training commitments and now controlled a variety of operational signals units and the extensive ground signals communications network that was being built up at airfields throughout the country. One of the Group's more important units, the Signals Development Unit (SDU), moved into the airfield on 15th April under the command of Wing Commander C.C. McMullen. It operated a rare mixture of aircraft from Ansons, Masters and Oxfords to Whitleys. Some of these aircraft had been acquired when the SDU had absorbed No 1551 Flight – a Blind Approach Calibration Unit – which had been operating from Bicester since the previous November.

A new Flight, No 1478, was also formed at the airfield on the same

No 1478 Flight used Armstrong Whitworth Whitley Vs. (RAF Museum)

day as it moved into Hinton-in-the-Hedges, and it was provided with Armstrong Whitworth Whitley Vs. This two-engined heavy bomber had been in the Service since 1937, and although rather slow and ponderous with a cruising speed of about 200 mph, it was an immensely rugged aircraft, which had played a major part in Bomber Command's bombing operations from the outset of the war until finally withdrawn from the Main Force at the end of April 1942. They were now operating in several OTUs as well as serving with Coastal Command and were also employed to tow gliders. Ultimately almost 1,900 were produced in a variety of marks and despite its size and bulk – 72 feet long with a wing span of 84 feet and an unladen weight of $8\frac{1}{2}$ tons – it could still operate from quite small airfields carrying its maximum weight load and with a high degree of safety, which made it a most useful and versatile aircraft.

A handful of the Flight's Whitleys would be literally filled with a mass of radio equipment – very high frequency, radio telephony, and medium frequency/direction finding – all fitted by Marshalls of Cambridge, which made the aircraft virtually airborne radio stations. The Flight's task was to operate over forward battle areas to maintain radio contact with the ground assault troops and to relay vital and up-to-date battle information speedily back from the battlefront. The aircraft were also fitted with long-range fuel tanks in the bomb bays as they were scheduled to serve in North Africa. The crews were given an extensive course of radio training before the first four Whitley crews left for Portreath in Cornwall in early June en route to North Africa. The Flight was eventually disbanded and ultimately three of its Whitleys made their way back to Hinton-in-the-Hedges towards the end of the year.

The Signals Development Unit was engaged in checking and developing the various electronic airborne landing and navigation aids, as well as installing radio transmitters and receivers in both aircraft and ground vehicles. It comprised just two Flights. One was mainly involved in the calibration and testing of the accuracy of the various defence radars and other similar equipment then in use at airfields. The other Flight was employed on work of a more secret and sensitive nature – the development and trialling of a new beam approach system. Since its entry into the European air war the USAAF had been less than impressed with the Standard Beam Approach system, which was then in universal use at Service airfields, including those used by the Eighth Air Force. The Americans felt, with some justification, that their Signals Corps System, which had been conceived and developed since 1939, was a much superior, more accurate and far safer system. In response to considerable pressure from the Eighth Air Force chiefs, the American system, which had been abbreviated to ILS or Instrument Landing System, was being tested at Hinton-in-the-Hedges by the SDU's Flight using Wellingtons and Beaufighters for the airborne trials.

In very simple terms the system was based on two ground transmitters, which provided an approach path for the aircraft's exact alignment and also produced the correct glide-slope for the aircraft's final descent onto the runway. The two transmitted radio signals were visually represented by two intersecting needles on the aircraft's instrument panel and when these needles crossed at right angles and furthermore remained in that position, the approach and landing would be accurate. Despite the very marked improvement of the Instrument Landing System over SBA and its proven success in all weather conditions, ILS was not introduced into the RAF until after the war; the first ILS receivers were fitted into aircraft of Transport Command. Of course, highly developed and very sophisticated Instrument Landing Systems are now in universal use at commercial airports and Service airfields throughout the world.

At the end of July 1944 the Signals Development Unit moved out to

The unusual defence pill-box awaiting restoration work.

Honiley in Warwickshire and its departure brought wartime flying at the airfield to a conclusion. In the autumn the airfield was used for the storage of radio and signals vehicles. However, over 50 years later the airfield still maintains its aviation links whilst other more famous operational airfields have long since disappeared. The remaining runways are now used for private flying although much of the

150

surrounding land is farmed. The airfield had an unusual control tower, which was quite unlike the standard design of the time, but alas this tower has now been demolished. One other unusual wartime feature has however survived – a defence pill-box. It has a pagoda-shaped observation tower on the top of the box, possibly for camouflage purposes, and at the time of writing it is awaiting restoration work.

12
HUSBANDS
BOSWORTH

In a search for a county's wartime airfield sites it is somewhat disconcerting to discover the number that were constructed across county boundaries; for example Castle Camps on the Cambridgeshire/ Essex border and Silverstone, which neatly crossed Northampton-shire's boundary with Buckinghamshire. Husbands Bosworth airfield proved to be a prime example. It was built right across the boundary with Leicestershire, and indeed the surviving part of the airfield is actually in that county whereas the land that was on the North-amptonshire side has now returned to agriculture.

The airfield site, to the east of the A1599 road, met all the essential pre-conditions for a wartime airfield. It was relatively flat, had a reasonable standard of drainage, and was situated about 500 feet above sea level, some 100 feet below the recommended maximum. This limit had been introduced because there was less likelihood of a low-cloud base that would restrict flying, especially during the winter months. No serious natural or man-made obstructions on or close to the proposed airfield or its planned flight paths were evident, and furthermore the nearest airfield was at Market Harborough, which was about six miles away, the normally accepted distance between airfields being at least five miles for quite obvious safety reasons. Thus with all the various preliminary conditions being satisfactorily fulfilled, detailed and exact surveys were made of the site field by field, before the initial legal steps were taken to requisition the necessary land under the Emergency Powers (Defence) Act 1939. From thence the development of Husbands Bosworth airfield, named from the nearby town in Leicestershire, went ahead and by the summer of 1943 a Class A standard bomber airfield was ready for occupation. It actually opened on 28th July as a satellite for No 14 OTU stationed at nearby Market Harborough.

This Unit had only recently moved into Market Harborough from Cottesmore in Rutland and Husbands Bosworth took the place of the Unit's previous satellite airfield at Saltby. Husbands Bosworth had become operational at a time when OTUs were hard pressed to provide a sufficient number of crews for Bomber Command. It was in 1943 that over one-third of the Command's total losses of the war occurred: the Battle of the Ruhr, the Hamburg raids and the first phase of the long and bitter Battle of Berlin would bring in their wake heavy aircrew losses. Flying Training Command estimated that some 3,000 crews were needed to replace those lost and wounded in action or made prisoners of war, and this figure did not take into consideration supplying crews to replace those that had completed their operational tours. During the whole of 1943 and well into 1944 all OTUs would be stretched to their full training capacity to maintain Bomber Command up to its maximum operational strength, especially as a Flight Engineer and a mid-upper gunner had been added to a crew's complement.

It would be perhaps stating the obvious to say that the Unit was equipped with Wellingtons – Mark Is and IIs – because only three out of the 22 OTUs were equipped with Whitleys and by mid-1944 they would also change to Wellingtons. The Wellington II had first flown in March 1939, and came into service in late 1940. It was powered by

No 14 OTU was inevitably equipped with Wellingtons. (RAF Museum)

Rolls-Royce Merlin X engines, which had been specially selected to provide a secondary source of power plants should the original Pegasus engine production falter or fail. The new engines gave the aircraft some slight improvements in speed, service ceiling and maximum weight, although its operational range had been slightly reduced. The Mark IIs had a relatively short operational lifespan as they were quickly replaced by the Mark IIIs, which had been resupplied with Pegasus engines.

In the early days of OTUs there was an almost continual shortage of experienced flying instructors, and this situation only worsened as the number of Units rapidly increased during 1941/2. However, in March 1941 a fixed number of missions to constitute a operational tour was introduced – 30. This decision had two immediate effects, on the one hand it released a number of battle hardened and experienced crews from operational squadrons, who then became available for instructional duties, but on the other hand it placed even greater pressure on OTUs to produce trained crews to replace them. The tour-expired crews would be given well earned leave and then they were posted to one of the Flying Instructors Schools for a four to five weeks instructors course. The syllabus closely followed that of the Central Flying School and was intended to train them in 'the standard methods of flying instruction', though many believed that the course was mainly to eradicate the bad flying habits they had acquired during their time on operational squadrons! After passing out of these schools the airmen either moved on to an OTU, a specialised aircrew category school or a Heavy Conversion Flight.

On average their stay on training duties could be anything between 18 months to two years, and almost without exception all these experienced airmen, whatever their special aircrew category, found themselves seconded to training duties. Judging by wartime recollections many of them found it rather difficult to adjust to the more steady and, at times, very monotonous regime of a training unit after the pace, excitement and fairly relaxed discipline of an operational squadron. One described his spell at a OTU as 'a tour of circuit-bashing with sprog [recruit] crews – a living hell', though not all would subscribe to such a damning view! Many airmen did volunteer for a second operational tour, but there was always a fine balance to be maintained by the Air Ministry between the need to keep the training staff up to a full complement and the almost constant demand for experienced airmen to serve in operational squadrons, especially from August 1942 onwards when the Pathfinder (PFF) Force was established.

To take one such flying instructor at random – Flight Lieutenant H. Thom, DFC, who arrived at Husbands Bosworth in May 1944. Although it must be admitted that Flight Lieutenant Thom was perhaps not the normal candidate to serve a bomber OTU because all his previous flying and training experience had been gained with Fighter Command. He had first flown Hurricanes with No 87 squadron, both in this country and in North Africa, where he had finally commanded the squadron. Since that time he had instructed at two fighter OTUs and arrived at Husbands Bosworth to take over the command of the Fighter Affiliation Flight. He stayed with the Unit until October. He later became a staff officer in Fighter Command.

The problems of simulating enemy fighter attacks for trainee crews had taxed the ingenuity of Flying Training Command for several years. In earlier days both operational fighter squadrons and fighter OTUs had at times been given the task of making mock attacks on training aircraft but operational duties and the sheer logistics in mounting such exercises regularly meant that the Units had to mostly fall back on their own rather limited resources. Quite frequently the Units' smaller aircraft – Lysanders, Martinets and Masters, all target-towers or trainers – were called upon to double as 'fighter' aircraft. However, by 1943 some outmoded Defiants, Hurricane IIs and Master IIs began to find their way into OTUs, and as was the case at Husbands Bosworth a special Flight was formed. The trainee gunners operated a 'camera gun', the films of which could be studied by the instructors to judge not only the standard of the trainee gunners' marksmanship but also the pilots' speed of reaction to take evasive action. With the increase of Heavy Conversion Units this aspect of the crews' training became increasingly devolved to this final stage of their operational training. However, in June 1943, Bomber Command introduced what were known as Bomber (Defence) Training Flights, the first six of which were numbered from 1681 to 1686. They were equipped with Curtiss Tomahawks, which had never made their mark either as escort or offensive fighters, and these Flights made regular tours of OTUs and HCUs to mount fighter affiliation exercises.

It was during the last few weeks of the course at OTUs that the crews' training became as realistic as was possible in artificial or make-believe situations. The crews were engaged in long cross-country flights by night, which inevitably led to some serious accidents. Also the trainee crews made several 'war load' flights, which was when the Wellingtons were loaded with their maximum permissible all-up weight. The 'bombs' that were carried on such flights were bomb

Bomber (Defence) Training Flights were equipped with Curtiss Wright Tomahawks.

canisters filled with sand, usually six 500 pound canisters. These exercises enabled the trainee crews, especially the pilots, to gain experience of handling the Wellingtons under normal operational conditions. But each crew flew at least one major exercise to give them a little taste of operating under simulated combat conditions, known as 'Bullseyes'.

They were basically night navigation exercises, which involved the crews flying to a 'hostile' area of the United Kingdom where the searchlight batteries attempted to illuminate the training aircraft for the anti-aircraft batteries, thus also providing training for the ground night-defences. At times the night-fighter forces were also engaged in these Bullseyes. The first daylight Bullseye was ordered on 17th July 1942 with London as the target. It was a large-scale exercise involving all the City's defence units and it was considered so successful that the first night Bullseye was flown on 4/5th August with London again as the target. From that time onwards night Bullseyes became an important and integral part of the latter stages of operational training. Special infra-red devices were set up at various targets throughout the country – Northampton, Bristol, Cardiff, Newcastle and London – where strike cameras could record the progress and effectiveness of the operation. There were several varieties of these exercises: a Command Special Bullseye involved a concentrated stream approach to a target from the sea to simulate a full-scale Luftwaffe raid, whereas a Local or

Colour Bullseye described a small exercise held at the request of an individual OTU. All such exercises were as close as possible to the real thing but they did result in quite a crop of accidents. As will be noted under Silverstone, several other exercises or operations were mounted by OTUs in an attempt to add a touch of reality to the crews' training.

In mid-June 1944 Husbands Bosworth became an independent station with the formation of No 85 OTU on the 15th of the month, commanded by Group Captain D. J. Eayrs. By now most of the Units were equipped with Wellington Xs and the pressure to provide crews had eased somewhat as Bomber Command's losses were lessening. The Unit was one of the last two to be formed, and they effectively replaced two OTUs that had been disbanded earlier in March, although by the end of 1944 another three OTUs would have closed down. No 85 OTU operated for exactly twelve months and during this period only one aircraft was lost due to accidental causes. On 24th September 1944 a Wellington X came down in the Spencer family estate at Althorp Park after the pilot had lost control of the aircraft.

Shortly after the end of the European war Bomber Command authorised Station Commanders, on a strictly informal basis, to allow their crews to fly over northern Germany and mainly over the Ruhr. The reason for these flights was to show ground personnel what damage had been inflicted by the Allied Air Forces. Some of the Unit's

The present day airfield.

Wellingtons flew to the Ruhr and these trips generally became known as 'Cook's Tours'. Sometimes the aircraft flew as low as 50 feet, and the extent of the terrible destruction that had been inflicted on the German cities and towns was all too evident. Most of the passengers watched in silent awe as they passed over the devastated areas, and many later recalled that these flights provided the most vivid memories of their wartime service days. About a dozen 'Cook's Tours' had been made before the Wellingtons left the airfield on 14th June 1945. Training had ceased two weeks earlier.

Flying effectively ceased at the airfield for almost the next 20 years. In 1964 the Coventry Gliding Club acquired a segment of the old airfield and since then gliding has been conducted from part of the site.

13
KING'S CLIFFE

From rather humble beginnings as a second satellite airfield for Wittering, King's Cliffe developed into a fighter station of no mean standing. Not only did it house several marks of RAF Spitfires, but every type of fighter that was used by the Eighth Air Force in the Second World War flew from the airfield. Furthermore it remained an important operational fighter base right up to the end of the war, thus eclipsing its neighbouring and more famous airfield, Wittering, which was about three miles due north.

The grassed airfield opened in late October 1941 and was first known as Wansford rather than King's Cliffe, the nearest village. It was situated to the south of the old Roman road to Peterborough and the first fighters to use the airfield were Spitfire Vbs of No 266 squadron from nearby Collyweston. The squadron would only make a brief stay at King's Cliffe as it had been selected to be re-equipped with Hawker Typhoons; No 266 would become the third squadron of a new Typhoon Wing that was being formed at Duxford. Towards the end of January the squadron moved out, after serving in this corner of the county since May 1940.

It was immediately replaced by another Spitfire squadron, No 616, from Kirton Lindsey in Lincolnshire. This famous Auxiliary squadron, the last to be formed in November 1938, was possibly better known as the 'South Yorkshire', its badge, a white rose, proudly proclaiming its origins. The squadron's Commander was Squadron Leader Colin F. Gray, DFC Bar, although in February he was succeeded by Squadron Leader H. L. I. Brown, DFC. Grey was one of the famous fighter aces of the war, a New Zealand airman who finally completed the war with $27\frac{1}{2}$ victories to his name. An even more legendary wartime airman was

Spitfire Vb: several squadrons at King's Cliffe operated this Mark.

serving as one of the Flight Commanders – Flight Lieutenant J.E. 'Johnnie' Johnson, DFC Bar, who would ultimately claim 38 victories to become the RAF's top scoring pilot. According to Johnson, King's Cliffe was rather less than comfortable: 'our quarters were bleak, wooden huts and we sorely missed the luxury of our permanent centrally heated accommodation at Kirton.'

The squadron formed part of the Wittering Wing, which frequently used West Malling in Kent as an advance landing ground. The pilots would fly down in the early morning, refuel, regroup before setting off on offensive sweeps over enemy territory, and then return to King's Cliffe in the evening. On 12th February some of the pilots became engaged in one of the RAF's most inglorious operations of the war – the vain attempt to prevent the 'Channel Dash' from Brest of the German warships *Scharnhorst, Gneisenau,* and *Prinz Eugen* to more secure

160

German ports. A contingency plan, Operation Fuller, had been devised should the German vessels attempt to break out, and make it through the English Channel.

Six of the squadron's Spitfires were despatched to Matlaske in Norfolk to join No 137's Westland Whirlwinds in an attempt to locate the vessels. From late morning, when the flotilla had been first sighted, until darkness Bomber and Fighter Commands launched over 640 sorties but because of poor visibility most of the aircraft failed to sight the vessels and those that did bombed rather ineffectively. The German flotilla was heavily escorted by fighters and 17 RAF fighters failed to return, by coincidence the same number as the Luftwaffe's losses. The whole sad and sorry operation showed an abysmal lack of liaison between the three RAF Commands, and although the pilots and crews fought bravely and with great determination (one FAA pilot was awarded the Victoria Cross), it was all to no avail as the German vessels escaped almost unscathed. Adolf Galland, the Luftwaffe leader, commented on the RAF's performance: 'inefficient planning without a clear concept of the attack and without any systematic tactics'. The national press had a field day and was loud in its condemnation of the RAF, even *The Times* thought the action 'mortifying'! All six Spitfires returned to King's Cliffe.

During April the first Spitfire VI landed at King's Cliffe. This was a very rare mark, with only 100 being finally produced. It had been specifically designed to improve the aircraft's high-altitude performance and to counter the threat of the Junkers 86P, a new high-flying reconnaissance bomber that was thought to be able to operate at 40,000 feet. The Mark VI was the first British fighter to be provided with a pressurised cockpit, which was reported to become 'unbearably hot' when operating below 12,000 feet. Johnson said it was like flying 'in a Turkish bath', and as the cockpit was secured by clamps it also felt as if one was 'encased in a transparent coffin'! The delivery of the new aircraft was rather slow and it was not until a month later that the squadron had 14 Mark VIs on its strength.

The pilots had begun flying high-altitude patrols and on 25th May they claimed two Dornier 217s damaged. Because so few Junkers 86s appeared during the early summer the squadron returned to low-level sweeps and in early June were engaged over enemy airfields in northern France. From the middle of the month the squadron was taken off operations so that the pilots could concentrate on training. On 3rd July the squadron was detached to West Malling for several days and returned on the 7th of the month but only for an overnight stay,

NORTHAMPTONSHIRE AIRFIELDS IN THE SECOND WORLD WAR

leaving next day for Kenley. Two years later almost to the day No 616 became the first squadron to receive the RAF's first jet fighter – Gloster Meteor I.

The squadron's immediate replacement was New Zealand's first fighter squadron, No 485, which was commanded by Squadron Leader R. J. C. 'Reg' Grant, DFM. Its pilots had been heavily engaged in the operations of the Kenley Wing, often flying twice a day. Its arrival marked the return of Spitfire Vbs, and the pilots continued to fly a mixture of 'Rodeos' (fighter sweeps), 'Ramrods' (escorts for light bombers with the destruction of a specific target as the main object) and 'Rhubarbs' (small scale fighter sweeps on targets of opportunity). These various operations were the bread and butter of Fighter Command during 1942 though they were, of course, not mounted at quite the same pace or intensity as in the squadron's Kenley days. The squadron also became engaged in escorting the early Eighth Air Force bombing operations as well as RAF daylight bombing raids from a variety of advance bases.

For about six weeks during September and October the airfield had a surfeit of Spitfire Vbs when No 93 squadron arrived from the Isle of Man pending its move to North Africa in November. In October No 485 was given a well-earned break from operations when it was detached to Kirkstown in Northern Ireland; it did not return to King's Cliffe until 23rd November. Just four days earlier the Squadron Commander's younger brother, Flying Officer I. A. C. Grant, had joined the squadron. He was destined to be shot down and killed whilst on a fighter sweep in February 1943. His brother was also killed in action just twelve months later.

The first American aircraft landed on 8th December from Snailwell in Cambridgeshire; they were Bell P-400 Airacobras of 347th squadron of 350th Fighter Group. This rather rare (in the United Kingdom) and radical fighter had been designed around a large T-9 cannon which fired from the hub and had necessitated its Allison engine being located behind the cockpit. It was first flown in April 1939 and entered the Service two years later. There were incessant problems with the engines but nevertheless these fast and heavily armed fighters served successfully in North Africa. Only one RAF squadron, No 601, was equipped with this American fighter. In early January 1943 the American pilots moved to warmer climes and the New Zealand airmen also left for Westhampnett in Sussex to join the Tangmere Wing.

Within ten days (13th) King's Cliffe became inundated with

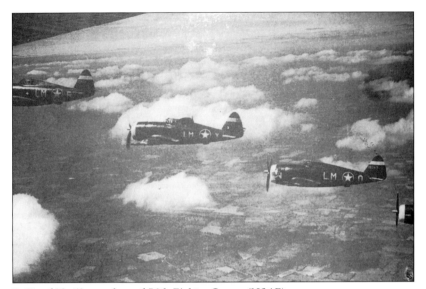

P-47s of No 62 squadron of 56th Fighter Group. (USAF)

American airmen when the 56th Fighter Group arrived from Gourock in Scotland. This Group was destined to become one of, if not the, most famous Fighter Groups in the Eighth Air Force. It achieved the highest number of enemy aircraft destroyed and had the greatest number of fighter aces of any Group as well as the two top pilots in the Eighth. It was also the only Group to fly P-47s (Thunderbolts) throughout the war and its pilots had been the first to train on P-47s in the United States back in June 1942.

The Republic P-47 was probably the most famous American fighter of the war and was built in greater numbers than any other. It was not built on particularly sleek lines and was variously described as the 'Jug', short for Juggernaut, or the 'Flying Milk Bottle'! The aircraft had first flown in May 1941 and yet just twelve months later it had entered service with the USAAF. The P-47 was heavy, very rugged and proved capable of sustaining considerable damage. Despite its bulk the aircraft was very fast, especially at high-altitudes, and possessed a quite fearsome firepower. Its main operational drawback was its range, though later with the provision of two drop tanks, this was greatly improved. Nevertheless the pilots of the Group amply demonstrated what an effective and destructive pursuit fighter it could be, and it served the Eighth Air Force admirably until the arrival of the P-51s (Mustangs).

The fighter was, however, in short supply and the Group's first P-47s did not begin to arrive until the beginning of February. Only then could Colonel Hubert Zemke, the Commanding Officer, get down to the serious business of bringing his pilots to operational readiness. Zemke proved to be one of the finest fighter pilots of the Eighth, as well as being a fine tactician and a most inspired leader. The Group left for Horsham St Faith in Norfolk on 5th April and eight days later its pilots started out on their long and very successful fighter campaign.

During early 1943 W. & C. French Ltd moved in to prepare solid runways constructed of tarmacadam and consolidated soil – one 5,490 feet and the other two at 3,900 and 3,690 feet respectively – a perimeter track and concrete dispersal pans. Twelve Blister hangars were placed around the perimeter of the airfield and extra accommodation sites were provided to the north-east, across the other side of the old Roman road in what was known as Bedford Purlieus. Although the newly refurbished airfield was already allocated to the Eighth Air Force, it was not officially transferred to the USAAF until late September, and meanwhile RAF Wittering utilised it to out-house a couple of Spitfire squadrons.

On 9th May No 91 (Nigeria) squadron, under the command of Squadron Leader Raymond Harries DFC, moved in with its Spitfire XIIs. The squadron had been formed in January 1941 and had spent most of its time engaged on 'Jim Crows' – coastal patrols to intercept enemy aircraft coming in low over the coast. Their new mark of Spitfires had been developed specially for such low-level interceptor duties. The aircraft was powered by a Griffon super-charged engine and it had clipped wings to improve its manoeuvrability and speed at low altitudes. The pilots mainly operated from an advanced base at Hawkinge in Kent and on one successful evening in late May its pilots accounted for six FW 190s that were approaching Folkestone, without losing a single pilot. In August the squadron moved to Hawkinge, near Folkestone, to join No 41 squadron, the only other unit to be equipped with XIIs. In the following month No 91 would become the top scoring squadron in Fighter Command.

The airfield was now ready for its next influx of American airmen, and on 26th August the 20th Fighter Group arrived. This Group had been scheduled to join the Eighth back in January 1942 but its overseas movement was delayed until August 1943. Despite the recent enhancement of the airfield there was still insufficient accommodation for the Group's three squadrons, so the 55th was out-housed at Wittering whilst 77th, 79th and the Headquarters settled in at King's

Cliffe, although the airmen considered the airfield to be 'one of the poorest in England ... the buildings were old and inadequate with facilities practically non-existent ...'. To add to their misery there was also a sad lack of aircraft. The Lockheed P-38s (Lightnings) were in desperately short supply, the aircraft took far more man-hours to build than other fighter, and when some P-38s finally arrived in the United Kingdom most were transferred to the 55th Group at Nuthampstead, whose pilots were more experienced and closer to operational readiness.

The P-38 was a brilliant aircraft in concept and at the time of its design it was far in advance of contemporary fighters. This large twin-boom and twin-engined aircraft was revolutionary for 1937. It was Lockheed's first military aircraft and its trials during 1939 had proved so impressive that the US Army Air Corps immediately placed an order, though the first P-38s did not see service until 1941. Perhaps its major attraction was its operational range – the first P-38s to come to Britain were flown across the Atlantic – and the aircraft was seen as the solution to the Eighth's heavy bomber losses. Unfortunately its Allison engines proved to be somewhat unreliable in the cold and damp north European climate and especially at high altitudes. The cockpit heating was also less than satisfactory, making combat flying decidedly uncomfortable for the pilots. But without doubt the aircraft was fast, about 410 mph at 25,000 feet, and with extra fuel tanks it had a range of more than 600 miles. With its armament of four .50 machine guns and two 20 mm cannons grouped together in the nose, it was a formidable fighter, but it did not make such an impact in Europe as it did in North Africa and the Pacific.

Because of the aircraft delays the Group took rather a long time in reaching an operational standard, though during November the three squadrons took it in turns to operate with the 55th Group. However, the Group's first operation left King's Cliffe on 28th December for a sweep of the Dutch coast and on this occasion the 37 pilots were led by Lieutenant Colonel Jack S. Jenkins, then the Deputy Commander of 55th Group. Two days later the Group went out on its first escort mission to Ludwigshafen. Already the first new P-38Js had arrived at King's Cliffe. They were distinguishable from the older 'Hs' by a flat panel windscreen and deep radiator intake housings to improve engine cooling, but they did have extra fuel tanks in both wings, which increased their operational range.

In the New Year the Group lost four pilots on two missions to Kiel and it had to wait until the 7th of the month, when in action over

P-38 coming in to land after a mission over Germany. (National Archives & Records Administ

Lt. Col. Johnson and other fighter pilots of 20th Fighter Group in front of a P-38. (Lt. Quinn – Capt. Morris – Lt. Col. Johnson – Capt. Williams) (National Archives & Records Administration)

Ludwigshafen, to claim its first victory. Towards the end of the month (29th) whilst on escort duties to Frankfurt twelve enemy aircraft were destroyed, but for the loss of five pilots – two in collisions. On this day Captain Lindol F. Graham added three victories to his total to become the Group's first 'ace'. This term dated from the First World War and had been reintroduced by both the Luftwaffe and the USAAF. The Americans required five positive claims in air combat to achieve ace status, whereas the Germans needed double that number. The USAAF were particularly quick to appreciate the propaganda value of its fighter aces. The British Air Ministry, on the other hand, refused to officially acknowledge aces as such as it was thought 'bad for squadron morale'. They were quite happy to publicise the exploits of their fighter pilots without actually calling them aces! Usually RAF fighter pilots were awarded the DFC after five victories in the air, and it is thought that over 1,000 RAF pilots during the war could have claimed to be aces. The Eighth Air Force had a total of 261 ace fighter pilots by the end of the war, of whom only five served with the 20th.

On 11th February the Group had another particularly bad time over Frankfurt, when eight pilots failed to return. By the end of the month although 23 victories had been claimed, each one was proving costly with 21 pilots missing in action and several more aircraft written-off in crashes. Not all the pilots were quite as fortunate as Lieutenant Albert Fogg when on 4th March he crashed into an opencast mine whilst attempting an emergency landing at Spanhoe. Although he had to be cut out of the wreckage of his aircraft he escaped with only minor injuries. His aircraft had suffered engine failure during the mission – a problem with the P-38s that was never really cured – only then to be attacked by a captured P-47 operating in Luftwaffe colours!

The first week of March saw the Eighth Air Force make its first bombing strikes against Berlin and the P-38s were the first American aircraft to fly over the German capital. It would prove to be a difficult month for the Group with nine pilots lost for just eight victories. Lieutenant Colonel Mark E. Hubbard, who had only taken over command of the Group on the 2nd of the month, was shot down on the 18th along with another three pilots; the Colonel survived the ordeal and was taken prisoner. He was replaced by Lieutenant Colonel Harold J. Rau, who would have two spells in charge. Rau was a very able commander, who led by his example. He would fly both a P-38 and P-51, each named *Gentle Annie*. Rau had started his service life as a private with the Group before the outbreak of war – such a rapid promotion speaks volumes for not only his abilities as a fighter pilot but also his innate qualities as a leader.

During the following month the Group's pilots were allowed to show the true metier of their P-38s – as low-level strike aircraft. On the 5th Colonel Rau led 50 aircraft to strafe airfields in the Munster and Berlin areas. However, the Group encountered heavy cloud and he decided to abandon the mission. One of the pilots, 1/Lieutenant Jack Yelton in *Cactus Jack*, was forced to crash-land at a German airfield. He deliberately crashed onto two parked Me 109s, and moreover escaped with his life, but he ended up as a prisoner of war. Three days later when fog had closed down King's Cliffe until noon, Colonel Rau gained permission to mount an independent fighter sweep of airfields in the Salwedel area to the west of Berlin. Each squadron separated to attack its own briefed targets. They created mayhem and it was a most successful operation. Over 35 aircraft were claimed in the air and on the ground, and at least 18 locomotives along with 50 rail wagons were destroyed as well as flak guns and oil and gas storage tanks, all for the loss of four pilots. The Group was awarded its only Distinguished Unit

Citation for this mission. This successful operation started the Group's reputation as a 'train busting outfit' and it gained the nickname of the 'Loco Group'!

On the 10th of the month, along with other P-38 Groups, the 20th launched its first fighter/bomber operation. Some of its aircraft had been modified with the installation of a plexiglass nose section to provide a cabin for a bombardier and sufficient space for a Norden bomb sight. These modified P-38s became known as 'Droop Snoots' and would lead the other aircraft into the bombing run. Ultimately the Group dropped over 340 tons of bombs throughout the war. During D-Day the P-38 Groups acted as escorts for the armada of Allied shipping crossing the Channel. Just before four o'clock on the morning of 6th June the first 18 pilots took off from King's Cliffe for the first patrol over the Channel and by the end of the day another eight had been mounted in strict relays. In the following days the pilots were heavily engaged over the Normandy beach-heads. It proved to be a little costly with nine pilots lost in action and several aircraft written off in crashes mainly on return to the airfield; not a single combat victory was recorded during this period. Colonel Rau left the Group on 24th June and he was replaced by Lieutenant Colonel Cy Wilson.

In July the Group began to exchange its P-38s for P-51s, although it still had one last successful mission with its P-38s. On the 7th of the month seven victories were claimed for the loss of one pilot, though unfortunately the missing airman happened to be the Group's leading ace – Captain James Morris. The final P-38 mission left King's Cliffe on the 21st flown by pilots of the 79th squadron (the other two squadrons had already converted to P-51s). In 133 missions the Group had destroyed 89 aircraft in the air with another 30 on the ground. Although 87 pilots had been lost, it still constituted the best record of all the P-38 Groups in the Eighth Fighter Command.

The North American P-51 had now developed into a magnificent pursuit fighter with a maximum speed of 440 mph at 30,000 feet, which was faster than both the FW 190 and Me 109G, and although it had the lightest armament of any Allied fighter with six .50 inch machine guns, it had nevertheless established a marked ascendancy over the Luftwaffe's day-fighters. The pilots scored their first successes (three) with their new aircraft on the 29th whilst on escort duties over Merseburg. In the next two weeks they added another 27 victims to their total as well as 37 locomotives, which brought their 'loco busting' total to over 200, then a record for the Eighth Air Force. However, on 27th August their Commanding Officer, along with three pilots, went

P-51D Sad Sack *of 77th Fighter Squadron testing chemical smoke over King's Cliffe.*
(Smithsonian Institution)

missing. Colonel Wilson ditched in the sea off the Danish coast, but he was fortunate to be picked up by a fishing boat and spent the rest of the war as a prisoner.

Colonel Rau returned to command the Group and would remain at King's Cliffe until almost the end of the year. On 11th September he led over 60 P-51s to Chemnitz as escorts for two B-17 Groups, and from there the pilots flew eastwards to land at Piryatin, a Russian airfield near Kiev. This was the third of the so-called 'Frantic' shuttle missions to be mounted by the USAAF, mainly at the behest of Stalin. One of the P-51s was shot down behind the Russian lines though the pilot escaped. A second pilot lost his way and ran out of fuel, making a crash-landing in Poland after almost $9\frac{1}{2}$ hours in the air. The pilots returned to King's Cliffe five days later via Hungary and Italy but minus another P-51, which had been forced to crash-land near Paris because of engine trouble.

On the afternoon of 3rd October 1944 the base was privileged to have a visit from the legendary Glenn Miller and his 40-piece American Band of the AEF. Major Miller and his band had arrived by road from their base near Bedford. The concert, which lasted about one hour, was held in one of the hangars, and the Group's pilots managed to return from an escort mission over northern Germany in time for the performance. It was said that over 2,500 people were in the audience. Because of the onset of winter, this concert was the last one performed by Miller's band at an American base. Since early July he and his band had made a long and exhausting tour of American bases, but from now on they played mostly in London. Their final concert was on 12th December, just three days before Glenn Miller's fatal flight to Paris.

Over the final months of the war the Group gained a fine reputation as a most efficient and effective unit under the command of Colonel Robert P. Montgomery. It managed to consistently get more aircraft into operations, with the lowest rate of aborted sorties due to mechanical failures. On 10th April in what the Eighth later called 'The Great Jet Massacre', the day when its fighter pilots took a heavy toll of the Luftwaffe's Me 262s, the Group claimed the biggest share – five. The Group's last mission (its 312th) left King's Cliffe on 25th April and sadly one pilot failed to return, he baled out over Dusseldorf, which had been recently captured by US troops. In over 310 missions the 20th had accounted for over 212 enemy aircraft destroyed in the air with over 230 on the ground, but in the process 132 aircraft had been lost in action.

During the next few months many of the personnel and aircraft were transferred out of King's Cliffe, although on 1st August there were still a sufficient number of P-51s to put on display when the airfield was opened to the public. One famous aircraft brought to the airfield was a rather aged B-17E which was not considered sufficiently airworthy for the long flight back to the United States. It had originally been called *Butcher Shop* and had left Grafton Underwood back in August 1942 on the Eighth's first heavy bombing mission. Since that time it had been used by several Groups as a training aircraft. Then it became the Group's communications runabout and was renamed *The Big Tin Bird*! When the 20th Group finally vacated the airfield in October 1945, this old B-17E was taken to the Air Depôt at Burtonwood where it was scrapped.

The airfield became a temporary base for German POWs awaiting repatriation, with this unit closing down in July 1947. Early in 1947 the RAF left the airfield and it was later sold. There is a fine and unusual memorial alongside the old Roman road, which uniquely commemorates the American, British, Belgian and Commonwealth airmen who lost their lives whilst flying from King's Cliffe.

14
PETERBOROUGH

When it opened on 2nd August 1932 Westwood or Westwood Farm aerodrome, as it was then named, was unique in several respects. Its gestation period had been fairly prolonged even judged by the more leisurely standards of the time – the original enquiry into the purchase of the land on behalf of the Air Ministry had taken place over five years earlier. Also few new Service aerodromes were being constructed at this period, this was several years before the rapid expansion of the RAF. Furthermore, it was not to be used basically for flying but rather for the receipt, storage and delivery of aircraft and equipment for the Home Defence Air Force by No 1 Aircraft Storage Depôt. Finally, and perhaps more unusually, the airfield was sited very close to a large built-up area – Peterborough. In those days, and indeed later, it was the normal and accepted practice for Service airfields to be situated well away from cities or towns for obvious safety and security reasons.

The Depôt, which was mainly staffed by civilians though commanded by a Squadron Leader, moved out to Waddington in Lincolnshire in early December 1935 to make way for a newly formed Flying Training School – No 7 – to train pilots for the now rapidly expanding Service. The student pilots would be trained on a mixture of Hawker Harts and Audaxes and many of the airmen that passed through the School during the pre-war years ultimately served with Fighter Command. Three well-known Battle of Britain 'aces' – Flight Lieutenant G. Eric Ball, DFC, Flight Lieutenant Wilfred G. Clouston, DFC and Flying Officer Paddy P. C. Barthropp, DFC – had all been trained at Peterborough.

The student pilots arrived from one of the many Elementary Flying Schools to start the second and important stage of their flying training. What had altered was the length of time they spent at these schools before receiving their coveted 'wings'. The duration of the course had

173

been originally six months but because of the pressure to supply pilots it was reduced to four months, though it was made clear to the schools that even this period could be shortened if favourable weather conditions allowed the requisite amount of flying time to be completed earlier. Although it must be said this rarely happened, as the vagaries of the British weather played a vital part in all types of flying training, and its uncertainty was one of the reasons for the establishment of the Empire (Commonwealth) Air Training Scheme.

The student pilots would certainly be aware of the vastly different environment of a Service Flying School. The rather relaxed and easy-going atmosphere of the EFTSs, which were normally housed on small and cosy airfields and run by civilian instructors, at least up until January 1940, had suddenly changed to the stricter regimes and firmer disciplines of the much larger Service schools. The training, both on the ground and in the air, had become more advanced and demanding, with extra and more complex theoretical subjects to study and more rigorous tests to pass. The training aircraft were faster, heavier and more complicated to handle, and a greater emphasis was placed on the physical fitness of the young airmen. Though, having said that, the students at Peterborough would fly Hawker Audaxes and Harts, which although they were quicker, still came from the same era as the Tiger Moths they had left behind at their EFTSs.

Both aircraft were two-seater bi-plane trainers with open cockpits that looked as if they belonged to a past era of flying, and had, in fact, served since the days of the pre-Expansion RAF. The Hawker Hart had been designed as a light bomber and had entered the Service back in January 1930, when it proved to be swifter than contemporary RAF fighters, with a maximum speed of 185 mph. Over 1,000 Harts were produced in a variety of different marks, more than any single aircraft in the immediate inter-war years. The Hart was probably the most successful aircraft of the early 1930s, and its excellent handling qualities along with its performance led the Air Ministry to develop a trainer mark – Hart Series 2.

The Hawker Audax was slightly later coming into operational service, not arriving at a squadron until February 1932. The Audax continued to serve mainly on army co-operation duties until 1937/8 when it was replaced by another Hawker aircraft – the Hector – and the Audaxes were relegated to flying training. It was slower than the Hart with a top speed of about 170 mph. However, in January 1939, the School took a step forward into more modern times when the first monoplane trainers arrived at Peterborough – Airspeed Oxfords. These

Fairey Battles were also used for training at Peterborough.

twin-engined aircraft had dual controls and would provide the student pilots with more advanced flying instruction and give those pilots destined to serve with Bomber Command experience of handling an aircraft a little closer to those they would encounter on their operational training.

When, in the summer of 1939, the School was switched to training Fleet Air Arm pilots, the twin-engined Oxfords were considered surplus to requirements and were transferred out in October. With the outbreak of the war the School had been redesignated a 'Service' Flying Training School and in January 1940 about 30 Fairey Battle trainers arrived. This single-engined light bomber had entered the Service in May 1937 as a replacement for the Hawker Hart, but by 1939 they were already obsolete in terms of performance and armament and these inadequacies would be cruelly exposed over France in May 1940. The heavy losses sustained during this period marked the operational end of the Battle as a day bomber, and they were then mainly used on training, with 100 specially built trainers provided with dual-control with separate cockpits. Over 2,000 Battles were produced in total and they were still operating with training schools abroad well into 1943.

At the height of the invasion threat during the summer of 1940 twelve Harts were ordered to be prepared in a state of readiness as part of the Air Ministry's 'Banquet Light' plan, a scheme to ensure that all available resources were ready to counter any German invasion. The

Harts would be bombed up, flown by instructors and, if called upon, would operate in support of the home forces from Stradishall in Suffolk. The operation, which of course did not materialise, seemed to be a little hazardous to say the least, especially as it was ordered that 'bombing practice should be undertaken at the home training school'!

No 7 SFTS was one of the first seven schools to be transferred to Canada under the new Empire (Commonwealth) Air Training Scheme, becoming part of No 31 SFTS based at Kingston, Ontario. Although it came under RCAF administration, it was still operated by RAF personnel so really it was a by-product of the scheme rather than part of it. The first personnel left for Canada towards the end of August on the first EATS convoy, travelling on the *Duchess of York* from Greenock to Montreal. It proved to be anything but a comfortable journey, with the continual threat of attack from U-boats and the German battleships that were particularly active in the north Atlantic at that period of the war. The School's personnel moved out during the latter months of 1940 and when the 15th and last FAA course finished in mid-January 1941 the School was closed down.

Now the airfield became flooded with Tiger Moths of No 13 EFTS, which had moved in from White Waltham. Certainly the skies around Peterborough would soon literally buzz with Moths flown by young airmen mastering the basics of flying training. Since July 1940 No 7 SFTS had acquired a relief landing ground at Sibson, which was a couple of miles to the west of Peterborough and south of Wansford. However, with the departure of No 7 School this small grassed airfield had been transferred to another elementary training school at Cranfield, so for the relatively short period – about five months – that No 13 School operated from Peterborough, the majority of the flying was conducted from the airfield. The School was disbanded on 31st May 1941 and its Tiger Moths were moved to Booker in Buckingham-shire to form the basis of a new EFTS – No 21.

The following day they were replaced by yet more Tiger Moths. This time they belonged to No 25 Elementary Flying Training School, which had been specially formed at Hucknall in Nottinghamshire to provide training for Polish airmen, though there was a sprinkling of other Allied airmen on the courses. However, there was only time for two courses to be completed at Peterborough before that School was also on the move, back to Hucknall in mid-July. There was no let-up for Peterborough because yet another EFTS moved in from North Luffenham, forced out of this airfield because it was to become an operational bomber base. No 17 EFTS was operating under contract to de Havilland Aircraft Company and it remained at the airfield for almost twelve months. During this period it had an amazingly low accident rate. The only serious mishap came on 17th September 1941 when a wing fell off one of its Moths; the aircraft was abandoned and it crashed in Willesden Avenue, Peterborough. The School was ultimately disbanded in June 1942.

Peterborough was now to get its longest surviving wartime unit when No 7 (Pilots) Advanced Flying Unit was formed there on 1st June. The intention of these Units was to bridge the gap between the advanced flying training undertaken overseas and the operational training courses. When the Air Ministry had recognised that there was an urgent need for such refresher courses, they realised that in many cases the facilities and nuclei of the old Service Flying Training Schools still existed at the airfields and they could now be fully utilised by these new Units. Thus the reason Peterborough was selected and why the Unit was numbered '7' from the school that had left for Canada back in late 1940. By the end of 1942 there were 13 of these Advanced Flying Units in operation. No 7 AFU was equipped with Miles Masters trainers, which was a sure sign to all the pilots posted to the Unit that they would ultimately serve in Fighter Command, which indeed seemed to be the ambition of most trainee pilots.

The Master was probably the best designed single-engined advanced training aircraft of its day. It possessed very similar handling

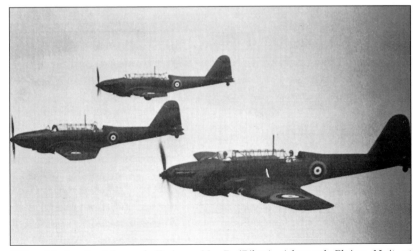

Miles Master I: Advanced Trainer. No 7 (Pilots) Advanced Flying Unit at Peterborough used Masters.

177

characteristics to both the Hurricane and Spitfire, it had a sliding canopy and gave the pilots their first taste of high-speed flying. The first Master had flown in March 1939 but just a handful had entered the Service by the outbreak of the war. The Miles Aircraft Company, formed by the brothers F. G. and G. H. Miles, had been building military aircraft since 1936, and perhaps their most successful model so far had been the Magister or 'Maggie'. The Master II trainer was a development of the Mark I but powered by a Bristol Mercury XX engine instead of the Rolls-Royce Kestrel, which gave it a maximum speed of some 240 mph and an initial rate of climb of 2,000 feet per minute. The aircraft was constructed of wood and covered with plywood. It proved to be a most reliable trainer with over 1,700 being produced. All had an instructor's seat in the rear cockpit which could be raised to give better vision over the head of the pupil in front, which was especially beneficial on practice take-offs and landings. The Master could also be adapted to tow gliders and it led directly to the Martinet, the RAF's first specially designed target tower.

The importance of the new Unit can be seen by the upgrading of the station, now commanded by a Group Captain – J. Norwood – rather than a Wing Commander. The first intake of pilots, proudly displaying their newly acquired 'wings', arrived at Peterborough on 15th June for the initial course. The satellite at Sibson had returned to Peterborough's fold and most of the night-flying was conducted from there. Ultimately three of the Unit's Flights were based there on a fairly permanent basis when the facilities had been improved and three landing strips provided.

The courses were planned to be completed in four weeks, covering advanced flying techniques and procedures, navigation and map reading. This timescale would allow for about 30 or so flying hours with at least ten of these flown at night and another ten of advanced flying by day. Nevertheless the nature of the British weather demanded a certain flexibility in the courses and in the winter months they were often extended to six weeks. The Unit originally comprised four Flights and was ultimately equipped with 130 Masters, mainly Mark IIs, and just a handful of Avro Ansons, although in March 1944 a Flight of Hurricanes was added to the Unit's complement. The intake of pilots rose steadily from 90 to over 200 at one stage although the average number was perhaps closer to 150. With this number of trainees airfield space was at a premium and King's Cliffe was used briefly for night-flying during the summer of 1943. In the following year Sutton Bridge in Lincolnshire was used and by August 1944 it had become

Peterborough's satellite airfield with Sibson almost closed down for flying. The Unit lost one of its aircraft, a Master II, to enemy action on 21st April 1944 when it was shot down by an intruder about a mile-and-a-half from the airfield; the pilot, Flying Officer J. Bannister, was killed.

In December 1944 No 7 Service Flying Training School was once again reactivated and it had a heavy bias of French airmen, who were being trained for their new post-war air force. The first French course, 36 pilots, passed out in February 1945, having been trained mainly on Oxfords but also on some rather old Spitfire IIs. Later in the year the School was re-equipped with North American Harvard IIbs – the training aircraft that had been used almost universally in the overseas training schools. During this period some of the night-flying was taking place at Wittering.

In early April 1946 No 7 SFTS moved north to Kirton Lindsey, thus bringing to an end almost eleven years of continuous flying training at the airfield. No 259 Maintenance Unit moved in but stayed for only two years before the airfield was placed under care and maintenance. The fact that the airfield had remained grassed throughout its existence, allied to its close proximity to Peterborough, meant it was not considered suitable for post-war flying despite having been a permanent pre-war station. However, for about two years British European Airways used Peterborough as a helicopter base for a regular mail service.

The airfield has today almost disappeared under housing develop-ment, although some of the old permanent blocks have survived and are still used for various purposes. In October 1993 a plaque was unveiled in the old Officers' Mess, now used by Cambridgeshire County Council, to mark its former use. On the other hand Sibson, which formally closed in October 1946, is still being used for civilian flying as well as sport parachuting.

15
POLEBROOK

In September 1939 it was estimated that the Air Ministry's Aerodromes Board had identified over 4,000 possible airfield sites in the United Kingdom, although perhaps less than 10% were ultimately developed. No suitable land was considered sacrosanct, as Sir Archibald Sinclair, the Secretary of State for Air, made clear in 1940: 'There are many large private estates and large parklands, which if trees were taken down, would be suitable as landing grounds, if not aerodromes. We are out to win this war and should not be put off by a desire to maintain intact the stately homes of England.' And the Rothschild family was no exception to this diktat. Part of their estate near Polebrook and Lutton was requisitioned for the site of this airfield, and Ashton Wold House, a rather splendid mansion to the north of the airfield, had some communal sites placed within its grounds.

The airfield was built during late 1940 and early 1941 as a bomber base, though even before it was completed, No 17 OTU, then based at Upwood near Huntingdon, used the new runways for training landings and take-offs to ease the pressure and wear on its grassed airfield. It was just one of two Units providing operational training for Blenheim crews destined for squadrons in No 2 Group. During March and April 1941 there were two mishaps at the new airfield involving training Blenheim crews, and during the year the Unit would lose 40 aircraft in a variety of unfortunate accidents.

Towards the end of May 1941 the airfield was officially taken over by the RAF as a station in its own right, though it was still not completely finished. Nevertheless its new and pristine runways seemed to be heaven-sent for the newly re-formed No 90 squadron, which was experiencing considerable difficulties operating from West Raynham and its satellite at Great Massingham in Norfolk with the RAF's latest heavy bomber – the Flying Fortress I or B-17C.

The squadron had been absorbed into No 17 OTU in April 1940 but 13 months later it had been reactivated to trial these American heavy bombers in daylight high-altitude bombing raids. Their unique appearance in the RAF had caused quite a stir and the British press were most complimentary: 'a good looking aeroplane ... perfectly streamlined, its wings have easy curves on leading and trailing edges, and the four powerful air-cooled radial motors are housed in well-proportioned nacelles that run back half-way across the wing'. One celebrated air correspondent, though very impressed with the aircraft, thought 'they might not be suited to operations in northern Europe'. The squadron's crews, who had all been hand-picked for their youth and the high standard of fitness considered necessary to contend with the rigours of operating at 32,000 feet, were delighted with the aircraft and its interior refinements – carpeted floors, ample space, comfortable seats, fitted thermos flasks and ash-trays. It was quickly dubbed 'the aircraft for gentlemen'! One of the squadron's pilots, Pilot Officer 'Freddie' Stokes, reckoned it was 'a lady and a graceful and elegant one at that.'

Before Wing Commander J. MacDougall brought his Fortress squadron to Polebrook towards the end of June, one aircraft had crashed whilst on an air test killing all but one of its eight-man crew, including Lieutenant Bradley, a USAAF adviser. Another aircraft was lost within days of their arrival at Polebrook, when it caught fire at the dispersals and burnt out. This left just 18 out of the original allocation of 20 Fortress Is. On 8th July just three aircraft left for Wilhelmshaven, where two crews managed to bomb the target but the other attacked Nordeney instead. Only six more sorties were flown in the month to Brest, Emden and Hamburg. Then on the 28th another aircraft was lost on an air test when it came down at Wilbarston near Corby killing all of the six airmen. Five operations were launched in August, and over Brest on the 16th one aircraft was attacked by enemy fighters at an altitude of 32,000 feet, the highest fighter interception of the war. The damaged aircraft crashed on landing at Plymouth with three men killed.

In the first week of September the squadron was detached to Kinloss in Scotland to launch an attack on the *Admiral Speer*, then in Oslo harbour. Of the four aircraft sent on the mission two were shot down by Me 109s before reaching the target and a third crashed on return. Only three more sorties were made from Polebrook, the final one on the 25th to Emden, but the crew were forced to return early because of a technical fault. The Fortress experiment had proved to be a dismal

Flying Fortress of No 90 squadron. (Imperial War Museum)

failure. Only 51 sorties had been made, half of which had been abandoned and less than 50 tons of bombs dropped. Bomber Command decided to withdraw the squadron from operations but training flights still continued. In mid-October five aircraft were sent out to the Middle East but in early February 1942 the squadron was once again disbanded. Later models of the Flying Fortress would operate with some success in RAF Coastal Command and No 100 (Special Duties) Group of Bomber Command.

The need for heavy bomber conversion training had been recognised by Bomber Command back in 1941 and the first Units, as opposed to Flights, were formed in January 1942, the first being No 1651 at Waterbeach in Cambridgeshire, followed by No 1653 at Polebrook. The intention of this Unit was to train, in the first instance, crews of Nos 159 and 160 squadrons on another American heavy bomber – the Consolidated Liberator II – a version which did not have a USAAF counterpart. The first RAF Liberators had operated with Coastal Command as long-range reconnaissance aircraft but it was planned to use the Mark IIs as heavy bombers, as they had an increased armament and a bigger bomb load. The aim was that No 1 Group of Bomber Command would exchange its Wellingtons for Liberators and the Unit began operational training in earnest in February, which, of course, included night-flying. But the RAF's days at Polebrook were now numbered as the airfield had been reserved for the USAAF, and the Unit moved away to Snaith at the beginning of June, where it only survived until October before it was disbanded.

The first USAAF airmen arrived at Polebrook on 13th June. They were part of the 97th Bomb Group (Heavy) equipped with B-17Es, which would have its headquarters there along with two of its four squadrons – 340th and 341st (the other two were housed at Grafton Underwood). The Group was commanded by Colonel Cornelius W. Cousland but he was soon replaced by Colonel Frank Armstrong Jr. Polebrook's thunder was somewhat stolen when B-17s of the other two squadrons – at least bar one, *Butcher Shop* – were engaged in the Eighth's first heavy bombing operation on 17th August, but it should be noted that six aircraft in two flights left Polebrook about an hour earlier to make a diversionary flight over the French coast. In its first eight operations during August the Group *was* the Eighth Bomber Command – its sole representative.

No aircraft were lost in action but several were damaged. The first combat fatality came on the 21st when the Group was attacked by FW 190s. In one of the damaged B-17s the co-pilot, 2/Lieutenant Donald A.

Walter, was killed and the pilot, 2/Lieutenant Richard F. Starks, though wounded, still managed to make an emergency landing at Horsham St Faith in Norfolk. The first aircraft lost in action by the Eighth Air Force went down on 6th September at Flasselles in France after an attack on an aircraft plant at Meaulte. The pilot, 2/Lieutenant Clarence W. Lipsky, and his crew were the first heavy bomber airmen to go missing in action.

The Group's other two squadrons moved in from Grafton Underwood on 8th September. On the previous day a damaged aircraft had returned from the shipyards at Rotterdam with one of the crew dead and another two seriously wounded, and the B-17 only fit for salvage, the first of literally hundreds of heavy bombers to be written-off. On 14th September the 97th was allocated to the Twelfth Air Force and for the next two weeks the crews concentrated on operational training for their impending move to North Africa. Before the Group would finally move out of Polebrook in November two crews had made the trip to Gibraltar and back, one carrying General Mark Clarke, General Eisenhower's deputy, and other senior officers. Then on 5th November both Generals were taken out to Gibraltar. Twelve days later when a B-17 piloted by Major John Knox, CO of 341st squadron left Predannock in Cornwall, it caught fire early into the flight and crashed in the English Channel with a total loss of life; on board the aircraft was Brigadier General Duncan.

After the crews' two week break from operations they returned to the Eighth's air battle on 26th September. The mission on that day was to airfields in the Cherbourg area but it proved to be abortive because of heavy cloud. Just three more operations were mounted from Polebrook in October, with their final and fourteenth mission with the Eighth Air Force being directed against the U-boat pens at Lorient. The three other Bomb Groups taking part in this operation failed to locate the target, only the 15 crews of the 97th managed to bomb and three of them failed to return – they had paid the ultimate price for their determination to complete the mission. By the end of November all the B-17s and airmen had left Polebrook for North Africa, and the airfield was now ominously quiet.

The opportunity was taken to bring the airfield up to Class A standard with the runways being lengthened, extra hard standings put down and more living quarters provided. It would be another five months before the next influx of American airmen – the 351st Bomb Group. Their first B-17Fs began to arrive on 15th April 1943 with the ground crews and support personnel appearing some weeks later. The

Group was assigned to 101st Provisional Bomb Wing and it was led by Colonel William A. Hatcher Jr, who proceeded to weld his crews, both air and ground, into a most efficient and effective fighting unit. The aircrews quickly gained a high reputation for their determination and the accuracy of their bombing.

Before the Group became operational there was a tragic accident on 7th May when two B-17s collided on their approach to the airfield after a practice mission. Twenty-two airmen were killed, including Major Keith J. Birlem, who was the CO of 508th squadron. The Group's first mission was mounted on 13th May to Ft Rouge airfield at St Omer, but because of the crews' inexperience they failed to form up properly and the operation was abandoned in mid-Channel. The following day the Group joined crews of the 96th (at Grafton Underwood) in an attack on the air depôt at Courtrai – the first time that the Eighth Air Force had managed to despatch 200 bombers on a single operation. Unfortunately two crews went missing, including Captain William P. Forsythe, the CO of 510th squadron. In less than a week the Group had lost two of its senior and most experienced officers.

Attached to the 351st at this time was one of the most famous faces of the day – Captain Clark Gable. The film star had joined the Army Air Force as a private in August 1942 and had been seconded to the Group whilst it was still training in America. Although Gable was 42 years old, which was well above the normal age for flying duties, he had passed out of the Gunnery School in Florida as an air gunner, and had been engaged to appear in a film designed to help train air gunners as well as to encourage their recruitment. During 1943 there was an acute shortage of air gunners, largely because the size of the B-17 turrets imposed a physical limit on the height and girth of prospective candidates!

The famous film star had flown on a couple of operations with the 303rd Group at Molesworth whilst the 351st was preparing for operations, but on 12th August Captain Gable was in the Group's lead aircraft on a mission to Gelsenkirchen. He could not have been in better hands, because the aircraft was piloted by Major Theodore 'Ross' Milton, a most able and experienced pilot who would later command two Bomb Groups – 384th and 91st. Clark Gable, along with an ex-MGM cameraman who had enlisted at the same time, managed to get some real live air-to-air action for the film. His last operation was on 23rd September to Nantes when he was aboard *The Duchess* of 510th Squadron.

Whilst Gable was at Polebrook the airfield became the centre of

A publicity photograph of Captain Clark Gable as an air gunner. (Smithsonian Institution)

considerable media attention with the film star's universal appeal ensuring there were plenty of publicity photographs. One of the photograph captions stated that he had wanted 'to become an aerial gunner because he believed it was the quickest and surest way to strike at the Axis', and that when he had received his wings it was 'one of the greatest honours of my life'. The film, entitled *Combat America* was not released for public viewing until October 1944.

It was perhaps rather appropriate that the Group should be directly involved in a film about the techniques of aerial gunnery because its own gunners had already made quite a mark with the accuracy of their fire-power. By the end of September 1943 they had claimed over 140 enemy aircraft destroyed and although it is now generally accepted that the claims by the Eighth's gunners were perhaps on average at least double those of the actual enemy losses, the Group's figures were nevertheless most impressive. The Eighth attempted to impose a strict criteria on the assessment of gunners' claims: the pilot must be seen to abandon his aircraft, or else the aircraft should be seen to crash or explode in the air. However, the nature of the Eighth's air battles with close bomber formations resulted in many gunners claiming the same fighter destroyed, while the speed and ferocity of air combat made accurate claims almost an impossibility. By the end of the war the

187

Group's gunners had claimed 303 victims, the fifth highest total in the 1st Division, and the other four Groups that had managed to surpass this total had all been in operations at least six months longer. It was a fine performance notwithstanding the fact that the total figure was probably over-assessed.

By the end of October 1943 in almost 50 missions the Group had lost 27 aircraft, which considering the nature of some of the operations was a most commendable record. For instance, only three crews had been lost in the two horrendous Schweinfurt missions. Also in the month the Group had been awarded its first Distinguished Unit Citation for its part in the raid on the 9th to a FW 190 components plant at Anklam, to the north of Berlin and near the Baltic coast. Not only was it the deepest operation into Germany so far but it also produced some of the fiercest air battles yet seen. The Luftwaffe opposed the Division in great strength, it was thought that upwards of 200 single and twin-engined fighters were in action firing cannons and rockets. Out of a total force in excess of 110 B-17s, 18 were lost (15%) and the Group bore the brunt (along with the 91st). Each had five crews missing, of which two came from the 511th squadron including its CO, Captain Harry Morse, but at least 26 enemy fighters were claimed by the Group's gunners. Despite this fierce fighter onslaught and the heavy and accurate flak barrage, the bombing was very accurate and all the targets were bombed inflicting heavy damage and causing considerable production delays.

As the year drew to a close Colonel Hatcher Jr must have been pleased with the performance of 'his boys'. In some six months 60 operations had been made and although 34 crews had been lost in action, this was quite a moderate figure compared with other Bomb Groups' losses. The crews had only added to their bombing reputation and furthermore the gunners had almost reached the 200-mark. Two squadrons – 509th and 511th – had gained a certain fame. The first because it had not lost a single crew in action since 13th June – an amazing record – and the 511th because all of its aircraft were given names ending in 'ball' – *Speedball, Cannon Ball, Screwball, Snowball, Fireball, Thunderball* etc. This practice had originated with its first Commander, Major Clinton Ball, who had christened his aircraft *Linda Ball* after his daughter. Ball later became the Group's Operations Officer and ended the war with the Group with 32 missions to his credit. The squadron appeared to be always in the thick of the action. Perhaps the only blemish over the previous six months had been the tragic accident at the airfield on 10th November which has already been described (see Collyweston).

188

B-17 Linda Ball *of 511th Bomb Squadron of 351st Bomb Group. (Smithsonian Institution)*

However, this reasonably happy state of affairs was about to be turned on its head on the last day of the year, when 31 crews, led by Colonel Hatcher Jr, set off for Bordeaux in south-west France. The crews were only too aware that it was going to be a long and exhausting operation, which was made more difficult by the bad weather that continually plagued the mission. They found the target obscured by cloud and, when turning away to find a secondary target, the lead aircraft was hit. The crews bombed Chateaubernard airfield at Cognac. The Division lost 15 aircraft over France with another seven crashing in England mainly because of fuel shortages. Colonel Hatcher Jr along with Major John R. Blaylock, the 510th's squadron commander, failed to return together with another six crews. On the return to England one B-17 crashed at Burnham-on-Sea with another coming down at Whitewell near Oxford after the crew had baled out. Yet another aircraft, *Speedball*, ditched off the Channel Islands and only two of the crew survived, the others died of exposure. The Colonel managed to bale out safely and was taken prisoner.

This mission was the Group's most costly operation to date. Colonel Eugene A. Romig, who was a Staff Officer at the 4th Wing headquarters, arrived to take over the Group and remained in charge until October 1944. Just eleven days later another six B-17s went missing over Oschersleben. This operation was led by Lieutenant Colonel Theodore Milton, who was now serving with the 91st Group, and he was wounded during the mission. Like all other Groups in the Division the 351st gained a DUC. It was on this operation that No 509 squadron's remarkable long run of good fortune finally came to an end. During the Eighth's 'Big Week' in February the 351st was in action over Leipzig, Achmer airfield, Bernburg, Schweinfurt and Augsburg. Five crews were lost with another two aircraft coming to grief on return – one went down in the sea off Cromer and the other crashed in Northamptonshire. The latter B-17, *Ten Horsepower*, had taken a direct hit in the cockpit, which killed the co-pilot and severely injured the pilot, 2/Lieutenant Clarence R. Nelson, who lost consciousness. The crew were ordered to bale out but the navigator, 1/Lieutenant Walter E. Truemper, and the ball-turret gunner, Staff Sergeant Archibald Mathies, managed to fly the damaged aircraft back despite the intense cold because of a broken windscreen. When they made contact with Polebrook they were advised to abandon the aircraft but refused to do so because of the injured pilot on board. They made an unsuccessful attempt to land at Molesworth. Colonel Eugene A. Romig went up to fly alongside them and attempt to guide them down safely, but three attempts failed and the B-17 finally crashed near Denton. Both airmen were killed. The injured pilot survived the crash but he later died in hospital. Truemper and Mathies, who were both aged 26 years and had only served with the Group since December, were posthumously awarded Congressional Medals of Honor.

Pre-dawn briefing for crews at Polebrook before the Berlin mission of 6th March 1944. (Imperial War Museum)

The Group managed to survive the four Berlin missions in March with just a single loss, really quite an amazing performance. The solitary missing B-17, *Blonde Bomber*, was not seen to join the formation after take-off from Polebrook on the 22nd. One of its engines had failed and it crashed at Hemington, killing four airmen with another four severely injured. Early in April the 100th mission milestone was passed and in the following month when the Eighth was operating at full stretch, the 351st completed 21 missions with the crews getting precious little respite from almost continuous combat flying. Perhaps it was not surprising that in May the Group suffered its worst monthly losses of the war, when in just eight days 15 aircraft were lost in action, which proved to be 12% of its total casualties for the whole of the war. For the next four months, operations would be mounted with great rapidity and most of them passed reasonably smoothly except for two disastrous days. The first occurred on 6th August at Brandenburg to the west of Berlin when six crews were lost. Almost five weeks later, on 12th September, another six aircraft went missing over oil targets at Lutzendorf with two damaged aircraft crash-landing in Belgium.

Early in October (7th) the 94th Combat Bomb Wing, which had its headquarters at the airfield, despatched 150 aircraft to oil targets at Politz near Stettin. The Eighth were well aware of the strength and power of the flak defences surrounding this vital target and the operation was planned and timed so that the crews would only spend eight minutes on the bomb-run. Nevertheless 17 B-17s were destroyed and the Group lost seven aircraft – four of them crashed or landed in Sweden.

The whole question of aircraft landing in neutral Sweden was quite a concern for the Eighth Air Force chiefs. Most of the aircraft that landed there were genuine, they were so badly damaged that there was little chance of them surviving the North Sea crossing. But there were several instances of apparently undamaged aircraft landing in order that their crews could seek sanctuary in a neutral country – a way to get out of combat flying. All the crews were interned and their aircraft sequestered by the Swedish government. In the early days the crews were under strict orders to set fire to their aircraft should they land in a neutral country. There were a sufficient number of the Eighth's aircraft ending up in neutral Sweden that quite an 'American colony' had been established there and subsequently a special Air Attache was appointed to the country to look after the interned airmen's interests. They still received flying pay and were housed in quite comfortable internment camps. Towards the end of the year a party of American

A B-17 of 509th Bomb Squadron landed in Sweden after a mission to Politz on 7th October 1944. (National Archives & Records Administration)

ground personnel were allowed in to repair the damaged aircraft. Ultimately an agreement was reached whereby the aircraft and crews were released provided that they were not again used in any operations over Europe.

From now onwards up until the end of the war the Group managed to achieve the lowest operational losses in the Division with only seven aircraft missing in action, although several damaged aircraft were forced to crash-land on the Continent, most of them coming down in Belgium. However, there were several unfortunate accidents on or near the airfield. The most serious one happened on 6th February 1945 when two aircraft, whilst in the landing pattern, collided and 19 airmen were killed. Then on 25th March when the Group was leaving for a mission, which was subsequently recalled because of bad weather, a B-17 caught fire, exploded and destroyed another aircraft.

The last operation left Polebrook on 20th April, the crews attacked the railway yards at Brandenburg and all returned safely. In 311 operations the Group had lost 125 aircraft in action, which was one of the lowest loss rates in the 1st Division. Several Groups that had come into operations later had suffered more heavily. The Group was one of the first to leave for the States, the first B-17s moving out on 21st May. Sadly one B-17 crashed at Barmouth in North Wales whilst making for RAF Valley, killing all ten crewmen and the ten passengers on board.

The RAF resumed charge of the airfield in July and in September of the following year the airfield was one of 60 RAF stations to be opened to the public on Battle of Britain Day, but the poor weather restricted the attendance to about 600. Before the airfield became inactive in

October 1948 it was used as a satellite for Upwood, echoes of the days of 1941. Eleven years later a Thor missile squadron of Bomber Command was based at Polebrook for almost four years, but by January 1967 the land had been handed back to the Rothschild estate. There is a fine triangular memorial stone to the 351st airmen, which is sited on concrete at the north-east end of what was the main runway, and close by there is another memorial inscribed: 'In memory of Lt. Gen. James T. Stewart 1921 – 1990, USAF Commanding Officer of 508th Sq. 351st Bomb Group who flew 60 combat missions against the enemy from this airfield 1943 – 1945'.

16
SILVERSTONE

Silverstone has became synonymous with motor racing in the United Kingdom and is famed worldwide as the venue for the British Grand Prix. Few of the thousands of spectators who visit Silverstone throughout the year are aware that the splendid race circuit has been fashioned from the site of an old wartime airfield. The circuit almost faithfully follows the lines of the old perimeter road with 'Hangar Straight' recalling the site of the two T2 hangars, and 'Abbey Curve' as a permanent reminder that the airfield was built on Luffield Abbey Farm, close to the site of an ancient abbey. The wartime control tower still stands in reasonable condition and flying has not been altogether edged out because on certain race days civil aircraft can still land there, with prior permission, and the circuit boasts a heliport facility.

The airfield, which was sited due south of the village from whence it gained its name, was set across the county boundary with Buckinghamshire. It was built by John Mowlem & Co Ltd to a classic A standard design, with three intersecting runways – the main one 6,000 feet and the other two of 4,200 feet and 3,900 feet in length. The technical sites were placed to the immediate west of the airfield, along with the living and communal quarters, which were sited farther west, in and around Lodge Copse and The Straights on the edge of Hazelborough Wood. The bomb storage area was to the far south of the airfield, which was finally completed in the early spring of 1943, and was allocated to No 92 Group of Bomber Command to house an Operational Training Unit.

The Unit selected to open up the airfield was No 17 which was then based at Upwood in Cambridgeshire. It was one of the first OTUs to be formed back in April 1940, and had, since that time, trained pilots, air observers and gunners as crews for the light bomber squadrons of No 2

Clubmans Race Cars compete at Silverstone with the old control tower visible in the background (BRDC Archives/Harold Barker).

Group. From its inception the Unit had been equipped with Bristol Blenheims, however by 1943 these aircraft had long passed their sell-by date – their last operations had taken place in August 1942 – and the decision had been taken to convert the Unit to Wellingtons. Although Upwood was a permanent pre-war station, it was at the time still a grassed airfield and the far heavier Wellingtons really required concrete runways to maintain the training programme during the autumn and winter months, hence one of the reasons why the Unit moved to Silverstone. Although, in fact, No 17 was officially disbanded on 30th April, only to be re-formed on the following day.

The move of an Operational Training Unit was a large undertaking and caused a major upheaval for all personnel. It began on 13th April and was not finally completed until the 29th. Two days later Group Captain K. P. Lewis was appointed Station Commander and he would remain at Silverstone until August 1945. The very first Wellingtons arrived on 6th May from No 11 OTU at Westcott in Buckinghamshire. They were two rather outmoded ICs, which had seen far better days and were destined to be grounded, that is turned into 'instructional' aircraft and used to familiarise the trainee crews with the layout of the aircraft they would later fly. During the next two weeks Wellington IIIs began to arrive with due regularity and the first training at Silverstone commenced on 1st June with Course No 62, which effectively meant

An early Wellington 1A: No 17 OTU was equipped with later Wellington marks. (RAF Museum)

that some trainee crews were forced to change from Blenheims to Wellingtons in mid-course. By the end of June there were 54 Wellingtons on strength, with a handful of Ansons and a couple of Martinets and Lysanders for target towing and fighter affiliation exercises.

Since the early days of operational training the format of the course had undergone many changes and enhancements but by mid-1943 it had been refined into two separate categories – basic and applied. The former was now undertaken by two identical Flights and a small Gunnery Flight, which were normally out-housed at the satellite airfield, responsible for the conversion, practice bombing and air firing. The applied part of the course covered cross-country flights, and operational exercises by two Flights based at the parent airfield. What had not changed over the passage of time was that all the crews underwent two weeks of ground training at the main base.

At the beginning of July Turweston, a grassed airfield about three miles to the north-east of Brackley but sited in Buckinghamshire, became Silverstone's satellite. Since November 1942 this airfield had been used by two different OTUs (Nos 12 and 13) as well as by Douglas Bostons and North American Mitchells of No 307 Ferry Training Unit for a short period. However, from early August the Unit's crews would undertake their initial conversion training and

The odd Westland Lysander could be seen at training airfields, used mainly for target towing.

basic handling flying at Turweston, both by day and night. And from November a special Gunnery Flight was formed there with some of the older Wellingtons and Martinets. The satellite would remain in use until late August 1945. It closed on 23rd September and in the following year was taken over by the War Office.

The initial two weeks of ground training, as has already been noted, saw the individual airmen coming together for the first time as crews and receiving ground training as an entirety. The instructional site at Silverstone was situated near the administration buildings, and like all operational training airfields comprised a number of buildings where the 'synthetic' or ground training was conducted. The three most important buildings were the AML Bombing Teacher, the Turret Instructional Trainer and last, but not least, the Gunnery and Crew Procedure Centre or 'Airmanship Hall'.

The first two buildings were very similar in design, brick-built and both two-storeyed. The AML Bombing Teacher comprised three units, and this method of ground bombing instruction had been first developed back in 1925. A film projector was housed in the top floor, which projected an image of slowly moving landscape onto the ground floor; it gave the same impression as if the trainee crew were flying at about 8,000 feet and the image could be adjusted to simulate the effect of different wind speeds and directions. The trainee crew with a bomb sight and navigation instruments would gather around the edges of the top floor and practise simulated bomb runs. The Turret Trainer used a similar photographic technique but in this case the image was normally projected onto a curved wall. The Trainer was also used for practising aircraft escape procedures.

The largest instructional building at the airfield was the Crew Procedure Centre and the type of ground training undertaken there had been first devised by Air Vice-Marshal A. T. 'Bomber' Harris, when he was the AOC of No 5 Group in 1939/40. He had utilised the fuselages of three written-off bombers to put the trainee airmen into a simulated operational environment. As he later recalled: 'the whole crews were put through this hoop time and time again, *ad nauseum* if necessary, until they were procedure perfect.' Since those days this system of crew 'synthetic' training had developed and been refined to take place in specially designed large halls, and it had become very realistic.

One airman recalled his impression of the Procedure Centre. 'The Grope [as the test was known to trainees] was basically an exercise that simulated the navigational and other problems a crew could expect to encounter on an operation. It was carried out in a large gymnasium-type building that was divided at the back into half-a-dozen twin-level studios each one housing a different member of the crew . . .' The noise of the aircraft engines was amplified so that each crew member had to communicate by intercom and there was an added complication that the large clock that controlled the test operation travelled at a faster speed than normal (about 50% quicker), thus giving the crew members far less time to undertake their normal duties, which added to the stress. Various emergency situations were artificially created such as icing, engine failures, crew injuries and emergency landings to add a further touch of reality. Accurate courses were required to be plotted and steered according to certain information supplied by the instructors over the intercom. Even fighter attacks were simulated by the sounds of amplified gunfire to test the crews' reaction and speed of evasion. The Centre was also used for reproducing ditching in the sea and practising dinghy procedures. The original building that housed the 'Airmanship Hall' at Silverstone has survived and is now used for storage purposes.

Nevertheless, however convincing such ground exercises were, they were no substitute for the real thing. Since July 1940 it had been the policy to send training crews on what were known as 'Nickel' operations during the final week of their course. These had been introduced as a result of an order from the Air Council that operations should, whenever possible, take precedence over training. Nickel was the code-name for the dropping of propaganda leaflets over enemy occupied territory, which was considered a very valuable part of the psychological battle. These operations fulfilled two objectives. First they enabled Bomber Command to maintain a regular despatch of such leaflets without seriously impinging on the activities of their operational squadrons. And secondly and more importantly, they gave the trainee crews their first experience of live operational flying.

These Nickel raids became known to the crews as their 'graduation' operation. Normally four crews per Unit were sent to selected areas in France, such as Paris, Lille or Brest. The operations were mostly controlled from Group headquarters, but later the Units were given a certain discretion to mount Nickel operations on their own initiative, although they should not be more frequent than one a week. On these Nickelling operations each aircraft usually carried about 20 packs of leaflets and occasionally a couple of bombs were carried, but these could only be dropped providing the military nature of the target had been clearly established. By the end of 1943 the Unit had completed 33 successful Nickel operations.

The most regular simulated operations were 'Bullseyes' and 'Erics' – the first was a night exercise involving trainee crews and the ground defences and the second was undertaken by day involving fighter units. The first Bullseye was mounted from Silverstone on 30th July, followed three days later by the first Eric exercise.

Early in September 1943 OTUs became involved in Operation Starkey – the Allies' large-scale air offensive against the Pas de Calais as an attempt to convince the enemy that an invasion on that part of the coast was imminent. The first in a series of small raids was mounted on the night of 30th/31st August when 33 training Wellingtons bombed an ammunition dump in the Forêt d'Eperlecques to the north of St Omer; just two crews left from Silverstone. The target had been marked by Pathfinder aircraft, so the raid had the additional purpose to accustom the crews to bombing on a variety of markers, which was now the Command's standard operational procedure. Two of the Group's training crews were lost on this night. Over the next few nights other ammunition dumps in northern France were bombed and in total eight of the Unit's trainee crews gained valuable experience without suffering any casualties.

During 1944, and more especially after the invasion of Normandy, training crews were sent out on diversionary sweeps over the North Sea and the English Channel. Often these sweeps were flown on nights when no major bombing operation was being carried out, with the objective of drawing up the German fighters, causing them to waste fuel and also to add confusion to the German fighter control. Some of these operations were mounted in considerable numbers, and on several nights over 100 Wellingtons were involved. Also some of the trainee crews were tasked with dropping 'Window', the thin strips of aluminium foil which interfered with the German ground and airborne radar. The diversionary flights by OTUs continued well into 1945, the last being flown on 3rd/4th April. During the war over 4,000 operational sorties were made by OTUs for the loss of 120 aircraft, and the lion's share was undertaken by Wellingtons – over 3,200 with the loss of 95 aircraft or a loss rate of 2.9%, which was only slightly higher than the Command's total rate of 2.6%.

Like all Operational Training airfields Silverstone was used on occasion by operational aircraft returning from bombing raids, diverted because of poor weather conditions over their home bases or because they were heavily damaged. In July 1943 alone there had been 54 such diversions at No 92 Group's airfields. For this reason and because of the number of training accidents at night, the airfield lighting at OTUs had been brought up to the standard provided at operational airfields.

The first serious accident involving an operational aircraft attempting to land at Silverstone occurred on 15th March 1944 when a Stirling of No 90 squadron, based at Tuddenham in Suffolk, burst into flames on its approach to the airfield. It finally crashed at Astwell Park killing the seven airmen; the pilot, Flight Sergeant J. V. Spring, was only 18 years old. The Stirling had collided with a training Wellington from Westcott, which came down near Aylesbury in Buckinghamshire. At the end of the month a Halifax III of No 578 squadron at Burn returning from the very costly raid on Nuremberg was attempting an emergency landing on three engines when it hit the masts of the wireless station to the south of the airfield and crashed. The pilot, Squadron Leader M. McCreanor, was killed along with six of his crew, only one escaping with injuries; the crew was on its fourteenth operation. Particularly bad weather during the latter days of July resulted in a rash of diversions, especially on the 30th, when over 100 aircraft sought refuge at training airfields after a daylight operation in support of ground troops in Normandy. Later in September (21st) no less than 17 Halifaxes landed safely at the airfield. All were carrying bombs – their operation had been aborted and rain and low cloud had closed their home base. The Unit's own safety record was about average; during 1943 nine Wellingtons had been lost in accidents, and another 16 were written-off in 1944.

After the end of the European war the Unit still soldiered on with its courses though operational training was now being greatly reduced. The airfield opened its gates to the public on the first Battle of Britain Day, 15th September 1945, and over 2,000 spectators were treated to an aerobatic display by Gloster Meteors. The following year the airfield was again opened on Battle of Britain Day but poor weather reduced the attendance. On 1st November 1946 the Unit moved away to Swinderby and the airfield, like so many others, was placed on a care and maintenance basis, but unlike many wartime airfields the site was sold in the following year.

During the summer of 1948 the disused airfield was selected to host the first RAC Grand Prix, the 3.67 mile track mainly using the perimeter road and the runways, and in October 100,000 people flocked there to see the Italian driver, Luigi Villoresi, win in a Maserati. This successful meeting revived the enthusiasm for motor racing in the country. Since those early pioneering days Silverstone has become one of the world's greatest racing circuits. Some of the old wartime buildings have survived and the British Racing Drivers Club, which has owned the circuit since 1971, has erected a small and easily accessible memorial near the main entrance, which remembers all the airmen who were trained at Silverstone and Turweston from 1943 to 1946.

The memorial at Silverstone.

17
SPANHOE

Spanhoe was the last wartime airfield to be built in Northamptonshire, another Class A standard. It was first known as Wakerley from the village to the north-west, but during its early stages of development it was renamed Spanhoe from the nearby farm and wood, where most of the ten living and general services sites were eventually erected. However, most of the locals referred to it as Harringworth as much of the airfield lay within that parish, and sometimes this led to a certain amount of confusion with the other American base at Harrington. To the USAAF the airfield was known simply as 'Station 493'; all American air bases were so numbered and the number appeared on all official reports and correspondence. The airmen were also actively encouraged to use the station number rather than the airfield name.

The airfield opened in the first week of January 1944 when a small station complement arrived to prepare the base for its future residents – the 315th Troop Carrier Group of the Ninth Air Force. This Group had served briefly at Aldermaston with the Eighth Air Force during 1943. It would be another month before the 315th made an appearance, and then with only about 650 men and just eight aircraft. The remainder were still on detachment in North Africa where they had been since May 1943. The Group was commanded by Colonel Hamish McLelland and would operate under the Ninth Troop Carrier Command, allocated to the 52nd Transport Wing, which had its headquarters at Cottesmore. Even when the detachment arrived from abroad in early March the Group was still under strength with just two squadrons, 34th and 43rd, and equipped with less than 30 aircraft. With the invasion of Europe imminent the Group was strengthened by the transfer of two squadrons, 309th and 310th, directly from the United States, although the crews had to be found from other Troop Carrier Groups serving in the Mediterranean. In fact the 60th, which had served briefly at Chelveston in 1942, supplied some of the crews and aircraft.

Douglas C-47B of the Ninth Air Force. (H. Holmes via D. Benfield)

The Group was equipped with Douglas C-47s of course, the work horses of the USAAF. This aircraft was the military version of the very successful twin-engined DC-3 civil airliner, which had first flown in January 1935. It was then far in advance of its time, built to a simple but very robust design and offering speed and comfort to its passengers. The military model was first ordered by the Army Air Corps in 1940 but it was not until 1942 that the C-47s began to come off the Douglas production lines in any great number. It proved to be an excellent and reliable transport aircraft, able to carry up to two tons of supplies and stores, which could be handled quite easily because of the double roller tracks on the floor of the fuelage. The aircraft doubled as an airborne troop-carrier, capable of carrying up to 20 fully equipped troops, who could jump safely and quickly from its large side door, and it could also carry five to six 'pararacks' of supplies under its wings. To add to the aircraft's versatility it operated quite successfully as a glider tower. To the American airmen the C-47s were universally known as 'Gooney birds'! The C-47 had a rather limited operational range and furthermore it was unarmed and also lacked armour plating for its crew, while the fuel tanks were not self-sealing; all factors that made the aircraft and its crews vulnerable to both flak and fighters. In reality, C-47s needed to operate where the Allied air forces commanded complete air superiority. Nevertheless the aircraft played a major role in all the airborne operations of 1944/5.

After the war the C-47 or Dakota, as it became universally known, was operated by many commercial airlines and cargo freight companies throughout the world. Indeed over 60 years later the Dakota is still flying, and considering that over 20,000 Dakotas, over half as C-47s, were built, it is probably the most remarkable and prolific aircraft ever produced. By April 1944 the 315th had 60 C-47s at Spanhoe and this figure increased by one-third four months later – the full complement was 24 to each squadron.

Also at Spanhoe were several C-53s or Skytroopers, another version of the C-47, but they had a smaller cargo door and a lighter flooring. The aircraft only saw limited production, at least compared with the prolific production of C-47s. About a dozen or so Waco CG-4A gliders were attached to the Group. This was the main American assault glider of the war; 48 feet long and with a wing span of 84 feet it was often described as 'an ugly blunt-nosed dragonfly'! The Group never towed gliders into action, it operated solely delivering paratroops and transporting supplies and passengers.

During May the Group was engaged in a number of paratroop dropping exercises. The first took place on the 6th with 48 aircraft involved, and it was a successful operation, but two days later a night-drop was attempted, which proved to be less than satisfactory. Another night-exercise was undertaken on the 11th but with little marked improvement. It was not until the 26th of the month that a much better result was achieved, and two days later the crews conducted an exercise with Waco gliders.

On 3rd June troops of the US 82nd Airborne Division, who were based around Leicester, began to arrive at Spanhoe, and they were accommodated in the two large T2 hangars sited to the south of the runways. The aircraft were now painted with their broad black and white 'invasion' stripes around the wings and the rear of the fuselage as an aid to identification for the Allied ships and troops below, as well as in the very crowded and confused skies over Normandy on D-Day. The ground crews referred to the imminent and highly secret operation as the 'cake walk'. This was taken from the words on the tins of paint, which, for some reason, bore the American legend 'for the cake walk'! Perhaps it was a matter of wishful thinking or supreme confidence on the part of the powers-that-be that this major air offensive would be accomplished with ease?

The crews were briefed on the afternoon of 5th June and then the airfield was sealed. At eleven o'clock on the evening of the 5th, 47 C-47s left Spanhoe with troops of the 505th Parachute Infantry Regiment.

There should have been 48 aircraft taking part but a grenade had exploded in one aircraft killing three men, with another dying in hospital later, and injuring some others. These were the first American D-Day casualties. Another C-47 was substituted because the troops involved were part of the Headquarters Company. The 82nd Airborne Division was taking part in Operation Boston, which had as its main objective the capture of the town of Ste Mère-Église, situated directly behind the US beach-head 'Utah', and as a secondary aim to establish crossing points over the Merderet river. Major General Matthew B. Ridgeway, the Commanding Officer of US 82nd Airborne Division, was originally going to land by glider but instead he flew from Spanhoe with the 315th. He later recalled: 'I climbed heavily up the little ladder of the plane that was to take me to France. In the doorway, I turned for one last look at the sweep of the English Midlands, now grown soft and green with spring . . .'.

The aircraft crossed the English coast over Weymouth and flew in tight 'V' formations across the Channel in a strictly prescribed ten mile corridor at about 500 feet, with their navigation and cabin lights switched off. They were following their own Pathfinder crews – two to each Group – who would lead them within visual distance of the dropping zones (DZs). Their planned approach to the DZs was to cross the French coast over the west of the Contentin peninsula, mainly to avoid the heavy concentrations of flak batteries known to be protecting the beach-heads. At this stage they should have climbed to between 1,000 to 1,500 feet but as they neared the DZs the pilots reduced speed to 110 mph and came down to 500/700 feet – the jumping height.

It was now that things began to go awry. Despite the weather forecast of a clear moonlit night the crews flew into a heavy blanket of clouds which obliterated the ground and the beacon markers laid by the Pathfinder crews. As a result the parachute drop became rather scattered and unfortunately many of the troops landed on the deliberately flooded fields surrounding the rivers Douve and Merderet, which the air reconnaissance photographs had not revealed. Furthermore, most of the troops of the 82nd Airborne Division landed in the midst of the Wehrmacht's 91st Infantry Division, and the American losses were quite horrendous; the battle for Ste Mère-Église has passed into the legends of the US Army. All the Group's crews managed to return safely by 5 am, although two aircraft were forced to land elsewhere, and another had returned earlier with its troops as enemy flak had injured seven men. The Ninth's Troop Carrier Command lost 21 aircraft in the paratrooping operations.

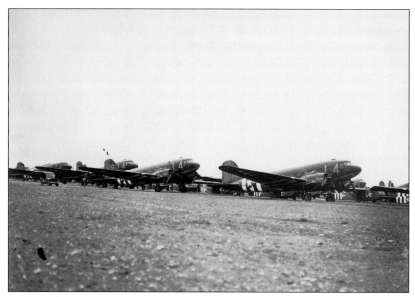

C-47s & C.G.-4 Gliders lined up along a runway – 7th June 1944. (National Archives & Records Administration)

For the rest of the month and into July the Group was involved in transporting ammunition and supplies into the beach-heads, as well as returning with wounded troops. They also became involved in a number of training exercises, which were mostly conducted over Wittering. On 8th July two C-47s collided and one of the aircraft crashed near Stamford. One crew survived but eight airmen and 26 Polish paratroopers were killed. They belonged to the Polish Independent Parachute Brigade, which had its headquarters in Stamford. These training exercises with the Polish troops were a prelude to the Group's next live operations in September. However, on 26th August, the Ninth Troop Carrier Command became absorbed into the newly formed First Allied Airborne Army under the command of Lieutenant General Lewis H. Bretherton, who had hitherto been the Commander of the Ninth Air Force. There had been a number of airborne operations planned but these were cancelled, mainly because by their rapid advance the Allied ground forces had already taken the intended objectives.

However, in early September two further Allied airborne operations were scheduled. On the first of the month Operation Linnett II – the crossing of the river Meuse – was planned to leave, but it was postponed and two days later the operation was cancelled. Then

Operation Comet – the crossing of the Rhine in the Wesel area – was prepared for 8th September but this was also postponed until the 10th, and then cancelled only four hours before the scheduled take-off time. Comet was not completely shelved, it effectively became the nucleus of a greatly enlarged operation, code-named Market Garden with similar objectives – the seizure of the bridges over the waterways in Holland between the existing frontline and the north German plain. The fame, or infamy, of Market Garden resides in the ferocious and costly battle at Arnhem. This operation has since been described as 'one of the most seriously flawed of all major operations in World War II'.

The reason for the two words in the new code-name was that 'Market' would be the airborne forces' part of the operation, with 'Garden' being the ground forces' offensive to advance and join up with the airborne forces. The launch of the new operation was planned for Sunday 17th September, and it was to be an airborne assault on a massive scale with almost 34,000 Allied troops going into action by air, 60% by parachute and the rest by gliders, along with over 5,000 tons of equipment and some 2,500 armed vehicles and guns. More than three-quarters of the transport aircraft involved would be American and Major General Paul L. Williams, the Commander of the Ninth Troop Carrier Command, was appointed overall Air Commander for 'Market'. The first problem was that there were an insufficient number of transport aircraft to carry this large airborne force in one lift, and ultimately it was decided that the force would be taken in three air-lifts on separate days. Nearly all the American airborne troops would depart on the first lift, whereas the despatch of the British and Polish airborne troops was to be spread over three lifts.

The 315th Group at Spanhoe would be heavily involved over five days transporting American, British and Polish troops. On Sunday 17th September 90 C-47s in two formations left with men of US 82nd Airborne Division and dropped them south of Nijmegen. Only one aircraft failed to return. On the following day 54 aircraft, with about 900 men of the British 4th Parachute Brigade (mainly 10th Battalion) and including their Commander, Brigadier J. W. Hackett, were due to leave Spanhoe at seven o'clock in the morning but the air-lift was delayed some four hours because heavy night-mists had been forecast for the various airfields involved.

The same flight path as the previous day's operation was taken. The formations assembled over March in Cambridgeshire, crossed the English coast at Aldeburgh and then the Dutch coast at Schowen Island and from thence it was about 100 miles (some 40 minutes flying time) to the dropping zone at Ginkel Heath about six miles west of Arnhem. The two formations of the 315th were flying behind the lead aircraft of 314th Group from Saltby, so the flak defences would be already well prepared. In any case the German defences had expected further airborne landings and had already strengthened their flak batteries. One of the Group's C-47s was hit by flak before the DZ. It burst into flames but all the paratroopers managed to escape. The pilot, Second Lieutenant J. Spurrier, attempted to crash-land but the aircraft hit a pylon and was engulfed in flames. Only the co-pilot survived but he was severely burned. Shortly afterwards a second C-47 was struck by flak, all the troops jumped and Lieutenant Tucker managed to make a successful crash-landing with no crew fatalities.

One of the Group's navigators, Lieutenant B. Coggins, described the scene over the dropping zone: 'I don't know just what hell will be like, but I think we got a preview ... the DZ was a solid ball of fire. At the command to jump, our troops had exited from the plane without any hesitation. My admiration, already at an extremely high level where paratroopers were concerned, went even higher as these brave men dropped into that preview of hell ... the tales of that mission lasted a long, long time.' An idea of the human costs of the Arnhem operation can be gained from the losses of the 4th Brigade – out of some 2,100 men that were dropped almost 1,800 were killed or taken prisoner, and only 327 were finally evacuated!

On the following day (19th) the Group, along with the 314th, was detailed to take the first batch of Polish airborne troops into battle, but because of bad weather over the English airfields, the operation was delayed for two days. The worsening situation at Arnhem and Oosterbeck persuaded the Airborne Army chiefs that the parachute air-lift should go ahead despite poor weather conditions. A total of 114 C-47s left in the early afternoon of Thursday the 21st. Due to the heavy cloud the pilots had great difficulty in assembling and completing the formations and it was fortunate that there were no collisions. The southern route via Belgium, which was considered to be much safer, was used. However, the weather had so deteriorated over both Spanhoe and Saltby that it was decided to recall the formations before landing conditions at the airfields worsened further.

No less than four recall messages were sent out but many of the radio operators on the aircraft had the wrong codes and only 41 C-47s turned back and landed at the nearest available airfields. The remaining aircraft ploughed on regardless and as they were approaching the dropping zone – the village of Driel on the south bank of the

C-47s line 'an airfield somewhere in England' — November 1944. (Imperial War Museum)

Rhine about a mile from Oosterbeck – they encountered fierce and heavy flak. Five C-47s from the 315th were shot down but all the Polish troops managed to jump before the aircraft crashed, with ten crewmen killed and another 14 rescued by Allied ground troops. The surviving crews complained bitterly about the apparent lack of fighter escorts.

One of the pilots, Lieutenant Cecil H. Dawkins, though severely wounded in the head and face remained at the controls whilst his crew baled out, and he was still in the aircraft when it exploded. Miraculously he survived and was taken prisoner. In January 1945 this brave and intrepid airman escaped from captivity and after walking for two weeks in snow and surviving by living off the land, finally met up with an advance party of Russian troops, by whom he was welcomed and royally received. Lieutenant Dawkins was later awarded the Distinguished Service Order, the second highest American decoration for valour.

The Group had another dropping mission to complete, when on 23rd September 41 aircraft left Spanhoe with over 500 Polish paratroops for Driel. On this operation all the aircraft survived. Three days later a total of 72 crews were in action when they transported over 300 British troops and equipment as well as urgent supplies to an emergency airstrip at Grave to the south of Nijmegen, and they all returned to

209

Spanhoe. On the three main dropping operations over 310 sorties had been made for the loss of eight aircraft with twelve airmen killed in action, 19 taken prisoner and another 19 rescued.

Towards the end of September Colonel McLelland was replaced by Lieutenant Colonel Howard B. Lyons as Commander. He would remain in charge until 9th January 1945 but would return to the Group just in time to lead his airmen on their last wartime operation. In November there were strong rumours circulating around Spanhoe that the Group was about to move to an airfield in Essex – Birch. This airfield had been completed in the spring of 1944 but had never been permanently occupied. For whatever reason the proposed move did not take place, but in March 1945 the Group did make a temporary move to another Essex airfield for its final operation of the war.

On 21st March 81 C-47s made the short flight to Boreham airfield, just outside Chelmsford, to take part in the last airborne operation of the war, 'Varsity': the crossing of the Rhine. The mistakes that had been made on Operation Market had been assimilated and the entire air-lift was planned to be completed within a matter of hours. On the 24th the Group transported almost 1,300 British troops of 6th Airborne Division, and it proved to be a most costly operation for the 315th – six aircraft were shot down and seven more crash-landed on the Continent with heavy battle damage. In total the Group lost 19 aircraft either missing in action or written-off, with 36 airmen killed. The Group's CO, Lieutenant Colonel Lyon, managed to escape by parachute. He was taken prisoner but was released five days later by troops of the 6th Airborne Division. Three days later the crews returned to land petrol, supplies and passengers.

In April the Group moved out to Glisy airfield near Amiens in France, though at the end of the month the crews returned to Spanhoe to take part in the final training exercise of the war – 'Amber'. By June the American airmen had left Spanhoe and the airfield was handed over to the RAF, and in early July No 253 Maintenance Unit arrived to assemble surplus RAF transport for sale by auction. The Unit remained at the airfield until 1947 when it closed down. Nowadays much of the old airfield has disappeared under quarrying, but there is a fine obelisk memorial, which commemorates the 315th and also lists those airmen who were killed in action.

The fine obelisk memorial at Spanhoe.

18
SYWELL

A visit to Sywell Aerodrome – yes, even the old-fashioned name has been retained – was a rewarding experience. After days of travel through the Northamptonshire countryside searching out old abandoned airfield sites, it was such a pleasure to find this delightfully neat aerodrome that was so obviously flourishing. Then to enter the old terminal building was like taking a nostalgic step back into aviation history. This building has been developed into a hotel complex, aptly named 'The Aviator', and its walls are lined with photographs of old aircraft and various items of aviation memorabilia that splendidly recall those exciting days of pre-war flying, a vivid reminder of the era when the RAF links with the airfield were first forged.

In April 1935 Brooklands Aviation Ltd was granted a contract by the Air Ministry to provide elementary flying instruction to RAF airmen. On 10th June the School opened, later becoming known as No 6 E & RFTS, the 'R' recognising that the flying instruction also included members of the RAF Volunteer Reserve – the so-called 'weekend airmen'! It was laid down that each student pilot should be given at least 50 hours of flying time within a period of two months, which was extended to ten weeks during the winter months, as well as ground instruction in a variety of subjects. The Chief Flying Instructor and Manager at Brooklands was Ian W. C. Mackenzie, who had left the RAF in 1929 as a Flight Lieutenant, but had qualified as a flying instructor whilst in the Service. For the next 18 years Ian Mackenzie would be in command of the flying training at Sywell.

At the outbreak of the war there were 25 Tiger Moths and three Avro Ansons and the School was staffed by 16 instructors. The Ansons were used by No 8 Civilian Air Navigation School, soon to move away to Squires Gate near Blackpool to allow No 6 EFTS (the Volunteer Reserve had been absorbed into the Service) to concentrate on elementary flying training. The first wartime course commenced on 23rd October 1939 although in the meanwhile a few short courses had been provided for flying instructors. Like other civilian flying schools, No 6 was made into a full RAF unit in January 1940, with the flying instructors resuming their previous RAF ranks. The 50 or so Tiger Moths would slowly lose their civil identification numbers, although in Sywell's case not until September. The upper surfaces of the aircraft were camouflaged, given RAF rondels and serial numbers, and the wing undersides and tips were painted in training yellow.

The initial course still lasted two months and 60 students arrived for each course with an average wastage rate of about one-third. At any given time two courses were being run concurrently, which meant that about 120 student pilots were under instruction, and to cope with these increased numbers a relief landing ground at Denton was brought into use. By the summer of 1940, largely as a result of pilot losses over France and during the Battle of Britain, as well as to man the new squadrons that were being formed, the initial course was reduced to five weeks. This cutback in training time put increased pressure on the flying instructors, the use of airfield space and the maintenance and servicing of the aircraft.

Before the introduction of the Empire Air Training Scheme, No 6 was just one of 46 such Elementary Flying Training Schools that were operating in the summer of 1940. The students would arrive from one of the four Initial Training Wings, where they would have already been inculcated into Service traditions and discipline. Besides pure flying tuition and practice, the students would receive ground instruction in the theories of navigation, armaments, signals, engines, aircraft rigging and photography with more general subjects such as mathematics, service organisation and law, and they would be given written examinations. They were also introduced to their parachutes, and instructed in how to use and to take good care of them; they would be constantly reminded that these were their 'life-lines', and it was emphasised that they were very expensive (about £70)! Their ground training would include hours spent 'flying' in the covered cockpit of the Link trainer, which was effectively a miniature aircraft, with its hooded fuselage complete with tail and wings, and it fairly accurately simulated flying whilst still on the ground. The pupils would respond to instructions from the instructor and the Link's automatic recorder, known as the 'crab', faithfully traced all their actions and errors! As an Air Ministry official hand-out stated, 'The Link trainer saves valuable hours of instruction in the air, as well as lives and aircraft.'

For most pilots their abiding memory of these early training days was the magical moment when they were finally allowed to fly solo for the first time. On average most students managed to reach this stage after about ten hours of dual instruction. From then onwards if the instructor was satisfied with the student's landings and take-offs, it was a matter of improving and refining the newly acquired skills, both by day and night, and including cross-wind and forced landings with some simple aerobatic flying thrown in for good measure. It was felt that such manoeuvres promoted self-confidence in the air. Throughout the course the students' progress would be carefully monitored and assessed as to their initiative and leadership qualities, along with their overall flying skills, and they were marked accordingly. After five weeks of highly concentrated training, both on the ground and in the air, they would pass on to the next stage of training at one of 17 Service Flying Schools, which were then still situated in the United Kingdom. However, by 1943 the majority of student pilots would be posted overseas for their second stage of flying training.

Little did many of the flying instructors at Sywell realise when the first Free French airmen arrived in January 1941 what an impact they would have on the airfield and school. They proved to be just the forerunners of the many French and Belgian airmen that would receive their early flying training at Sywell. Ultimately a special Free French Flight was formed with its own French flying instructors and with a First World War pilot, Lieutenant Colonel Edouard Picôt, in charge. Even when 'grading' courses became the norm at Sywell, the Free French airmen were still given the full course of elementary flying training. Probably about one-third of the total output of pilots were either French or Belgian. Even by the end of 1944, when the demands for flying training were decreasing, there were over 60 French airmen still in residence.

During 1941, because of the rapid growth of operational requirements there was a demand for a higher standard of pilot training. Flying Training Command was also deeply concerned about the wastage rate at the Elementary Schools, which was proving to be such a drain on valuable resources, so it was decided that another check would be added to the pilot selection procedure with the introduction of a 'grading' course. The first of these courses started at Sywell in November 1941. Under this new system the aspiring pilots were given twelve hours' dual instruction to bring them up to the time they would be ready to go solo, and only if they were then assessed as suitable for further flying training would they progress to the next stage. Three

A de Havilland Tiger Moth II – 1942. (RAF Museum)

weeks was the time set aside for these courses.

By June 1942 Sywell was operating mainly as a Grading School, and would do so for the rest of the war. There were five Flights, three of which were based at Denton. However, another Flight was formed, which brought the complement of Tiger Moths to over 120. This Flight was solely for the use of the flying instructors, in order that they could maintain their flying skills, especially at night, because so much of their instruction was now of a very basic nature. Nevertheless the airfield was very busy with nearly 8,000 hours being flown during July and an intake of over 300 pupils. Perhaps one of the most famous airmen to pass through the Grading School was Walter 'Wally' Hammond, the celebrated Gloucestershire and England batsman, who after his short course at Sywell went to the USA for his flying training and, in 1943, served with No 103 squadron of Bomber Command.

In January 1943 the School was called upon to mount yet another type of flying training – the refresher courses. With the Commonwealth Air Training Scheme in full stride, trained pilots were arriving back in the United Kingdom and forced to kick their heels until there were vacancies at one of the Advanced Flying Units. These refresher courses, three weeks in length, were introduced to ensure that the new pilots were given the opportunity to practise their skills over blacked-out Britain. They also allowed them to familiarise themselves with the take-off and landing procedures in operation at Service airfields, as well as giving them some valuable experience of map reading and navigation. Whilst these courses were being mounted, the intake of airmen for grading was reduced by about a half.

On 26th February 1942 the Canadian pilot, Pilot Officer Murray Peden, first noted under Chipping Warden, arrived at Sywell for his refresher course. It was his first experience of Northamptonshire and little did he know that over the next five months he would get to know the county very well, at least from the air! He described Sywell as 'a tiny hamlet and our aerodrome was a barren grass and mud field just clear of the bush that lay south of the town ... We were billeted in private houses in Northampton ... at 7.15 in the morning an old bus trundled us the six or seven miles over to the drone at Sywell ...' He found that his time at the airfield proved to be most congenial. 'It had been the closest thing to membership in a flying club for the idle rich that we had experienced ... the common privilege of having a fleet of Tiger Moths as our own playthings had the best of all possible worlds.'

The airfield at Sywell was not solely devoted to flying training nor indeed was it the exclusive preserve of Tiger Moths. Wellingtons were

Wellington having undergone refurbishment at Sywell Aerodrome. (Sywell Aerodrome Ltd via Chris & Mavis Parker)

216

Besides Tiger Moths & Wellingtons, Lancaster IIs were also in evidence during 1942/3. This Mark II served with No 514 squadron at Waterbeach. (Imperial War Museum)

very much in evidence from 1940 onwards, up to the end of the war and beyond. Brooklands Aviation Ltd of Weybridge had been granted a contract to repair damaged Wellingtons. The company was just a part of the nationwide Civilian Repair Organisation, that had been set up by Lord Nuffield, and which made such a vital contribution to keeping the operational squadrons flying. Five factory hangars had been erected by the end of 1939 and the first Wellington to be repaired and returned to the Service left Sywell in April 1940. Many local sub-contractors, from premises in and around Northampton, Kettering and Desborough, were also engaged in the project. In total over 1,800 Wellingtons had been overhauled and repaired up to 1951 when the contract finally came to an end.

During 1942 and 1943 especially, Avro Lancaster IIs could also be seen around the airfield. In August 1942 the first Lancaster II was assembled at the Armstrong Whitworth facility, which was based in two large hangars in the south-west corner of the airfield. The Mark II had been developed in 1941 and the prototype first flew on 26th November 1941. Unlike the earlier mark it was powered by four Bristol Hercules IX or XVI engines rather than Rolls-Royce Merlins. During the war Lancasters were built under licence by Metropolitan Vickers, Vickers Armstrong, Austin Morris and Armstrong Whitworth, along with a myriad of sub-contractors throughout the country. Production of Mark IIs started in May 1942 at Armstrong Whitworth's factory at Coventry but it was delayed for about four months because of bomb damage. So the facilities at Sywell were used merely as a temporary expedient, mainly because of the smallness of the airfield and the fact that it was grassed. The first Lancaster II left Sywell on 12th August 1942 and perhaps another 100 or so were assembled there until a larger production centre at Bitteswell to the north of Rugby, which was provided with concrete runways, was opened towards the end of 1943. Only 301 Lancaster IIs were produced in total and only a handful of squadrons operated them until September 1944.

Like all flying training schools Sywell had its share of accidents. The worst year was 1941 with seven. One of these, on 12th September, resulted in the death of an instructor, Flight Lieutenant G. Brembridge, AFC, and his pupil, LAC B. W. Lavan. Their Tiger Moth collided with an Oxford of No 15 SFTS at Kidlington as it emerged from clouds at 600 feet, and the two airmen in the Oxford were also killed. Although there were some unfortunate accidents during 1944, including the death of another instructor and his pupil in July, the safety record at Sywell was probably better than most other Elementary Schools – a testimony to Wing Commander I. W. C. Mackenzie and his staff of instructors and the ground crews that serviced and maintained the School's armada of Tiger Moths.

Over 2,500 British and Allied airmen passed through Sywell on some part of their flying training, and it is perhaps rather invidious to pick out just a few individuals from such a large number. However, there were four airmen who made quite a mark in their subsequent Service careers and they are worthy of mention. Anthony C. Bartley had already had experience of civilian flying when he joined the RAF in 1939. He completed his initial training at Sywell in May and was later posted to No 92 squadron. After the Battle of Britain he was awarded the DFC, gaining a Bar in February 1942. After service in the Middle and Far East, he left the Service in 1946 to become a test pilot with Vickers Armstrong. He married the film actress Deborah Kerr, and his Service experiences are recalled in his book *Smoke Trials in the Sky*.

Robert D. Elliott was a local man from Northampton, who joined the RAFVR in 1938, completing his early flying training at Sywell. He served with No 72 squadron over Dunkirk and in the Battle of Britain, had four victories to his name and was awarded the DFC. After a distinguished Service career he retired in 1968 at the rank of Air Vice-Marshal. Another pre-war trainee at Sywell was the South African

Present day aerial view of Sywell Aerodrome. (Sywell Aerodrome Ltd via Chris & Mavis Parker)

airman, Petrus H. Hugo, who entered the RAF in February 1939. He served in France and in the Battle of Britain with No 615 squadron, and later became Wing Commander (Flying) at Tangmere when he had already been awarded the DSO, DFC with two Bars. Hugo retired from the RAF in 1950 at the rank of Group Captain.

But perhaps the most famous 'old boy' of No 6 School was Brendan E. F. 'Paddy' Finucane. He joined the RAF on a short-service commission in August 1938. On completion of his elementary training at Sywell he was only rated 'average', and when one considers his relatively short but brilliant flying career, it might suggest that he was a late developer! By June 1942 he was a Wing Commander Flying at Hornchurch, but sadly he failed to return from an offensive sweep over France in July. He also had been awarded the DSO, DFC with two Bars and had 32 victories to his name. The AOC of Fighter Command wrote of him, '[his] courage, skill and powers of leadership were a great inspiration of Fighter Command. He was the beau ideal of the "fighter boy".'

No 6 EFTS finally closed its doors in May 1947, the last course passing out on the 21st of the month. However, flying training instruction still continued from June with No 6 RFS, which provided refresher courses for the RAF Reserve and by 1951 the Tiger Moths had

Memorial to those that trained at Sywell between 1937 and 1945.

been exchanged for Percival Prentices, the Service's basic trainer. In late 1951 No 4 Basic Flying Training School opened to give elementary flying instruction on Chipmunks to National Service pilots. By the summer of 1953 both Schools had closed, thus bringing 18 years of RAF flying training to a close.

Although the ban on civil flying was lifted in January 1946, the Northampton Aero Club did not return to the airfield for another year, and on 21st May 1949 the first flying display since the war was held. In 1997 the aerodrome proudly celebrated 70 years of aviation – a really remarkable and memorable milestone. In June of the same year a memorial stone was dedicated to the memory of all the airmen that had trained at Sywell.

19
WITTERING

It is now over 70 years since Wittering reopened as an important RAF station, a history of Service aviation that can be hardly bettered; from the days of fragile bi-planes through to Harrier 'Jump Jets' and beyond. At the outbreak of the Second World War Wittering was the only RAF operational station in Northamptonshire. It was under the control of No 12 Group of Fighter Command with two fighter squadrons, Nos 23 and 213, based there, equipped with Blenheim Ifs and Hurricane Is respectively.

The Hurricane had been designed by Sidney Camm and first flew in 1935, entering the Service in December 1937. Powered by a Rolls-Royce Merlin II engine and armed with eight .303 machine guns, it ushered in a new era for the RAF as its first monoplane fighter. Although slower than the Spitfire, it was a steady, reliable and highly manoeuvrable aircraft, which became the mainstay of Fighter Command during the Battle of Britain, destroying more enemy aircraft than all the other defences combined. The 'Hurry', as it was fondly known, was greatly admired by all its pilots, and it proved most adaptable, later operating with great success as a fighter/bomber.

In October the station complement was increased to three squadrons with the result that No 610 'County of Chester' Auxiliary squadron arrived on the 10th with its newly acquired Spitfire Is. Thus the airfield housed Fighter Command's three major fighters, and in March 1940 the new Boulton Paul Defiants made a brief appearance at Wittering. During November 1939 the aircraft would be camouflaged and their squadron identification codes applied to both sides of the fuselages, in most cases to the aft of the RAF rondels with the aircraft's individual letter on the other side of the rondel. In the majority of cases these codes were different from those carried pre-war. For instance, No 23's

Spitfires of No 610 squadron.

code was changed from MS to YP, 610 from JE to DW, but No 213 squadron unusually retained its pre-war letters AK until the squadron lost its identity in 1945.

The squadrons were mostly engaged on east coast patrols using both Bircham Newton and West Raynham in Norfolk as forward operational bases. By early December, along with other squadrons in the Group, they would begin covering the fishing trawlers from Lowestoft and Great Yarmouth, some of which had been attacked on 8th December to the utter condemnation of the British press, who called it 'an unprovoked attack on unarmed and harmless fishing boats.'

The Spitfires left for Biggin Hill on 10th May and they were replaced by another Spitfire squadron, No 266, which would remain in the area for twelve months except for periods of detachment farther south. Collyweston opened as a satellite but both airfields were really too far north to become directly involved in the air battle over the Dunkirk beaches and the Battle of Britain. Various squadrons left for action in the south, whilst others arrived at Wittering for a rest and regrouping. In June the Station Commander, Group Captain Harry Broadhurst, DFC, AFC, led what was known as the Wittering Wing – two squadrons of Hurricanes and Spitfires. This was a couple of months before the large Duxford Wing under Douglas Bader became such a contentious issue in the Battle of Britain. In December Broadhurst left to take over the command of Hornchurch and after a most distinguished Service career he retired in 1961 as a highly decorated and greatly respected Air Chief Marshal.

On 9th August twelve Spitfires of No 266 squadron left for Northolt and after operating from there, Eastchurch, Manston and Hornchurch, returned to Wittering on the 21st. Eleven aircraft had been lost and eight pilots killed or wounded, including its Commanding Officer, Squadron Leader R. L. 'Wilkie' Wilkinson, who was killed in action on the 16th. The squadron had claimed ten victories with another six probables. The new Commander, Squadron Leader D. G. H. Spencer, an ex-Cranwell graduate, was left with very little to command until the squadron was re-equipped and replacement pilots drafted in.

During August a famous Spitfire squadron, No 74, arrived for a rest and to replace the heavy casualties it had suffered whilst operating from Hornchurch. It had just been taken over by Squadron Leader A. G. 'Sailor' Malan, DFC Bar, but about a week later the Spitfires moved a little farther north to Kirton Lindsey. They were replaced, on 9th September, by Hurricane Is of No 1 squadron, which was one of the oldest RAF squadrons, having been first formed as a balloon unit in May 1912. The squadron had earlier served in France and had been fully engaged in the Battle of Britain from Tangmere and Northolt. Amongst its leading pilots was Sergeant Arthur V. Clowes, DFM, who had at least eight victories to his name. He was commissioned in September and within weeks was given command of 'A' Flight. Clowes

Flying Officer A. V. Clowes, DFM, with his Hurricane of No 1 squadron at Wittering, October 1940. (RAF Museum)

added to his score in October, and ultimately went on to command two squadrons, ending his service as a Wing Commander with the DSO, DFC.

Sadly, in November Squadron Leader D. A. Pemberton, DFC, the Squadron's Commander, was killed on the short-hop from Collyweston to Wittering. He was replaced by a Canadian airman, Squadron Leader M. H. 'Hilly' Brown, DFC. Brown had already experienced two lucky escapes. He had been shot down over France and had managed to escape via Brest, then in August he had to bale out again and was rescued from the sea. He was killed in action over Sicily in October 1941 whilst leading a Wing, with 18 confirmed victories to his name. By the middle of December the squadron had moved back to Northolt. However, almost 30 years later (July 1969) it would return to Wittering to become the first squadron to be equipped with the famous Hawker Siddeley Harrier GRI-VSTOL ('Jump Jet'), and at the time of writing the squadron is still serving at Wittering.

The heavy and incessant night-bombing raids during the autumn had highlighted the need for a much stronger night-fighter force allied to a properly co-ordinated night-defence system. Wittering was moving inexorably towards becoming a specialist night-fighter station for the defence of the Midlands. Towards the end of November, No 25 squadron moved in from Debden in Essex with its newly acquired Bristol Beaufighters. The crews, when operating Blenheim Ifs, had been in the vanguard of trialling the AI system, but they had already claimed their first victory with their new aircraft. On 22nd December the squadron was joined by the Hurricanes of No 151 squadron, which had just completed a spell of night-flying training at Bramcote and was being re-equipped with Defiants. Wittering was designated a Sector control station and would be provided with its own Ground Control Interception stations at Orly and Langtoft in Lincolnshire. Perhaps the final piece in the jig-saw was the appointment of Group Captain Basil Embry, DSO, DFC, AFC. as Station Commander to replace Harry Broadhurst. Few RAF officers during the Second World War would have such a varied experience of both operational flying and senior command as Basil Embry, and became probably the most able of RAF wartime commanders.

Earlier in the year Embry had returned to the United Kingdom after being shot down over France whilst leading his Blenheim squadron from Wattisham. He had managed to evade capture and had made his escape via the south of France. For the previous two months he had commanded RAF Rochford in Essex, where he was specifically appointed to establish the first night-fighter Wing; in fact No 151 squadron had been destined to be part of this Wing. Eventually Embry considered that Rochford airfield was less than ideal for night-flying and he was also rather forthright about the qualities of the Defiant, which he thought was a 'thoroughly bad night-fighter'! By December 1940 the Rochford Wing project had been dropped and Embry was moved to Wittering to command its night-fighting force. He was destined to make a lasting impression on Wittering.

During the early months of 1941 both squadrons began to make their mark in the night skies, and more especially No 151, which was now operating with Defiants and Hurricanes. One of the squadron's pilots, Pilot Officer Richard P. Stevens, DFC Bar, became the most successful Hurricane night-fighter pilot of the war. Although he operated without the benefit of AI radar, Stevens still managed to account for 14 enemy aircraft during the year with maybe another six probably destroyed. On January 15/16th he shot down a Dornier 215 and Heinkel 111, only the third time a pilot had claimed two enemy aircraft in one night. He would later repeat this feat but sadly Stevens was killed in action on 15th December 1941 when attached to No 253 squadron at Manston. He was then an acting Flight Lieutenant and had been further decorated with the DSO.

But the squadron was not just a one-man band. On 4/5th February a Defiant crew claimed a Dornier 17C, which crashed at Weldon and was the first enemy aircraft to be shot down in the county. Other successful pilots were Flight Lieutenant Irving Smith DFC, a New Zealander, who would later command the squadron, and Flight Lieutenant Desmond McMullen, DFC Bar, who along with Sergeant Fairweather made a most successful Defiant crew. They managed to claim two Heinkel 111s on successive nights in April and in the following month they downed a Junkers 88. In June the squadron received Hurricane IIcs, which were armed with four .20 mm cannons.

The Beaufighter squadron had no success at night until April 1941. It was now commanded by Squadron Leader H. P. Pleasure, DFC Bar, who had flown Blenheims under Embry's command back in his Wattisham days. The crews were mainly operating on ground controlled sorties, and in May six victories were claimed followed by seven in June. Group Captain Embry also managed to get some operational flying, almost a hundred hours, first with No 25 and later with No 151. His AI operator was Peter Clapham, who had been a controller in the Sector Operations room. As Embry later explained, 'When crews know their station commander is sharing their difficulties

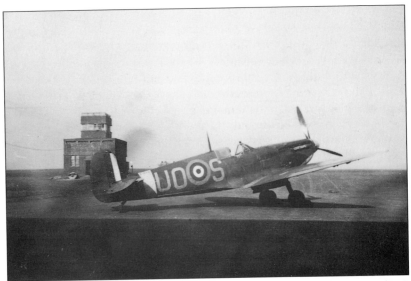

Spitfire of No 266 squadron at Wittering. Note the pre-war control tower. (RAF Museum)

and dangers, it helps them to withstand the strain of operational flying and gives them just that extra something which makes a man try to do better than he ever thought or hoped he could.'

The Spitfire squadron, No 266, which was now commanded by a New Zealander, Squadron Leader Pat G. Jameson, DFC, also managed to get into the night action by flying some 'fighter nights'; they brought a modest success in March and April. Jameson had previously served with No 46 squadron in Norway, and had been one of the first pilots to undertake the hazardous task of landing a Hurricane on an aircraft carrier. He was one of only five of the squadron's airmen to survive the tragic sinking of HMS *Glorious* in June 1940. He would later be promoted to Wing Commander (Flying) at Wittering.

The Luftwaffe was well aware of the growing importance of Wittering as a night-fighter station. On New Year's Day 1941 the airfield was bombed, followed by another raid on 14th March when five airmen were killed. On four nights in May (7th to 10th) it suffered further attacks with six aircraft destroyed and several fatal casualties.

It was still a grass airfield with a main landing run of about 1,400 yards, of which the last 150 yards or so, on the eastern boundary, 'sloped steeply to the Great North Road'. Embry was well aware that it was far from easy to land the heavy Beaufighters (10 tons) there and he was also concerned at the number of accidents that had occurred – nine in twelve months. He therefore devised a plan to extend the landing run by joining it to the satellite airfield at Collyweston. The Air Ministry Works engineers came to examine his proposal, concluding that the construction work would take about nine months. In typical style Embry decided to undertake the project 'in house'. As he later recalled, 'it only needed the removal of about fifteen hundred trees and the filling in of two or three ditches with the minimum of grading...'!

Within a month the construction work was completed, including the erection of a flare path, which had been made from locally purchased cable. The airfield now boasted an extremely long and well lighted landing strip, which would officially become known as a 'Master Diversion Airfield' and within a couple of months had been used by over 70 damaged aircraft for emergency landings. In fact, a special Bomber Command Service Unit was later formed at Wittering to deal with the damaged aircraft. The landing strip became the forerunner of the three Emergency Landing Grounds or 'Prangdromes' that were ultimately sited near to the coast at Carnaby, Woodbridge and Manston.

For some time Bomber Command had appointed Wing Commanders to command their operational squadrons, and Group Captain Embry felt strongly that the responsibilities of commanding an AI night-fighter squadron were equally arduous and responsible. He continually petitioned the Air Ministry to upgrade the post to Wing Commander with the Flights being commanded by Squadron Leaders. Ultimately this was agreed and the command of No 25 squadron was given to Wing Commander David F. W. Atcherley, DFC, who had previously served as an instructor at the CFS at Wittering with Embry. He was rather fortunate to survive a serious flying accident at the airfield in August 1941, suffering a fractured spine.

In July 1941 one of the ten Turbinlite Flights in Fighter Command was formed at Wittering – No 1453 – commanded by Squadron Leader Kenneth Blair, DFC, who had previously served in No 151 squadron. The idea behind these Flights was that aircraft equipped with AI equipment and operating under Ground Control Interception were also fitted with a large and powerful airborne searchlight in the nose. They would be accompanied on their night patrols by single-seat fighters, normally Hurricanes, which would move into the attack once an enemy aircraft had been intercepted, located and then illuminated with the searchlight. The Flight was equipped with Douglas Havocs, and its first Turbinlite operation was mounted on 22nd October. It would be fair to say that the Turbinlite experiment was not particularly successful, with little to show for all the hard work and effort put in by the crews and pilots. Though the Flights were up-graded to squadrons in September 1942, and No 1453 became No 532 squadron, in early 1943 all were disbanded.

In 1942 the Luftwaffe's night-bombing raids began to tail off and in late January No 25 squadron left for Northern Ireland. The other night-fighter squadron, No 151, which would continue operating Defiants until May, was now mainly engaged in flying convoy patrols along the east coast, but it still managed to claim the odd victory. The squadron had been selected as only the second unit to be supplied with the new Mosquito night-fighters, or at least it would be once these scarce 'wooden wonders' became available. Group Captain Embry, who had returned to Wittering in March 1942 after a temporary spell of duty in the Middle East, strongly urged the Air Ministry to provide his squadron with what he considered to be 'the finest aeroplane, without exception, that has been ever built in this country.'

The first Mosquito NFII arrived at Wittering on 6th April and was allocated to 'A' Flight, and by the end of the month 16 Mosquitos were on hand. Although a Heinkel 111 was possibly destroyed by Flight Lieutenant Pennington on 29th May, the first positive victory by a Mosquito night-fighter was recorded on 24/25th June when the squadron's CO, Wing Commander Irving Smith, DFC Bar, shot down two Dornier 217Es over the North Sea. From then on the crews began to add to these initial successes. Group Captain Embry had his own personal Mosquito, and when he was put in charge of No 2 Group of Bomber Command later in 1942, he actively encouraged and authorised some of the daring and successful low-level Mosquito missions that so captured the imagination of the British public.

In April 1942 the recently formed No 486 squadron, which was New Zealand's second fighter squadron, arrived from Kirton Lindsey under the command of Squadron Leader C. L. C. Roberts, with the intention of operating its Hurricane IIbs with the Turbinlite Havocs. The pilots made their first night sorties on the 27th of the month, but by July the squadron had resumed a day-fighter role. It was now beginning to exchange its Hurricanes for Hawker Typhoon IBs – yet another aircraft designed by Sidney Camm. This aircraft had first flown in February 1940, but its development had been rather hastily advanced in order to counter the potent threat of the Luftwaffe's new FW 190. The Typhoon, which entered the Service in September 1941, was a large and brutish aircraft, powered by a Napier Sabre engine giving it a top speed in excess of 400 mph, and was armed with twelve .303 machine guns or four 20 mm cannons. It was plagued with various teething problems but once these were resolved, the Typhoon developed into a most impressive and destructive ground-strike aircraft, which really came into its own over the battlefields of northern France after D-Day. The squadron moved away to North Weald in September, and it was replaced by No 152 squadron flying Spitfire Vbs, although the squadron was in the process of being transferred for service in Malta and the airmen left for overseas in November.

It was perhaps with some surprise that on 7th September 1942 Wittering was allocated to the US Eighth Air Force as a fighter base, and although this decision was confirmed two weeks later, the order had been amended to 'joint RAF/Eighth Air Force use'. The first American fighters did not arrive at Wittering until the following January; they were P-47s of No 63 squadron of 56th Fighter Group, which had moved into King's Cliffe. The Americans stayed until 5th April, by which time Wittering had become rather congested with aircraft. The Mosquito crews of No 151 were still operating from the airfield but they were now mostly engaged in night-intruder raids or 'rangers', although they had claimed their first night-victory of the year on 15/16th January 1943 over Lincoln.

On 25th March the Air Fighting Development Unit, along with its Royal Naval equivalent, No 787 RNAS squadron, arrived from Duxford. This Unit had been formed at Northolt back in 1940, to undertake trials on new versions of fighters as well as testing their armament. It also acted as a centre for the development of fighter tactics to provide a cadre of fighter expertise to train potential squadron commanders. During its time at Wittering the Unit would be commanded by several famous fighter pilots such as Wing Commanders W. F. Blackadder, DSO, DFC, and Myles Duke-Woolley, DSO, DFC, and was manned by very experienced fighter pilots, several of whom became test pilots after the war.

Occasionally the Unit was allowed into the action, not only flying defensive patrols but also to mount offensive sweeps. On 29th June Squadron Leader James MacLachlan, DSO, DFC two Bars, along with Flight Lieutenant Alan G. Page, DFC, set off in two Mustang Is on a daylight foray over France and they managed to account for four Henschel HS126s and a Junkers 88. However, in July (18th) they repeated the operation but MacLachlan was shot down and later died in a prison hospital from his injuries. He had lost his left arm below the elbow in February 1941 and flew with a special artificial forearm and hand. Page returned safely, although he subsequently left the Unit and later became a leader of a Fighter Wing in France, being awarded the DSO. Page was a most talented and brave pilot, who had been badly burned in August 1940 during the Battle of Britain and had spent over two years in hospital, becoming one of the founder members of the Guinea Pig Club – those that had undergone plastic surgery at East Grinstead.

At the end of April, after almost $2\frac{1}{2}$ years at Wittering, No 151 squadron moved to Colerne in Wiltshire to be closer to the action over France. It was immediately replaced by a Beaufighter squadron, No 141, which was commanded by one of the most successful fighter pilots of the Second World War, Wing Commander J. R. D. 'Bob' Braham, DSO, DFC Bar. He was only 22 years old when given command of the squadron and in the words of a colleague, '[his] 100% dedication and commitment to the task, whatever it may be, set him apart from other people and lesser mortals.' With his AI operator, Squadron Leader W. J. 'Sticks' Gregory, DSO, DFC, DFM, they formed the most successful night-fighter crew, and when Braham was shot down over Denmark and taken prisoner in June 1944 his total stood at 29 confirmed victories and he had been awarded a Bar to his DSO with a second DFC Bar!

Nos 25 and 141 squadrons operated Bristol Beaufighters from Wittering. (via V. Mathews)

The squadron was equipped with Mark VIf Beaufighters, which were powered by two 1,670 hp Bristol Hercules engines and had been equipped with a Vickers gun to fire aft of the navigator's hatch. The crews had become deeply engaged in the trialling of a new aircraft interception device, which was code-named 'Serrate'; the name came from the serrated images portrayed on the radar screens. This new electronic device enabled the crews to home onto the enemy's night-fighter radar emissions from a distance of about 100 miles, and used in conjunction with AI MkVI sets provided very accurate range indications. The squadron became engaged on intruder raids over the Continent and later on bomber support duties, flying ahead of Bomber Command's Main Force with the express purpose of tempting the Luftwaffe night-fighters into the air. This was especially effective on 17/18th August in the Command's famous Peenemunde operation, when three victories were claimed – two by Wing Commander Braham. Towards the end of their stay at Wittering the crews began converting to Mosquitos but with the establishment of No 100 (Special Duties) Group of Bomber Command in November 1943, the squadron was transferred into the Group and left for West Raynham early in December.

In the same month No 438 squadron moved down from Digby. It had only recently been formed from an RCAF squadron and was unusually equipped with Hurricane IVs. These aircraft were able to carry eight 60-lb rocket projectiles and it was said to 'pack a punch equivalent to the broadside of a destroyer.' This massive fire power extended the aircraft's operational life beyond the Second World War; in total over 14,000 Hurricanes were manufactured in this country and in Canada. The squadron left Wittering early in January 1944, and now the operational days of the airfield were fast drawing to a close. The only operational fighters using the airfield were P-38s of the 55th squadron of the 20th Fighter Group. They would remain at Wittering until almost the end of May.

By October 1943 the airfield had become the base for the RAF Bomb Disposal teams in the area. The RAF was responsible for the disposal of all unexploded bombs (UXBs) on their own airfields, their own and Allied aircraft as well as all enemy aircraft that had crashed in the country. There were now six RAF Bomb Disposal squadrons and 29 Flights, and during 1943 alone RAF teams cleared over 43,000 UXBs of which only 3,000 or so were of enemy origin!

The intense build-up of aircraft to D-Day had created considerable pressure on all airfields in southern England, and as a result the Fighter

Interception Unit and its Royal Naval counterpart, No 746 squadron, was forced to move out of Ford in Sussex and into Wittering at the beginning of April. The Unit had been formed in 1940 to study the problems of fighter interception, both by day and at night, and was engaged in trialling new fighters as well as evaluating various electronic devices. The pilots were also testing the high-altitude Westland Welkin, which although it had first flown in late 1942 never came into operational use, and less than 100 were produced. The Unit had a very varied selection of aircraft – Mosquitos, Beaufighters, Typhoons, Tempests, and Fireflies. It was also testing one of the Luftwaffe's most successful intruder aircraft – Messerschmitt 410. One of the Naval pilots, Lieutenant Peter Twiss, would become the first pilot to fly at over 1,000 mph in March 1956. By late August the Unit was able to return to Ford.

With both Wittering and Collyweston being deeply involved in experimental and testing work, it was not a great surprise that when Sir Roderic M. Hill, AOC-in-C of Fighter Command, proposed the establishment of a Central Fighter Establishment in August 1944, it should be first based at Wittering. The CFE, which was authorised on

Nos 141, 151 and 68 squadrons operated various marks of Mosquito night-fighters. (via J. Adams)

3rd September, was effectively an amalgamation of all the various experimental and training units into one centre of excellence for advanced training for fighter leaders, the development of fighter tactics and technical enhancements. The Day Fighter Leaders School was commanded, in November, by Wing Commander E. P. Wells, DSO, DFC Bar, yet another New Zealander, who had started his operational career with No 266 squadron at the airfield in September 1940. The CFE left for Tangmere in February 1945, but it rapidly expanded in the immediate post-war years and had an important influence on Service flying as the RAF entered the jet age.

For a brief few weeks during February No 68 night-fighter squadron used the airfield, its Mosquito crews making a number of sorties before they departed for Coltishall. The airfield's wartime operational life had ended. It was reckoned that 151 enemy aircraft had been destroyed by squadrons operating from Wittering with another 50 as probables. Although Wittering was not so famous or glamorous as other wartime fighter airfields such as Biggin Hill, Hornchurch, North Weald and Duxford, it could probably lay claim to having the greatest number of famous fighter pilots serving there during the war; unfortunately, the pressure of space has meant that only a mere handful of all these courageous airmen have been noted here.

Wittering was transferred to No 21 Group of Flying Training Command and a Flying Training School operated from the airfield until the station returned to the fold of Fighter Command in April 1946 with the arrival of No 41 squadron and its Spitfire F21s, one of the final versions of this remarkable fighter. That Wittering would become an operational V-bomber base and later *the* home of the Harrier 'Jump Jet' was then in the distant future.

20
CIVILIANS AT WAR

In August 1942 Lord Woolton, the Minister of Food, made a speech in which he voiced the prescient opinion that 'when the story of this war comes to be written it will be a family story – the story of the work and devotion of ordinary men and women everywhere. And no greater story will be ever told.' The Second World War has now passed into the history books as 'The People's War', indeed it touched every person in the country wherever they lived and whatever age they were at the time. Those who lived through the long ordeal have their own special recollections of the conflict – the ululating wail of the sirens, the incessant drone of aircraft, searchlights, barrage balloons, bombing, food rationing, blackout, evacuation of children, gas masks, endless queuing, *ITMA* … the list seems endless, and each reminiscence can still evoke sharp and vivid memories of those wartime days despite the long passage of time.

Few of the millions that crowded around their wireless sets on that fateful Sunday morning in early September 1939 to hear the grim news that the country was at war with Germany, would have expected, or even believed, that five years later the battle would still be raging, all the troublesome wartime restrictions would still be in force, and that the threat of death from the air would not have abated. The formal announcement of the declaration of war came as no surprise to most people, in fact it was more a matter of relief after months of anticipation and suspense, but the 'Phoney' or 'Bore' war that followed was quite unexpected. Air Raid Precautions had been put in place, sirens erected, and public air raid shelters dug in parks and erected in streets. The first

War is declared! (Daily Telegraph)

of the ubiquitous sandbags had appeared around official buildings and the armed forces had been mobilised. The massive evacuation of children had already begun and a complete blackout had descended on the country. The public had been warned to expect massive air attacks and the probable use of poison gas; after all, 38 million gas masks had been issued as early as 1938, and the tops of post boxes had been coated with yellow gas detector paint.

The first eight months of the war were remarkable for the lack of enemy activity over the country but nevertheless an increasing number of wartime measures and restrictions were put in force. National Registration Day was set for 29th September and identity cards were issued, which were required to be produced on demand to anybody 'in authority', followed shortly by ration books, which became the two most essential and important documents of the war. Petrol was rationed early in September followed by food in January 1940, with bacon, butter, sugar, ham, and later meat, tea and cooking fats, all being stringently rationed. Queuing had already become a feature of everyday life and would later almost become a national obsession. These irksome restrictions and shortages were all the harder to bear during the harsh winter of 1939/40 (the most severe since 1881) as there was an acute shortage of fuel. When Easter came at the end of March, people flocked to the coasts as they had done in pre-war days, almost as if they sensed that this would prove to be their last real holiday of the war.

The invasion of the Low Countries and France in May 1940, their subsequent fall and the Dunkirk evacuation suddenly changed the 'Strange War', as Neville Chamberlain, the Prime Minister, called it, into a very serious and real war. The threat of invasion became a grave and sombre probability and the formation of an all-party coalition government headed by Winston Churchill only emphasised the perilous and vulnerable state of the country. The issue of *Rules for Civilians in case of Invasion* to every household only added to the public's deep concern. This pamphlet gave instructions to 'stay indoors ... hide maps, food, petrol and bicycles ...', and most of the population were quite convinced that an invasion was imminent. Road signposts in country areas disappeared, as did the names on railway stations, and maps and guides were taken out of the shops. Strange constructions began to appear in the countryside, anti-tank traps, and the now familiar pill-boxes, many of which have survived to this day; indeed it has been suggested that they should now be preserved as historical buildings. Church bells were silenced and would only be rung again as a signal of an enemy invasion.

The extreme gravity of the situation was heightened by the broadcast on 14th May 1940 by Anthony Eden, the Minister of War, wherein he appealed for volunteers to come forward to defend the country from attack by airborne forces. The Local Defence Volunteers, as they were first known, should be between the ages of 17 and 65 years, they would not be paid but would be provided with a uniform and armed (ultimately!), and would be required to serve a minimum of ten hours per week. The Government had expected to raise a force of some 150,000, but it was quite overwhelmed by the public's response. Within two weeks double that number had enrolled and in another month over one million men had come forward. In Peterborough 400 had enrolled at their local police stations by 16th May with one third of them being ex-servicemen. It was not until the middle of July that they acquired their familiar name – The Home Guard – a name that Winston Churchill had suggested back in late 1939.

Almost every village had its own platoon and most Home Guardsmen took their duty very seriously indeed. They manned road blocks, patrolled their territory and inspected the identity cards of anyone moving during the hours of darkness. By 1943 there were over 1,100 battalions of the Home Guard throughout the country. By this time they were well supplied with arms, albeit mostly old American rifles, and their average age was now under 30 years. They had also become well trained and were quite professional, in reality belying the comic images later portrayed in the successful TV series *Dad's Army*. There are, however, such a wealth of amusing stories about the Home Guard, especially concerning exercise manoeuvres, as to suggest that certain of the comedy scenes had some basis of fact! For those men who felt that the Home Guard was not quite their cup of tea, they could volunteer for fire watching duties up to a maximum of 48 hours a month.

Also in May 1940 the Treachery Act was passed, which was designed to deal with enemy agents and 'Fifth Columnists'. Aliens were rounded up and taken into 'protective' custody, many destined for internment in the Isle of Man. Posters carrying such slogans as *Careless Talk costs lives* and *Be like Dad, keep Mum* could be seen everywhere and a spy mania overwhelmed the country. The carrying and use of cameras became most suspicious, as did any stranger asking too many questions. The famous American broadcaster, Ed Murrow, recalled that he had been arrested as a foreign spy in an Essex country pub because 'I asked too many questions about wartime life at a time when everybody in the country was looking for spies'!

It was in Northamptonshire that the first enemy spy was captured by members of the public. On Friday 6th September a man in civilian clothes, armed with a pistol and equipped with a small wireless in a suitcase, was discovered hiding in a ditch near Denton. He was captured by a farmer, who was also in the Home Guard, and three of his workers. The man, Gösta Caroli, was a Swedish citizen but was known by military intelligence to be a German agent. He admitted that he had landed by parachute and that his orders were to report on the damage done to airfields by the Luftwaffe's bombing, and that his ultimate destination was Birmingham. Eventually Caroli worked as a double agent for MI5 under the code-name 'Summer'. A second enemy agent was caught on 4th October close to Bozeat, and he too was arrested by a farmer and a member of the Home Guard. As the recently released official papers have confirmed, military intelligence were warned of the arrival of these foreign agents as MI5 had already managed to penetrate the pre-war German spy network in the country.

Although it would be only fair to say that Northamptonshire suffered far less than most central and eastern counties, nevertheless over 7,800 bombs fell on the county, the majority of which were incendiaries. Peterborough was the first to attract the attention of the Luftwaffe as early as 8th June 1940 when a few small capacity bombs fell in the Bridge Street area, breaking many windows but causing only slight structural damage. Over two months later (16th August) Kilsby, to the south-east of Rugby, was bombed, and 14 high explosives were dropped but with fairly minimal damage. A week later BBC Daventry was strafed by a solitary Dornier 17 and one civilian worker was injured. The anti-aircraft guns around the radio station were able to fire off some rounds but with no success. It is interesting to note that in March 1941 the three heavy A-A guns defending the station were removed and reallocated to seaports to strengthen their defences.

Northampton suffered its first air raid on the night of 26/27th August and an ARP warden was electrocuted whilst attempting to extinguish what he thought was an incendiary bomb. The first land mine landed at Pury End, Paulerspury near Towcester on 12th September. These mines were dark green cylinders over eight feet long and two feet in diameter, and came down by parachute. The blast from them could cause devastating and extensive damage, and the Ministry of Home Security called them 'an indiscriminate form of aerial attack against the morale of the people.' At Pury End the terrific blast from the mines seriously damaged over 50 houses and injured eight people. As the Luftwaffe's night blitz intensified from October onwards, Peterborough, Northampton, Kettering, Wellingborough, Oundle and Rushden all received bombing raids. It was the latter town that suffered the heaviest treatment, when on 3rd October 18 HE bombs and a dozen incendiaries resulted in eleven civilian deaths (including seven children) and another 43 were injured. In the following month Rushden was again bombed and this time there were five deaths and 31 injuries.

During the winter of 1940/1 when the night blitz was at its height the county escaped relatively lightly, but most nights were disturbed by alerts as enemy aircraft crossed the county for Midland targets. The dismal and dreaded wail of the 'Red Warning' or 'Raiders Approach', which since the previous September had been reduced in duration from two minutes to one, was followed some hours later by the blessed tones of the 'All Clear' or 'Raiders Passed'. However, on 15th January St Andrews Hospital in Northampton suffered heavy bomb damage, and in May, Corby, Peterborough and Irchester all were bombed. The heaviest raid occurred on the 20th of the month at Irchester, resulting in considerable damage to homes and a chapel with nine civilians killed.

It was during this period of the war that the country's fortunes could be said to be at their lowest ebb. The 14th January 1941 had marked the five hundredth day of the war and for most people the war now seemed to have lasted for an eternity. The civilian population had so far borne the heaviest brunt of the conflict, and by the end of 1941 over 40,000 had been killed in the bombing raids with another 50,000 injured. It would not be until the following year that it was possible to say that 'the enemy had killed more soldiers than women and children.' The Battle of the Atlantic was at a most critical stage and there was an acute shortage of food and other basic essentials. Although bread was never rationed during the war, the white loaf disappeared and the 'National Wheatmeal Loaf' appeared. It was universally detested and was called 'this nasty, dirty, dark, coarse, indigestible bread'! A black market in a wide variety of goods and foodstuffs began to flourish, and profiteering became widespread with the name 'spiv' entering the vocabulary.

During 1941 the Government was deeply concerned about the health of the nation, as it was considered that the diet of the people was now the poorest of the war. By November a 'points' system had been introduced for canned meat, fish and vegetables. The purchase of clothing and footwear was severely limited by the issue of coupons and petrol was now only available to 'essential users'. Against this background of extreme hardship and austerity on the Home Front, the news from the war fronts abroad was most dispiriting and disheartening, with defeats in the Far East and both Singapore and Hong Kong falling into Japanese hands. It would not be until late 1942 that the country was able to cheer the first Allied victory – El Alamein.

One of the most familiar, if rather unusual, wartime institutions to emerge from this dire time was the Community Feeding Centre, or 'British Restaurant' as Winston Churchill insisted that they should be called because 'everybody associates the word "restaurant" with a good meal, and they may as well have the name if they cannot get anything else'! The 'restaurants' were non profit-making and run by the local authorities with Government sponsorship, established to provide a good, wholesome and hot mid-day meal for one shilling per head. By 1943 British Restaurants had become an established feature of wartime life, certainly in urban areas, with over 2,000 in operation serving half a million meals each day. Rural areas were covered by the Women's Voluntary Service's Rural Pie Scheme, which was set up in 1942 and provided over a million pies and snacks a week to some 5,000 villages.

Since the outbreak of the war the civilian population had been constantly exhorted to 'Dig for Victory' and to turn their gardens over to the production of vegetables and fruit. The number of allotments had increased from 800,000 in 1939 to nearly one and a half million in 1943. Even parks, squares and golf courses were commandeered for the production of food. The beleaguered housewives were daily targeted in the press, on the radio, and by posters and leaflets on 'Food Facts' and 'Food Hints' as well being offered advice on ways to improve their families' diets; they were described as 'fighting on the Kitchen Front'! All these encouragements flowed from the Ministry of Food, which had a network of local offices nationwide, and its remarkable and enthusiastic Minister, Lord Woolton. Perhaps, other than Winston Churchill, he was the best known politician of the war. His flair for propaganda was considerable and it was largely due to his efforts that by the end of 1943 the Government could report that the diet of the public was now better than it had been in the 1930s.

Without doubt the nation's wartime obsession was saving – paper, rags, glass, jam jars, old saucepans, bones, books, bottles, aluminium and tins – with children being willingly engaged in the many and various salvage collections. A Government decree had made the wastage of paper an offence. However, the most successful wartime venture was the National Savings Movement, and it all really started with the Spitfire Fund in the summer of 1940. The Government announced that any town, locality or private firm could have a Spitfire specially named if they subscribed £5,000, then the estimated cost of one aircraft. All the towns in the county were involved in the Fund and all had Spitfires named after them, for instance *Peterborough District*, *Northampton*, *Higham Ferrers* and *Irthlingborough*. By the spring of 1941 the Spitfire Fund had reached £13 millions! Encouraged by this success the Government launched special savings drives throughout the war – War Weapons Week, Warships Week, Wings for Victory and Salute the Soldier Week. But it was the regular and on-going extent of National Savings that proved to be phenomenal, with over one quarter of the average weekly income being given up to savings, compared with about 5% before the war. There were savings groups in every street, office, factory and school, and such was the importance attached to National Savings the BBC reported details of each week's savings contributions.

The Luftwaffe's new bombing offensive that was launched during the spring and summer of 1942 brought back the horror of air raids to the county, especially so in August. On the 3rd, which was Bank Holiday Monday, Wellingborough received a number of bombs in the early evening. They fell in the Market Square area and extensive damage was caused to commercial property with the loss of seven lives

Bomb damage at Wellingborough, August 1942. (Northampton Chronicle & Echo)

241

Junkers 88 on display at King's School, Park Road, Peterborough in late 1940 as part of Peterbor(

and another 55 persons injured. Peterborough suffered on the night of the 9/10th, mainly from incendiaries, then on the 22nd Wellingborough, Kettering and Peterborough were attacked as were other places in the county. At Wellingborough an 18 year old Home Guardsman was killed. In June (13th) Peterborough sustained fairly considerable damage mainly around the North Station area as a result of a few HE

Veapons Week. (City of Peterborough Museum)

bombs and a considerable number of incendiaries.

It might be said that from now onwards the civilian population would be placed under greater risk from 'friendly' aircraft crashing in the county. Up to 1942 there had been at least 50 crashes, besides those accidents at or near airfields, and only two of these were enemy aircraft. Perhaps the most spectacular so far had occurred on the night

Cadbury's Cocoa Caravan was a welcome sight in all bombed areas. (Cadbury Limited)

of 14/15th July 1941 when a Short Stirling of No 7 squadron, returning with heavy damage from a raid to Hanover, ran out of fuel and the crew abandoned the aircraft near Northampton. It finally crashed onto Gold Street, Northampton, causing considerable damage to commercial properties but with no civilian fatalities. All but the pilot, Flight Sergeant B. K. Madgewick, survived; he slipped out of his parachute harness and crashed to his death. It was reported that the Chief Constable of Northamptonshire telephoned a protest to the Station Commander at RAF Upwood saying, 'I can't have this happening'! On 20th September a Wellington of No 101 squadron at RAF Oakington was lost in bad weather on return from a raid to Ostend. It crashed into a tree at Preston Deanery near Northampton and only one of the six-man crew survived.

As the number of operational and training flights steadily increased, the incidence of crashes rose dramatically with over 60 in 1944. The villagers living in the vicinity of the airfields were obviously at far greater risk, but there were a number of narrow escapes at villages well away from the airfields. For instance, on 20th March 1944, a training Wellington fell onto a rickyard in Yardley Gobion and the villagers joined firemen in fighting the fire to prevent it spreading to the rest of the village. There is a lectern in St Leonard's church dedicated to 'the eight brave airmen, and in thanksgiving for a Great Deliverance.' Towards the end of the year (5th December) a Halifax and Lancaster collided over Yelvertoft on their outward flight. The Halifax narrowly missed the village and a large crater was caused when the full bomb load exploded. Eleven days later a B-17 from Kimbolton caught fire in the air. All except the pilot, Lieutenant John Ahern, baled out. He remained at the controls to prevent the aircraft falling on the village of Bozeat and was killed in the subsequent crash. There is a framed testimonial in the local church from the Commanding Officer of the 379th Bomb Group acknowledging the villagers' appreciation of Lieutenant Ahern's sacrifice.

One of the features of the early war years was the number of women taking up voluntary war work – either in the Civil Defence, on the land or in the WVS. The Women's Voluntary Service was formed in 1938 by Lady Reading with the original intention of giving assistance to the Civil Defence forces, but their subsequent wartime duties became many and varied. They operated reception and rest centres and canteens, dealt with evacuees and manned telephones during air raids. In addition they organised the distribution of clothing and other items to bombed-out people. By 1944 there were over one million members and they made an immense contribution to the war effort. As did the members of the Women's Institute, who became fully engaged in the various salvage programmes, operating rest canteens in village halls, preserving fruits, making jam and knitting garments for the armed forces.

But perhaps the most conspicuous female war-workers were the girls of the Women's Land Army. Dressed in their distinctive uniform of a green jumper, khaki corduroy breeches and a wide brimmed hat, they became an essential part of the wartime farming scene. The WLA had its origins in the First World War but had been re-formed in June 1939 by Lady Denham. The Land Army girls were volunteers drawn from all walks of life, and after about one month's training at the Northampton Institute of Agriculture at Moulton most of them went to one of the 20 hostels in the county, where living conditions were rather basic and the rules quite restrictive. Their hours were long, and the work hard, dirty and poorly paid. They had to earn the respect of a largely suspicious farming community, where there still existed a considerable amount of mutual distrust and ignorance between town and country. At its peak in July 1943 the WLA numbered over 87,000,

Cleaning away aircraft wreckage was an all too familiar task in the county; the remains of a B

Bomb Group, 5th December 1943. (National Archives & Records Administration)

and it continued after the war, not being disbanded until October 1950. Conscription for women between the ages of 20 and 30 years was not introduced until December 1941. The conscripts were given the choice of serving in any of the three auxiliary armed services, the Civil Defence or in industry. The Women's Auxiliary Air Force had been formed in June 1939 and by 1943 WAAFs accounted for 22% of the RAF's strength in the United Kingdom. They were stationed at all the major RAF airfields in the county and were mainly employed on tasks that were traditionally associated with 'feminine' roles – clerking, operating telephones and radios, driving motor vehicles and, perhaps inevitably, catering. Women also filled the jobs vacated by men serving in the forces – bus drivers and conductors, milkmen, policemen, postmen and railway workers. By mid-1943 the number of women employed on war work was in excess of three million, and the mass employment of women was perhaps the major social change brought about by the war.

It would be stating the obvious to say that the peace of the Northamptonshire countryside and the even tenor of its ways were changed beyond recognition by the war. The construction of the various airfields from 1941 through to 1944 alone brought about this transformation. The invasion of the county's roads and lanes by heavy lorries and large earth-moving equipment brought major disruptions without the added desecration of hundreds upon hundreds of acres of the countryside, which were effectively lost for many years. Many local inhabitants considered this airfield construction work to be the greatest inconvenience of the war, bringing in its wake oceans of mud in the winter and clouds of choking dust in the summer.

The completed airfields brought in the first influx of RAF airmen and the beginnings of the foreign 'invasion' of the county. French and Belgian airmen were regular visitors to Sywell and Northampton, and during 1942 Wittering and its satellite airfields almost became an enclave of New Zealand. In May 1942 the first American airmen arrived at Grafton Underwood and they would be followed by their colleagues arriving at regular intervals until the spring of 1944, when almost 20,000 were serving at the seven USAAF airfields. Each of these airfields became effectively 'Little Americas' where the American way of life had been transferred into the English countryside – movies, hamburgers, hot dogs, doughnuts, baseball et al. The narrow lanes soon became congested with American lorries and jeeps and towns and villages echoed to the sound of American accents. The local pubs, of which there was no equivalent in the United States, became the

Private Hadyn C. Williams, a military guard at Deenethorpe, and a young visitor from the nearby village, 1st January 1944. (National Archives & Records Administration)

favourite places of recreation for the GIs (Government Issue) and it was here that the clash of the two different cultures was most noticeable. Although the Americans complained about 'the warm, flat and weak' beer, they still managed to drink enormous quantities, and with beer being in short supply this led to a certain amount of friction.

The antipathy and resentment felt towards the American airmen, who were far better paid, had smarter uniforms and were demonstrably far better fed, was ultimately melted by the friendliness, good humour, politeness and generosity of most American servicemen. Their boundless benevolence to local children and those in hospitals and orphanages gained them immense respect; their Christmas parties for children became legendary. The endless bounty of goods and foodstuffs from their PXs (NAAFIs) – ice cream (which had disappeared in Britain in 1942), Hershey chocolate bars, beef steaks, quality soap, tinned foodstuffs, nylon stockings, cigarettes (3d for a pack of 20) and the inevitable chewing gum – filtered through to the local communties. Certainly the American airmen brought a touch of glamour to wartime austerity Britain, and the appearance of such stars as Bob Hope, Bing Crosby, Glenn Miller, Frances Langford, Clark Gable and Marlene Dietrich at the nearby air bases, seemed to bring Hollywood that much closer than on the screens of the local cinemas. Strong and faithful links of friendship that were established with the local communities during these brief years have survived right up to the present day.

Perhaps the more unwelcome temporary foreign residents in the county were the German and Italian prisoners of war; quite a number of camps had sprung up throughout the county. Although it must be said that the Italian prisoners in their distinctive brown uniforms became more readily accepted, because they were found to be 'friendly and cheerful and often given to singing when they worked on the land'. By July 1943 nearly 40,000 Italian prisoners were at work in the fields. The fraternization with prisoners, especially the Italians, was frowned upon by the authorities and the local police were directed 'to stamp it out'! There was, however, a widespread if erroneous belief that the prisoners received better rations than the civilian population and this led to considerable resentment.

From 1943 onwards the public was well aware that the tide of war had begun to turn in favour of the Allies. Although the annoying wartime restrictions were still strongly in force and over 70% of the population was engaged in war work, it was confidently felt that it was merely a matter of time before the war would end. From April church bells could be heard again each Sunday, and the following month the first horse racing meeting at Ascot since the war was held. Some normality was returning! The vast increase in the number of Allied heavy bombers that passed overhead, and the news of the invasion of Italy were all welcome signs to the public of the changed fortunes, so much so that at the end of the year the *Daily Telegraph* could state: 'we may conclude that nothing but unimaginable blunders in strategy or unconceivable failure of national determination could prevent the victory of the Allies.'

In January 1944 the public could be forgiven for thinking that such sentiments were merely wishful thinking as the Luftwaffe launched its heaviest bombing offensive since 1941. The county escaped very lightly from the raids but in five months over 1,500 civilians, mainly in London and the south-east, were killed in the bombing. Nevertheless the country waited somewhat impatiently for the Second Front. As one correspondent remarked, 'England is expectant, almost hushed. Every time we turn on the radio we expect to hear that the great invasion of Europe has begun.'

The relief and euphoria of D-Day was not allowed to linger for very long before the first V1 rocket landed on Britain on the night of 12/13th June and within days the newspapers were reporting 'Pilotless planes now raid Britain'. The first V1 rocket landed in the county at Creaton on 22nd July, where it made a 24 foot crater and caused damage to several houses with five people injured. The next to fall landed on Christmas Eve, just one of the 31 V1 rockets that had been launched from Heinkels flying off the Lincolnshire coast with Manchester as their prime target. The V1 landed at Woodford and damaged some farm buildings. Just two more V1s were to land in the county, both in January 1945, but little damage was sustained.

By this time many of the Air Raid Precautions had been abolished. On 12th September 1944 fire watching had finished, five days later the blackout regulations were lifted and many of the Civil Defence forces had been transferred to other duties, either in the armed forces or factories. From the 11th of the month there was no longer any compulsion to attend the Home Guard parades, it could now revert to its original status as a volunteer force. Its strength now numbered over 1,700,000, and about 10% were employed on the anti-aircraft batteries. However, its days were numbered, and the final parade and march past of the Northamptonshire Home Guard took place in Market Square, Northampton on Sunday 3rd December 1944. The Home Guard was an experiment that had proved to be a tremendous success. Its very existence and increased strength had enabled the country to outlive the threat of a German invasion, while it also released regular armed forces to serve abroad in other theatres of war.

Despite the fact that most of the public believed that the war would be over by Christmas 1944, the country was forced to face another hard

The Home Guard stand down parade in Northampton Market Square, Sunday 3rd December 1944. (Northampton Record Office)

and cold wartime winter. The Allied drive towards Berlin had lost its impetus and the outlook was decidedly bleak with flying bombs, rockets, rationing and war work. The five years of war had taken its toll on the civilian population, 'they were physically and mentally exhausted ... in short utterly war-weary.' But as spring arrived the war situation changed rapidly and when victory in Europe finally arrived in early May the country erupted into celebration.

Every town and village celebrated VE Day with street parties, bonfires, sports meetings and fancy dress parades. Many had been collecting money and food for this special day for weeks upon weeks, and despite all the rigours of food rationing the spreads that were provided at these parties seemed like veritable feasts! The People's War had finally come to an end, and, as Winston Churchill said on 8th May, 'The lights went out and the bombs came down. But every man, woman and child in the country had no thought of quitting the struggle ... Now we have emerged from one deadly struggle – a terrible foe has been cast on the ground and awaits our judgement and our mercy.'

BIBLIOGRAPHY

During my research I consulted various books. I list them below with my grateful thanks to the authors.

Air Ministry, *Target: Germany. The USAAF's Official Story of the VIII Bomber Command First Year over Europe*, HMSO 1944.

Armitage, Michael, *The Royal Air Force: An Illustrated History*, Cassell, 1993.

Asworth, Chris, *RAF Bomber Command, 1936–1968*, Patrick Stephens, 1995.

Bartley, Tony, DFC. *Smoke Trials in the Sky*, Crecy Publishing. 1997

Birdsell, Steve & Freeman, Roger A., *Claims to Fame: The B-17 Flying Fortress*, Arms & Armour, 1994.

Bowman, Martin N., *The Bedford Triangle: US Undercover Ops from England in World War II*, Patrick Stephens, 1988.

Bowyer, Chaz, *Royal Air Force, 1939–1945*, Pen & Sword Books, 1996.

Bowyer, Chaz, *Fighter Command: 1936–1968*, Dent, 1980.

Bowyer, Michael J. F., *Action Stations: 6. Military Airfields of the Cotswolds and the Central Midlands*, Patrick Stephens, 1991.

Butler, Phil, *War Prizes*, Midland Counties Publications, 1994.

Calder, Angus, *The People's War; Britain 1939–45*, Pimlico, 1992.

Chorley, W. R., *RAF Bomber Command Losses in the Second World War*, Vols 1 to 5, Midland Publications, 1992–97.

Croall, Jonathan, *Don't You Know There's a War On?: the People's Voice*, Hutchinson, 1989.

Delve, Ken, *D-Day: The Air Battle*, Arms & Armour, 1994.

Delve, Ken, *Nightfighter*, Arms & Armour, 1995.

Embry, Sir Basil, *Mission Completed*, Metheun, 1957.

Falconer, Jonathan, *RAF Bomber Stations of World War 2*, Ian Allen, 1992.

Franks, Norman, *Fighter Command, 1936–1968*, Patrick Stephens, 1992.

Freeman, Roger A., *The Mighty Eighth*, Arms & Armour, 1989.

Freeman, Roger A., *The Mighty Eighth War Manual*, Janes Publishing Co, 1984.

Freeman, Roger A. with Alan Crouchman & Vic Maslen, *The Mighty Eighth War Diary*, Janes Publishing Co, 1990.

Gibson, Michael L., *Aviation in Northamptonshire: An Illustrated History*, Northamptonshire Libraries, 1982.

Golley, John, *Aircrew Unlimited: The Commonwealth Air Training Plan during World War II*, Patrick Stephens, 1993.

Harris, Air Arthur, *Bomber Offensive*, Collins, 1947.

Jackson, Robert, *Guinness Book of Air Warfare*, Guinness Publishing, 1993.

James, John, *The Paladins*, Macdonald & Co, 1990.

Johnson, J. E., *Wing Leader*, Chatto & Windus, 1956.

Lacey-Johnson, Lionel, *Point Blank and Beyond*, Airlife, 1991.

Longmate, Norman, *When We Won The War*, Hutchinson, 1977.

Marriott, Leo, *British Military Airfields: Then and Now*, Ian Allan, 1997.

Middlebrook, Martin, *The Schweinfurt – Regensburg Mission: American Raids on 17th August 1943*, Allen Lane, 1983.

Mondey, David, *British Aircraft of World War II*, Hamlyn, 1992.

Moyes, Philip J. R., *Bomber Squadrons of the RAF*, Hutchinson, 1981.

Northamptonshire Libraries, *Northamptonshire at War: 1939–1945*, 1978.

Parry, Simon W., *Intruders over Britain: The Luftwaffe Night Offensive 1940–1945*, Air Research Publns, 1987.

Paul, C. J., *Sywell: the Story of an English Aerodrome, 1928–1978*, Sywell Aerodrome Ltd, 1978.

Peden, Murray, *A Thousand Shall Fall*, Stoddart, 1988.

Price, Alfred, *Instruments of Darkness*, William Kimber, 1967.

Rawlings, John, *Fighter Squadrons of the RAF*, Crecy Books, 1993.

Ray, John, *The Night Blitz: 1940–1941*, Arms & Armour, 1996.

Richards, Denis, *The Royal Air Force, 1939–45*, HMSO, 1953.

Scutts, Terry, *Lions in the Sky*, Patrick Stephens, 1987.

Simons, Graham M., *Airfield Focus: 26. Peterborough*, GMS Enterprises, 1996.

Smith, David J., *Britain's Military Airfields, 1939–45*, PSL, 1989.

Thetford, Owen, *Aircraft of the Royal Air Force Since 1918*, (9th Edition) Putnam, 1995.

Townsend, Peter, *Duel in the Dark*, Harrap, 1986.

Turner, John Frayn, *VCs of the Air*, Harrap, 1960.